THE CRABB
ENIGMA

MIKE & JACQUI WELHAM

Matador
5 Weir Road
Kibworth Beauchamp
Leicester LE8 0LQ, UK
Tel: (+44) 116 279 2299
Fax: (+44) 116 279 2277
Email: books@troubador.co.uk
Web: www.troubador.co.uk/matador

ISBN 978 1848763 821

British Library Cataloguing in Publication Data.
A catalogue record for this book is available from the British Library.

Typeset in 12pt Perpetua by Troubador Publishing Ltd, Leicester, UK
Printed and bound in Great Britain by TJ international Ltd, Padstow, Cornwall

Matador is an imprint of Troubador Publishing Ltd

Contents

Acknowledgements

The authors would like to thank; Gary Murray, investigator extraordinaire and Nick Aarons, an executive film producer for his investigative help and continued attempts to put the project onto the screen. We very much value Sydney Knowles for his important contribution of personal knowledge and experiences. We were pleased to see that Knowles has published his memoirs. We are grateful for the interviews and letters with and from Robin (Harbinson) Bryans who knew Crabb in the 'art years' and allowed us to use valuable material. We extend thanks to Frank Goldsworthy, Cdr Stan Currie Davies and Pat Rose (all now deceased). Thanks also to Dr Svoboda for his interest and help with regard to the former Czchekoslavakia. There are many who do not want to be named and others who have contributed in some way and we offer our thanks to them. We wish to acknowledge the National Archives at Kew in London, who have made information available. Finally we would like to thank Joe Welham for creating the front cover image and the final title of the book.

Authors' Note

We have for more than 25 years continued to gather information about Commander L.K.P. Crabb and have have quoted from contemporary sources. In some cases accounts are woven together, in much the same way that a documentary film, enables the viewer to 'experience' events through participants narratives. These personal interviews, documents, books, articles and letters provide first-hand information, often set down while events were fresh in mind. They also offer personal insights no longer available.

Throughout the research into the man and his secret activities, we encountered events that emanated from the establishment to the extent that whilst researching the first book, *Frogman Spy*, we and witnesses were subjected to surveillance, telephone tapping and mail interception.

There have, throughout the years, been television programmes which have touched on the Commander Crabb disappearence as well as a number of publications. Much of the material used was first researched and published in our book *Frogman Spy*. Examples include the Karlovy Vary Sanatorium, the change to *his* headstone at Portsmouth and the link to the *Spetsnaz* (Soviet Special Forces) as well as the use of copyright photographs. In most of these cases we have never been referenced as the source of the material even though anybody researching the subject will readily find *Frogman Spy* on the web.

Following the publication of *Frogman Spy,* we made our debut on television, radio and newspapers, with particular focus on the south coast. The coverage was very wide and detailed and resulted in long queues at a well-known high street book shop, which did not have copies of the book. Most interesting was the fact that the book was not listed on the bookshop computerised ordering system. We received telephone calls identifying that people were seeking copies of the book, but none were available. One call came from a magazine who ran an article and wanted copies to sell through their bookshop. They could not obtain copies. The book was published by WH Allan, a respected publisher and there were copies available for distribution. We received more information highlighting the problem from Dr Svoboda, who had provided assistance and told us:

" ... *Most of the people who lived in Chichester and Portsmouth in the 1950s were extremely keen to read your book and I was unable to satisfy the great demand. I was surprised that the book did not appear in the Portsmouth bookshops, as it would certainly sell very well here. Should you wish to travel to Czechoslovakia again, please do not hesitate to contact me.*
Yours very gratefully, Dr V Svoboda F.R.C.R."

So the authorities would not stop publication but they could and did initially influence those who distribute and sell books in an attempt to stop or delay its availability. However, media interest and public demand sought otherwise!

Why all the fuss? It was an incident that occurred in 1956 and should have passed into history as a major cock-up, one of many made by the security services at the time. But it was not that simple because it was so serious and the implications so great that it is to remain a state secret for 100 years. The British Government will say nothing, the CIA consider it to be a matter of national security and the Soviet Union contacts have met a wall of silence.

There are many references in the book to homosexuals and homosexuality. The attitudes portrayed are historical and relevant because during the period, homosexuality was a crime and individuals faced prosecution and prison sentences. It was considered that anybody who was homosexual could not risk being exposed to blackmail.

By design, the contents of *Frogman Spy* have been greatly expanded upon and updated for this version, so as to allow the reader to have a full understanding of events as they occurred. The result is the most factual record of the life of Commander 'Buster' Crabb, not from us as the authors, but from those who knew him.

Preface

Tis strange-but true; for truth is always strange; stranger than fiction.

Lord Byron 1788-1824

It is said that when Ian Fleming created the character James Bond he based him on the real life exploits of Commander Lionel Kenneth Philip Crabb, GM, OBE, RNVR. The comparison involved them both being Commanders in the Royal Navy, and adventurers with no intention of following the rules. Both were expendable as far as the establishment was concerned. Fleming created 'M' as the controller of Bond and the person who sent him on secret operations. Interestingly, Crabb was also controlled by 'M', who in his case was Lord Louis Mountbatten, a member of the Royal family. However, Bond always returned having got the women, but Crabb did not return and he even lost the women.

Following our first book *Frogman Spy* in 1990 there were many unanswered questions and we continued to explore the life of a unique frogman, who was highly decorated for his underwater exploits during Second World War. He was, in the true sense, an adventurer who thrived in the alien underwater world. His real claim to fame which made the front page of every national newspaper, was in his disappearance in 1956 whilst undertaking a 'spying mission' under the Soviet cruiser *Ordzhonikidze*. The ship was visiting Portsmouth at the time, carrying Premier Khrushchev and Marshal Bulganin on a goodwill visit to Britain. It was the height of the Cold War and a very politically sensitive time. Just over a year after he disappeared, a body washed up headless and handless near Portsmouth. The Establishment took charge of the body and, at an inquest, declared it to be Crabb's body. However, vital evidence was omitted and key witnesses not called. It is now known that it was not his body and he was not buried in Portsmouth at that time.

The problem for the establishment was that Crabb worked for the then head of the Royal Navy, Lord Mountbatten, who, it is said, sent Crabb on many secret missions. This was during a time when US Government security agencies alleged that Mountbatten was doing 'unofficial' business with senior officials within the Soviet Union's Communist party. This of course would be a valid reason for keeping the whole Crabb story secret for 100 years.

Crabb has been described as a nobody wanting to be a somebody, who sought involvement with the ruling class and their illegal activities dabbling in the melting pot of art and currency smuggling in particular Nazi looted gold and treasure, homosexual blackmail and mysterious deaths. Crabb was certainly a frogman amongst vipers.

So what happened to Crabb? Was he captured and taken back to the Soviet Union, did he defect or, as the bizarre stories tell us, was he killed in Portsmouth by the Soviets, either by being shot by a sniper or having his throat cut whilst underwater? Was he killed by MI5? All could be classed as good James Bond material.

The reader may well consider after such a long period of time why all the interest about what the 'establishment' called an aged 'over the hill' frogman seeking a last glimpse of adventure. Well consider the legacy today when among official documents released was a hand written note identified as Top Secret and dated 24 January 1978. It identified that the authorities wanted to move documents relating to Crabb into records as a special category. The reason was determined with three criteria:

"1. *Exceptionally sensitive...disclosure of which would be contrary to the public interest on security grounds;*
2. *Contains information supplied in confidence, disclosure of which would... constitute a breach of faith;*
3. *Disclosures...could cause distress or embarrassment to living persons."*

The note concluded that the information should not be disclosed for 75 years, until 2031. We now know that the figure was extended to 100 years, meaning that the 'truth' will not be made public until 2056.

Mike and Jacqui Welham
2010

1

Agent 'X'

We never knows wot's hidden in each others heart's; and if we had glass winders there, we'd need keep the shutters up, some on us, I do assure you!
Charles Dickens 1812-70

This is a story that will not go away even though the authorities would like it to. Many have written about the mystery and most have followed the political line. However, we have not done that and, as a consequence, paid a price because throughout our research we have personally endured intercepted telephone calls, had mail tampered with and have been spied on for many years by a Government official, a spook we have named Agent X or *Crabb Watch*. When investigated, it was revealed that he was a *special person,* who claimed that he had access to military records. He claimed that, as a civilian, he had undertaken very specialised Naval diving courses and was a positively vetted Ministry of Defence contractor of many years' standing. He had investigated the Crabb affair in the 1960s interviewing anybody who had known or been involved with Crabb. As the story unfolds it will be shown that those who had offered us assistance were threatened and told not to talk to us, and there have been attempts on the lives of Sydney Knowles, Crabb's former diving partner and Gary Murray, a former Security Service operative and investigative TV researcher.

The Crabb story did not enter our lives until 1983, when Mike was visiting a military book publisher to discuss the possibility of publishing his book entitled *Combat Frogmen*. The publisher wanted to know what they would get for their money and so he was asked what topics would be included. It became very evident that the publishers wanted to include real life drama in it, without running foul of the Official Secrets Act, but if there was action and the story could be told they wanted it included. It was during this meeting that he was asked what he knew about Commander Crabb and his disappearance in 1956. At this time it was known that Crabb was essentially a wartime frogman and Mike was concentrating on the more modern aspect of underwater operations. He had to reply that he knew nothing about Commander Crabb, although he vaguely remembered the name. However, he knew people who did. Jacqui remembered hearing about his disappearance at the time, and whilst researching *Combat Frogmen* they had located photographs of Crabb at the Imperial War Museum photo library in London. We considered that there might be nothing new to add to the stories that already abounded about Crabb's dive in Portsmouth. However, it was approaching the expiration of the thirty-year rule, a period of officially enforced silence about the matter. The publisher was of the opinion that Crabb would be good for the book and asked if, through his contacts, Mike would enquire to see what, if any, information was available. They even proposed that if there were something new they would be interested in producing a separate book on the subject. If there was nothing new to add, then all would not be lost, as he could include Commander Crabb in *Combat Frogmen* anyway. It was agreed Mike should go away and review the subject and produce a detailed synopsis.

A few days after that meeting, an editor with the publishing house contacted us to explain that he had received a telephone call out of the blue from a man who said that he had a considerable amount of information about Crabb, most of which was unpublished. He had decided that he would like to use the material for the production of a book and with that in mind, sought an author with whom to collaborate on a joint venture. The editor thought that it was a remarkable coincidence and asked if he could pass on our telephone number for him to contact us. We thought that this was most opportune and readily agreed. We awaited developments.

It was only a matter of days before the man telephoned, to introduce himself as Agent X (for legal reasons we have not used the name he gave). He was, in his own words, the foremost expert on the subject of Commander Crabb and had followed the events since 1956, culminating in 1963 when he interviewed all the people concerned in the incident. He had, in fact, made a film of them telling their stories. With such vital information, he wanted to use the material in the production of a book, and therefore sought somebody with whom to collaborate. He wanted to know who we had contacted and what information we had. At that point, it was for us the beginning of research and we had little or nothing of value. He declared the next step should be a meeting and stated that he would drive up and visit us at our home, whereupon a date and time was agreed. It did not register any concern with us at this time as to why in the years between 1963, when he spoke to all of the 'witnesses', and 1985, a period of 22 years, Agent X had decided to pick that very same week to telephone the same publisher, to express his interest in writing a book about Crabb. Looking back, we initially suspected nothing untoward, after all we had no information and he said he had everything, so what was the harm in talking to him? In hindsight we would have suggested that it was not a coincidence but an interception which, as events unfolded, is just what it was. We had become the prey to our own real life spook.

At the one and only meeting we had with the man, he explained that during the 1960s he had been a filmmaker and had an interest in the subject of Crabb. He had followed the story over the years. His filming career found him involved in making military training films and he had undertaken a naval clearance diving course. This meant that he had been trained in the use of closed circuit breathing apparatus. This was interesting because such equipment was reserved for specialist military operations, and never for civilian use. It was at that point that alarm bells began to ring, because Mike knew that the only non-military people trained in the use of such equipment would have been the secret intelligence service. It was his statement about his training and use of such equipment that raised the question as to why a currently positively vetted Ministry of Defence contractor would be involved in a subject as sensitive as Commander Crabb. He did have knowledge of the diving equipment used by Royal Naval divers (frogmen). But on that Sunday morning events dictated that we watch the film, which he had brought with him along with a cine-projector.

As the film opened we were transported back in time to the mid sixties. Carnaby Street, mini skirts and hot pants opened the scene before the events surrounding that day in 1956 evolved before us. We saw and heard those who, until then, we had only read about in the limited number of books on the subject. They provided details of what they knew, which was not very much. From what we could remember of the film, it was black and white and by to-days standards very amateurish. There were no interviews with military people, only civilians. It portrayed a number of individuals describing Crabb and the last few days prior to his disappearance. The operation itself was not re-enacted, but was a monologue, "Yes I knew Commander Crabb, he often went away on diving jobs, and no, he never came back from this one". Whilst we only had the one viewing, we concluded that the film was nice to have but needed to be examined in detail. We concluded that there was nothing of real value. There was certainly nothing that we did not subsequently find disclosed in newspaper reports of the Crabb story, both immediately after the incident and in the ensuing years. We asked where the film had been shown, and were told that in Britain it was 'D' noticed, but had made the screens of other countries. This was yet another remark that gave us food for thought, for, in our opinion at the time, there was not a single item that would have stopped it from being shown. A 'D' notice would have specified that a certain item in the film be removed but not the film in its entirety, for it was seven years after the event and it gave away no secrets. Our views were to be supported in due course by Gary Murray when he watched the film as part of his investigation into the activities of Agent X.

From memory, the film lasted approximately forty-five minutes, by which time we were impressed that such a film had been made, but on the other hand, not really impressed with its contents. It provided no details of the events that followed Crabb's disappearance, which were of the greatest interest to us. When we raised the subject of Crabb having gone to Russia, Agent X declared that it was absolute rubbish and continued to state that he had died and had been buried in Portsmouth. It was perhaps his arrogance and overpowering insistance that Crabb had died and that made us more aware of the possibility that perhaps he had not. We continued to enquire as to how he thought we should proceed and again his very forceful character came to the fore and he stated that he would not discuss any proposals with us, but declared that he would contact our agent. He would determine the terms of the agreement and once that had been done, we would then exchange information, and that would enable a book to be written. It was the first and only meeting we ever had with Agent X, but not the only contact, for he was to become an integral part of our lives during the ensuing research and publication of *Frogman Spy.* He made contact with our agent on one occasion, but she was, to the best of our knowledge, never to hear from him again and we assumed that he was off to locate some 'well known' author to co-operate with, while we continued with our research.

Our first task was an attempt to locate two key figures: Pat Rose, Crabb's fiancée and Sydney Knowles, his former Second World War diving partner. We tracked down Rose, and Jacqui wrote to her seeking a meeting. That resulted in a telephone call from her and it was agreed that we would meet at her home in Bognor Regis. The following day we received a call from Agent X who asked if we knew where Rose was living. He claimed that she had moved from the address he had. We suspected that all in the garden was not rosy and said that we had not managed to locate her. The evening before we were due to travel to Bognor to meet Rose, a friend of hers telephoned to say that she had changed her mind and would not see us. There was no reason given. It was two weeks later that we received a telephone call from Rose herself who said that after some thought, she had changed her mind and decided to meet us. At her home during the first of many long interviews, we asked why she changed her mind about our meeting. We were told that a man who had interviewed and filmed her in the early 60s had arrived on her doorstep and asked if she had any up-to-date information about Crabb, and then told her that if the Welhams should contact her, she should have nothing to do with them. Initially she agreed because she feared the man, but then decided to meet with us, and from that meeting the basis of a working relationship was formed. The man who had visited Rose was Agent X.

During one telephone conversation, Rose told us that she had a tape recording of Sydney Knowles stating that the body washed up at Chichester was not that of Crabb. Before we could arrange a visit to Bognor, Agent X went to Rose's house and demanded to listen to the tape recording. A close friend of Rose's was at the house at the time and, while remaining out of sight in the kitchen, she heard everything. She told us that Rose was pressurised into playing the tape so that he could hear the content. Reluctantly she played a small part of the tape before she drew enough courage to ask him to leave. He was angry and again re-iterated that she should not give the tape to the Welhams. The only way he could have known about the tape was through telephone interception of either her telephone or ours.

We received information from a third person who had located Knowles and we asked him if he would speak to us. Because of the common bond with diving, Knowels telephoned and agreed to meet with Mike. The meeting was to be on neutral ground, at a golf club in the north of England. Knowles talked to Mike about Crabb and the tape recording and asked if he could have a copy to verify that it was his voice. Before parting, Knowels asked Mike if had ever met a filmmaker who had followed the Crabb story. Mike was intrigued at the question, and discovered that Agent X had telephoned Knowles a few days before their meeting. Knowles last saw him 1964 and was told that he should not speak to the Welhams, who were seeking information about Crabb. Knowles was more concerned as to how Agent X had found him because he had long since moved and had an ex-directory telephone number. Again it was through telephone interception. We were all being bugged!

A copy of the tape recording was made and checked before posting. When Knowles played it he found that it was blank, not the blank sound of a new, unused tape but that of one which has been used and had the contents removed from it. We made another copy, checked that it had recorded and sent it correctly stamped, addressed and by recorded delivery. He never received it. We pursued the loss with the Post Office but they failed to trace it. Knowles prepared a signed statement describing our original meeting, and that failed to pass through the postal system.

We know that Agent X had preceded our visits to both Rose and Knowles and attempted to stop them speaking to us. Both incidents with Agent X had occurred after we had made arrangements by telephone. He made the contacts more than twenty years after he had last seen them. For somebody who wanted to undertake a joint venture and write a book about Crabb, this was a strange way of going about it, unless of course his plan was to stop research and any publication. Rose summed it up in a letter to Jacqui:

"I expect that Agent X had got at him (Knowles) the day before you met, like he did with me."

Throughout a four-year period, we regularly received telephone calls from Agent X who made no moves to develop the collaboration. He always enquired as to our progress stating that if anybody did talk to us they could be breaking the official secrets act, and so he quizzed us for names and information of their whereabouts. It took no imagination to know what Agent X was and what he was doing and we christened him *'Crabb Watch'*, for it was evident that in the aftermath of Crabb's disappearance he had made contact with everybody who picked up the story.

Two other key players in the research of Crabb were Frank Goldsworthy and Gary Murray. Both proved to be invaluable in their own way. Frank Goldsworthy was a newspaperman, long retired from Fleet Street, but he had a very active memory. He had been a Naval Intelligence Officer during the Second World War and had served with Crabb. They knew each other quite well and were to meet in the post war era, when Goldsworthy was sent to cover naval matters, which involved divers. He was working for the *Daily Express* newspaper when the news of Crabb's disappearance broke and he was immediately dispatched to Portsmouth to get a story. Goldsworthy was good at his job and, with the help of a local man's knowledge of the area; they began to fill in many of the gaps. The *Express* editor saw that it was a hot story with potential and decided that a book should be produced. He passed that assignment on to the best man for the job. Goldsworthy followed the story as far as he could in Portsmouth before returning to London, where he began writing, leaving the local reporter to continue to ferret for information. He was more than surprised when the editor called him into the office to ask how the story was going and, after listening to the update, said that on orders from the top, the project was being stopped, and that nothing more was to be done, either in the writing or the investigation; the proposed book was dead. Goldsworthy told us that the directive had come from Lord Beaverbrook himself. Goldsworthy was devastated and, returning to his desk, he opened the bottom draw and dropped the unpublished pages in it. He closed the draw and so closed the Crabb story. That was until he responded to our advertisement nearly thirty years later and, at a meeting handed us those faded pages and told us to make best use of them.

Gary Murray is a private investigator who had served in the security services and was to become a very valuable colleague. His knowledge of the workings of the security service and use of electronic telephone devices, that could identify if a telephone call was being intercepted were invaluable to say the least. As we continued to undertake our research he told us on numerous occasions that his electronic device was picking up interference. That, combined with our own experiences with Rose and Knowles confirmed strange goings on, and in fact confirmed that our telephone calls were being intercepted.

Following the one and only meeting with Agent X we moved house. It was a temporary move and our phone was ex-directory. It was not long before a telephone call came asking how things were progressing. So Agent X had traced us and made contact. It was about two years before we found the house we wanted and moved. On the day the removal company loaded up our belongings, we told our neighbour where we were going and she was instructed to tell nobody. However, as the removal lorry moved down the road and round the corner with us following in our car, a man went to our old house and asked the new incumbents where we had moved to. They did not know. All they knew was that contact could be made through our neighbour. He went to our neighbour's house and demanded to know where we had moved to. He claimed he was an insurance agent and that he had to speak to us or our new house would not be insured. She was intimidated by the man and concerned about the insurance so she gave him our details. Our first telephone call at the new house was from her explaining what had happened. The second telephone call was from Agent X just wanting to let us know that he knew where we were.

Overcoming the obstacles as they arose we eventually produced a manuscript that could be delivered to the publisher. With only the last chapter to complete, we received a copy of an internal memo that clearly showed that they were very pleased with what they had been given. The editorial staff had determined that because of the potentially contentious nature of the subject they wanted it vetted by their legal advisers. We had no problems with that and agreed that it would be better to resolve any issues before going to print. In due course Mike was called to an *editorial* meeting with the publisher's lawyers. In normal circumstances this would have been a routine process, but nothing about this story is normal.

Mike was faced with an efficient legal machine whose aim was, without any shadow of doubt, to discredit the contents of the manuscript. The lawyers declared that the contents were not acceptable and the information provided by the many witnesses was not valid and, therefore, the publishing contract was null and void. Mike sat holding the internal memo whilst listening to the destructive comments. A new publisher was sought and on the 9 August 1988 W.H. Allen agreed to go ahead, but there was a major problem in that the manuscript was still held by the original publisher who would neither go to print nor release us from their contract. With no movement on the release of our manuscript we discussed the matter with Gary Murray. At the time he was undertaking some controversial research for a TV company. It was decided that a direct approach was best and Murray requested to speak to the man who was designated our editorial director.

He told him that he was undertaking research for a major television company (which was true) and had heard about a book based on Commander Crabb's disappearance in 1956, which was being held out of circulation, and were they (the publisher) prepared to go in front of the cameras to discuss it. The reply was to the effect that they did have the rights to a manuscript, which they were not going to publish, and yes, they still held those rights. The editorial director declined to get involved and became concerned that the publisher could be implicated with any stoppage of the book. He said that it was a matter for their legal advisors and as publishers they abided by their advice. Murray asked if he could bring a film crew to the publisher's office to undertake an interview. The editor made it clear that an interview was not acceptable. Murray telephoned the editor the following day and said that he was on his way to his office with a film crew. The editor stated that they no longer had the manuscript as it was being released back to the authors. Events then moved rapidly to a situation where the manuscript was released.

Within a matter of days, following the manuscript being handed over to the new publisher, WH Allan, Agent X telephoned us to renew the acquaintance and ask how we were progressing. In particular he wanted to know if we had found anybody to provide us with any information and when we would publish. He claimed again that he alone had all of the information and everybody else was dead, but he did not raise the issue of collaboration in producing a book. Presumably he would have been briefed as to the situation with the original publisher and just wanted to see if we would reveal anything.

Murray had never met or spoken to Agent X and so everything he knew about him had come from us, the authors. However, he knew that the events surrounding our investigations into Crabb and the legal problems with the original publisher could be identified as interference from a high level in the Establishment. However, after his car was tampered with and the failed attempt on Knowles's life (see below), he became determined to find out who and what Agent X was and who he worked for. Murray, through his own judgment, was convinced that Agent X was a spook, a Government agent, and in his words, not a very good one.

Murray's approach was to phone Agent X with the cover story that he was researching for a film about Crabb. The response from Agent X was cautious but as Murray continued to enquire as to what he knew about Crabb, Agent X suddenly offered his services to assist Murray for £200 per day.

There followed a series of telephone interviews with Murray, where Agent X declared that he had met everybody and recorded them. He said that among them were at least twenty Navy people who knew and worked with Crabb. Was this to be a dramatic new revelation? He continued to say that they told him everything, but there were no cameras or recording machines, and they would walk in the open where they could not be overheard or bugged. Agent X was saying that he, as a civilian, walked and talked with serving military people, who knew or were part of the Crabb operation, possibly Britain's greatest spy mystery. The reader must draw their own conclusion as to why those who, aledgedly having played an active part in Britain's most controversial underwater frogman operation, would speak in detail to Agent X, a civilian, and for what purpose? He then declared that most of them were still working under the Official Secrets Act, and that their information would remain with them until they died. It is worthy of note that by speaking about the operation to Agent X it would have meant that they had breached the Official Secrets Act anyway Murray was astounded at these revelations, particularly from what was believed to be a positively vetted Government contractor.

The reader must remember that we are referring to an old, over the hill former naval frogman off on some frolic. There was, according to the establishment, nothing to hide, so why would the authors have to pay people or buy them villas? Perhaps this is an indication that the truth warrants such payments for information.

Murray asked Agent X how he had managed to get on a Naval diving course, because he was a civilian at that time. Agent X replied that he was a *special person*. This clearly shows the absurdity of the man, who in one breath talks about the secrecy of naval diving and the Crabb operation, and how none of the naval divers will talk, but in another breath talks of resurrecting them for the *proposed* film because they liked him.

We all agreed that he had been trained in the use of naval diving equipment and techniques, outside of the normal military system. He was, to use his own words, a *special person*. He had throughout the years maintained a *Crabb Watch*, and contacted anybody who was investigating the Crabb story and offered assistance. He said he wanted to collaborate with the Welhams in writing a book, but that was a sham with no foundation.

Murray directed a statement at Agent X to the effect that there was an inference that he was a Government spook who was going around sabotaging everything. Agent X asked what was meant by 'sabotaging'. Murray said he would replace 'sabotaging' with 'monitoring'. Agent X seemed to be quite impressed with that and stated that he had always served his Queen and Country fairly honestly. Murray said that he understood that his diving instructor was still alive, and if that was the case, could he speak to him. Agent X was emphatic in the fact that he could not, as he did not want to involve other people, and that he did not have to qualify what he had done or who he had done it with.

Murray clarified the situation by stating that he was pursuing a story by speaking to a person who was an MoD employee, agent or contractor. He said that under the Official Secrets Act there is a question mark against the relationship that had developed between him and Agent X. He stressed the point by pointing out that Agent X had told him things that could qualify him for breaching the Act as a positively vetted person. It was a very indignant Agent X who wanted to know what he was supposed to have told Murray. He said that he had been offered information which was not 'off the record'. Agent X demanded to know what information. Murray described the fact that he had spoken to the entire Royal Navy diving team who he said had dived with Crabb, the team that in official circles did not exist because there was no *official operation*, according to the Prime Minister at the time. Agent X offered the defence that he was researching material for his film and there were a lot of people who told him things. Murray agreed but added that he, Agent X, was not a lot of people and by his own admission was somebody *very special*. Again, Agent X was defensive and now did a 'U' turn by saying that he was not *special*.

Then, in a twist, Agent X told Murray that he would not be

surprised if the telephone conversations had been taped and, in fact, would have been surprised if they had not, and he concluded that everybody did it. He then clarified the situation by saying that if a story were to be produced he would see his security advisor. He thought that his security advisor would consider that it was another of those media, sensational, scare-mongering events that rise and cause problems for a short period of time. Murray asked why it was that the equipment that he had connected to his telephone showed a decrease of power in the line indicating an interception system. Agent X stated that he did not have any recording equipment.

Murray asked him why he spent the majority of the time away from the address that he gave, to which Agent X asked how Murray knew how much time he spent at the house or away from it. Murray was direct and replied that he had arranged for the house to be kept under surveillance. He said that he had looked in through the windows and checked the dustbins to find a mass of convenience food packaging, both providing evidence that the house was not lived in as a 'home', a fact confirmed by the neighbours. Agent X was taken aback. Murray continued and told him that he did not believe that he lived at the address, which was a private house in a residential part of the country. He continued to say that he lived a lifestyle of an undercover agent, and that he conducted himself the way that Murray had done for several years while working for the security services.

It was to be the end of all of the authors contact with Agent X who we all agreed had been planted to monitor the activities of those researching the Crabb story as well as those who were able to provide information. However, others were not so lucky.

During the week of 12 March 1990, Murray experienced rough running of his Fiat Croma Car and took it to the supplying dealers, Savage & Sons of Englefield Green, Surrey, for a mechanic to examine it. The vehicle was two years old and had been regularly serviced by the garage, so Murray thought that it was a small problem. When he collected the vehicle, the Fiat trained motor engineer asked if he had any enemies, as the mixture control nut that holds the fuel line in place, and is part of the automatic fuel system, had been sawn through with a hacksaw. The objective of making such a cut would be for the fuel line to vibrate out and spray petrol onto the hot engine. Murrays's words spelt it out: "When driving at speed, the engine is hot, and with petrol sprayed onto it, you go up in smoke, in just one big fireball." Murray was given the nut, and it clearly showed, even to the untrained eye, that it was a saw cut and not a hairline fracture.

Murray made a sworn affidavit which states:

"I have identified a Ministry of Defence contractor (Agent X) who appears to be working under cover as a filmmaker when, in fact, his real role is a deep cover intelligence operative monitoring the activities of anyone interested in the Crabb / Blunt affair. I have collected considerable evidence illuminating the covert activities of this individual, whose conduct is dedicated to harassing and discrediting witnesses who have been helpful in the Crabb / Blunt investigation. It is significant to note that the trouble with the motor car only materialised after I became aware of my research into the Crabb link with Blunt and other homosexual Russian spies in London."

The incident was reported to the police and on 24 March 1990 a Detective Inspector and a Detective Sergeant visited Murray at his home and took a statement. They then asked him to withdraw his report, which he declined to do, and they departed, taking the nut for forensic examination and testing. On 5 April 1990 the Detective Sergeant called at Murray's home and explained that the forensic department had reported that the nut was not cut but had developed a 'fault'. He did not return the nut so that an independent test could be made but declared that Murray would have to apply to the Chief Constable and request its return. This was done and on 3 May 1990 the Detective Inspector telephoned to say that it was impossible to return the whole nut as it was cut up during forensic examination. The fact is, the Fiat trained engineer stated that it was a hacksaw cut and the photographic evidence shows it was not a fatigue crack, which would be difficult to see, but a wide, straight cut, the same size as a junior hacksaw blade. However, a forensic scientist made an examination and determined that the nut had a fracture that was probably corrosion, but could not identify any corrosive material, but equally important was the fact that the nut was not available for return to Murray for an independent examination.

While Murray had problems with an attempt on his life in England, in April of the same year Sydney Knowles was also subject to an attempt on his life. It began with a long telephone conversation with Mike about the contents of *Frogman Spy* and he said that, while the story was for the most part correct, there were some details that were not quite right, and he duly pointed these out. However, he said that there were things missing that he had not wanted to say before, but now he would make the revelations. While he had said many things over the telephone, what he now had to say had to be done face to face and that meant either we visited Spain or Knowles came to England.

The first real concern came when we became aware that Knowels's telephone was tapped. While Mike was speaking to him, Knowles had to leave the telephone to answer his front door. Because nobody spoke for a while, an English voice came onto the line and said, "Have they finished." Another English voice replied, "I don't know, I'm just routing it through Lyon." The first voice responded, "Ok, I'll leave the line open".

Now, the mention of Lyon means one thing, our telephone conversation was being intercepted by the world famous organisation INTERPOL, but why? INTERPOL, whose correct full name is 'The International Criminal Police Organisation' is the world's largest international police organisation, and comprises some 186-member countries. It was created in 1923 and facilitates cross-border police co-operation, and supports and assists all organisations, authorities and services whose mission is to prevent or combat international crime. INTERPOL's constitution prohibits any intervention or activities of a political, military, religious or racial character. The hub of the organisation is located in Lyon, France, and operates 24 hours a day, 365 days a year.

Each INTERPOL member country maintains a National Central Bureau (NCB) staffed by national law enforcement officers. The role of an NCB is to participate in all of INTERPOL's activities, providing constant and active co-operation with overseas investigations and the location and apprehension of fugitives. Member countries national police agencies provide officers, with specialists in terrorism, fugitives, high-tech crimes, or trafficking in human beings, drugs or stolen property. Officers working in the NCB's remain employed by their national administrations.

Each NCB is connected to INTERPOL's secure police communications network which enables them to share crucial information on criminals and criminal activities 24 hours a day, seven days a week. They can search and cross-check data in a matter of seconds, with direct access to databases of information on suspected terrorists, wanted persons, fingerprints, DNA profiles, lost or stolen travel documents, stolen motor vehicles, stolen works of art, etc.

Ah! Is this the missing link? Stolen works of art.

Neither the authors nor Knowles could by any stretch of the imagination be linked to any criminal activities especially as INTERPOL's mission is to prevent or combat international crime and prohibits any intervention or activities of a political or military nature. We know that the telephone call was intercepted and, from the evidence that we were to gather, we have to presume they were listening for any names of those who, in the past, may have been involved with stolen works of art.

However, telephone interception was not enough, and events became very serious when knowels had left his Spanish home at ten thirty on a clear Sunday morning and joined the many people who were out and about. For Knowles it was a normal day, although since the sabotage of Gary Murray's car, he had taken care to be watchful and to check his own vehicle. In no hurry, he crossed the road at a pedestrian crossing, fully aware of Spanish driving standards. He was halfway across when he became aware of a small, mustard yellow coloured van bearing down on him at high speed. In those split seconds he realised that the vehicle was being driven deliberately at him. Although then 68 years of age, Knowels was remarkably fit and agile, and it was this fact alone that enabled him to jump and roll clear. In those moments of recovery when he was lying on the ground, the van skidded to a halt and then reversed, again at high speed, straight towards the prone Knowles.

Again his awareness and sharp reflexes allowed him to roll clear and get to safety. But after failure of the second attempt, an individual got out of the van, ran to Knowels, who was still lying on the ground, and grabbed him by the lapels and said in Spanish, "Be careful, be careful, you understand, this is a warning." He then let Knowles go and ran back to the van, as did a second man who was the lookout and had been standing on the pavement close to the crossing during the entire event. The van, then departed at great speed. Although there were some twenty witnesses to the whole event, nobody took the vehicle's number, they were too shocked by what they had seen. There was one witness in particular, who was the wife of Knowles next-door neighbour Colonel Emica Enesfo, who wanted to take the matter to the police, but Knowles declined, knowing that this was beyond the scope of the Colonel and his wife's understanding and that of the local police force. The perpetrators of the attempt against his life were a law unto themselves, directed by a higher authority and at the time the best that we could do was to obtain a statement from the most credible witness. The English translation states:

"I was walking in the company of Mr.. S. J. Knowles on Calle Las Mercedes, Torremolinos, Spain. As we approached the pedestrian crossing he was a few metres ahead of me. The road was clear of traffic at that moment and he commenced to cross. Suddenly a yellow van came accelerating round the corner at very high speed and seemingly steered straight at him. Mr.. Knowles leapt

clear but fell onto the floor. The van braked violently to a halt and then went into reverse in an attempt to run over him, but he rolled clear. The driver then leapt out, bent down and grasped him by the lapels of his coat. He was speaking to Mr.. Knowles but I was unable to hear the brief conversation. Several people saw the incident but in the panic did not get the registration of the van before it drove away. In my opinion what I witnessed was a possible attempt to run down Mr.. Knowles.

Signed:
Maria Dolores Sanches Eznarriaga Rodriganez de Crepso
April 12 1990."

Knowles flew to London's Gatwick Airport where Murray and Mike met him and, for more than four hours in a hotel room, they talked over the new revelations, double checking and cross referencing, all of which was recorded on tape.

In an effort to reduce the threat against Knowles it was arranged for him to be interviewed by the media. An article appeared in the *Sunday Telegraph* on 6 May 1990. Whilst it mentioned the attempt upon his life, it was very low key and the so-called *Crabb experts* who remained solidly with the political line were given priority and dismissed Knowles version of events and set about discrediting his revelations, which were only revealed in part. The *experts* who condemned Knowles, could offer no constructive evidence, and there was no attempt to check the allegations that he made. The cover up continued even after a bungled attempt to kill Knowles.

* * *

Evolving from the publication of *Frogman Spy* was a strange twist to the story, when the authors received a letter from a former East German who, prior to the reunification, had escaped the Communist state system to live in the West. He had read every spy book that he could obtain; *Frogman Spy* was one of them and although he did not have any research experience he offered to assist us. He chose *Romeo* as a code name. With information in the UK a closed door, it was possible that the Eastern bloc could reveal important information. He knew nothing about diving but it had been reported that Crabb had been seen at an East German base, where he was said to have instructed a team of special frogmen. Romeo was to undertake research in both Germany and Czchechoslovakia.

There are very few events that have been placed under the 100-year rule, which means that in official terms the facts of the incident cannot be revealed for that period. The events surrounding Crabb are deemed so serious that information is withheld for 100 years. This alone is crucial because only activities involving Northern Ireland or Royalty find themselves in the 100-year category. This story is not connected to the troubles of Northern Ireland and so it leaves the only other option. The question falls back to what involvement Royalty played in the events. Is it Lord Louis Mountbatten, the First Sea Lord, to whom Crabb reported and who had lunch with the Prime Minister prior to his speech in Parliament when he said that it was not in the country's interest to disclose what had happened.

There is a link to the USA in the Crabb story, so we made an application to the CIA and FBI for information under the Freedom of Information Act. In the fullness of time a large box of paper arrived from the FBI. Mike had to go and collect it from the delivery company. Standing amid a group of others waiting to collect parcels Mike heard his name called and the man at the counter produced a parcel from the US Federal Bureau of Investigation. Upon the summons all eyes turned to look. Opening the box and examining the pages, it showed that the FBI had exhausted all the black marker pens that could have been available in the USA. What was left on the pages that could be read and was of the vaguest interest amounted to six pages and that was from a total of some 1,500 pages. Clearly the FBI had information about Crabb and/or Mountbatten, but was not willing to share it. The CIA sent nothing and just said that: "It was in the interest of US National Security not to make available any documentation for Crabb and/or Mountbatten". Applications to the KGB for information remain unanswered and a former KGB official acting on our behalf attempted to search for information but failed to make progress. In fact every contact we made with requests for official information, even under Freedom of Information Act's drew a blank. Then a former Soviet Admiral involved with military diving contacted us and was keen to help. This was great news and so we gave him the essential information to enable him to make enquiries. After a period of time and follow up communication he replied to say that he could not help. When we visited Russia he was unable to meet with us. A lady who did Russian translation for us had good contacts in Russia and we placed advertisements in newspapers and magazines searching for anybody who could help all to no avail. In the UK the Freedom of Information Act allowed requests for the information about Crabb and the incident to be made available. Some was forthcoming from the repository at Kew but one file had been sent to the Ministry of Defence. Upon application for access to the file we were informed that it was a file that had been close to asbestos. Along with many other files it had been sealed in bags and removed to an undisclosed location while officials decided what to do about them.

A report in the *Daily Telegraph* of 25 October 2004 revealed, that up to 10 million pages of vital military secrets have been rendered unusable by exposure to asbestos. Experts say the contamination threatens the operation of the Freedom of Information Act. The 63,000 files include many official versions of events. A decontamination expert said the cost of cleaning the files would run into tens of millions of pounds and could take years to complete. The Ministry of Defence says the files have been removed from the basement of the old War Office building in Whitehall to a warehouse in West London while it works out how to deal with them. Under the Freedom of Information Act, which came into force on 1 January 2005, all such files can be subject to requests by members of the public. Campaigners for open Government fear that the ministry will now be able to delay answering such requests. Historians who have asked to see some of the files under less sweeping open Government codes have been told it is impossible and that the ministry cannot say when normal procedures will be resumed. Under the Freedom of Information Act the ministry is allowed only 20 working days before having to say whether a researcher can get particular files. A ministry spokesman said:

"The immediate concern of those responsible for the records has been to protect the health and safety of staff and others. Therefore the records have been treated as potentially contaminated with asbestos and sealed into plastic sacks which were then packed into crates"

Prof Peter Hennessey, of Queen Mary's College, London, an expert in Whitehall secrecy, said:

"These are the crown jewels of the Cold War generation and we owe it to that generation of people who did many serious and secret things for their country to get this stuff out."

The ministry said that documents would not be destroyed unless they had been transferred to 'another medium', such as scanned into computers or microfilmed for permanent preservation at the National Archives. A source at the National Archives said:

"People are understandably suspicious because the Government generally and the MoD in particular do not have a very good record in handling secrets".

You can say that again!

2

Nazi Looted Art and Treasure

I suppose that writers should, in a way feel flattered by the censorship laws. They show a primitive fear and dread at the fearful magic of print.

John Mortimer 1923 -

By the beginning of the 1970s Nigeria had just endured a bloody civil war. The battered offshore oil fields became the focus of much effort to get production flowing and money exchanged. Mike was a diver and with two others embarked on a large oil tanker which was permanently moored in position off the coast. Oil to flowed from an onshore terminal and filled the tanks of the ship. The oil would then be pumped to other tankers, which visited at regular intervals. It was an ongoing process which passed the oil cargo to the ports of Europe or wherever the demand was made. Mike, as a member of the three-man dive team, were tasked with diving on the underwater pipes and control valves. It was the underwater element that transported the oil from the shore to the tanker. The team also checked the underwater inlets and outlets of the tanker and removed any marine growth.

The crew of the tanker were German and life aboard was quite formal. The German merchant mariners were disciplined and operated more like a military organisation than a civilian one. Whilst the crew were divided into officers and men, divers were just the *Englanders*.

They did their job and kept out of the way of those running the ship. The evening meal was a fairly formal event and everybody knew their place in the hierarchy, apart from the divers. They were placed away from the top table and shared one with the engine room oilers and deckhands who were, in the eyes of those on the top table, only just above them in the pecking order. Sitting at the table was one of the engine room crew, a Bavarian, and seemingly not a proper German. He spoke excellent English, so he could tell them what was happening.

Having undertaken a dive, they were basking in the sun when told that at the evening meal they were required to be more formal in attire. Ties would be worn as well as jackets. There was a problem as there was not a proper pair of trousers, shirt, tie or jacket between them. That said, they would do their best to conform. At the back of the room they joined the table where the crewmembers wore black trousers, white shirts and ties. All very smart. Once everybody was at their seat the captain and officers entered the room and went to their seats. They wore uniforms. Remembering that some of the senior members of the crew had served in the Second World War, it was not strange that they wore medals.

Glancing around the room, Mike became aware that many of the younger men were wearing the medals of their fathers. The captain gave a command and everybody stood. He then gave a toast and the crew raised their glasses in salute, a salute that was only ever seen in war films and news programmes about the war. Among the medals worn, those around the necks were the Iron Cross in its varied forms. There were more toasts and then the singing of 'Deutschland Ueber Alles'. They felt out of place, not just by their lack of dress code but the celebration we were privy to. The meal was a noisy affair and was, in effect, a sort of club where we could look in, but were not members.

It was evident that the Bavarian engineer was not really part of the gathering either and he was going through the motions so as to keep out of trouble. When the opportunity arose, Mike asked what the celebration was all about. When he was sure nobody was listening, he explained that in Germany there were those who kept the spirit of Nazi Germany alive. They celebrated certain dates that were important in the Third Reich. Some of the senior members of the crew had served in the war and wore their medals, while younger men wore those of their fathers who had not survived or had passed away. What Mike was being told and from what he had seen, the Nazi Party was alive and kicking, albeit in some form of underground movement. Mike was told that the party had money and that much of it was from the spoils of war, which had been looted and secreted away for the future. He was told that Bavaria, Austria and Switzerland were places where valuables were secreted, hidden from outsiders who sought its whereabouts. This was very intriguing and so the question of where such valuables might be found became a serious question. Caves, forests and lakes was the answer. Before the subject could really be explored, the tanker's second in command, who had been giving them the evil eye, walked over and spoke to the Bavarian. Not speaking German Mike did not understand what was said, but it was evident from the tone of the voice that the order was not to talk to us. Once the officer had gone the Bavarian confirmed their thoughts and, despite further questions over following days, he valued his job and probably his life and would say nothing more on the subject. It was to be a few years before the question of Nazi loot and lakes were the focus of Mike's conversations.

On 3 February 1997 Britain, France, and the United States agreed to freeze their remaining stores of looted Nazi gold bars, which were turned over to the Allies at the end of the Second World War. The gold at that time had an estimated value of $68 million and was collected from Switzerland, Sweden, and several other nations as part of a post-war reparations settlement. The gold bars are actually stored in the vaults of the U.S. Federal Reserve Bank in New York and the Bank of England in London. The frozen assets are what remains of the original 337 metric tons of gold collected from secret Nazi accounts, and are intended as the basis of a fund to compensate Holocaust victims who have unsuccessfully claimed for years that Jewish assets are still illegally tied up in Swiss banks and elsewhere.

A British Foreign Office report entitled 'Nazi Gold' accuses Swiss banks of accepting Nazi-tainted gold expropriated from persecuted Jews during World War II. It reinforces information contained in U.S. documents that indicate collaboration between Swiss bankers and the Third Reich in a type of money laundering plot. There is no doubt that Swiss banks received looted gold from the Nazis. So the Nazi gold scandal adds substance to the fact that the 'neutral' Swiss co-operated with the Nazis in accepting tainted money.

The Swiss Government-mandated publication of some 1,800 dormant Swiss bank accounts opened before the end of World War II, made the banks' previous reluctant efforts look even worse than before. In some cases the new estimated amounts of possible Holocaust victim deposits was double that of the earlier estimates. A list of inactive Swiss bank accounts was published and Switzerland's top three banks admitted that the amount of deposits in dormant accounts from the Nazi era was much higher than reported earlier.

The gathering of the illegal treasure came about as the Nazis ravaged various parts of Europe and senior military and political figures organised the looting of Jewish and other families and took their valuables. They attacked banks, depositories and art collections, in fact anything of value. They stole jewellery and even gold teeth from the victims they gassed and burned. It was packaged up and returned to Germany. If it was gold it was melted down and used for paying for the continuation of the war. However, as the war progressed and it became apparent that Germany was not going to win, a lot of the senior Nazis decided that they needed to have a nest egg outside Germany so that when the time came they could make good their escape and have a source of money. The hard line Nazis wanted to keep the movement going so that it could rise again with a Fourth Reich.

The stocks of gold and other valuable items were put in containers and moved to Bavaria or out of Germany. A lot went to Austria, where it was hidden. However, it is claimed that there is still a large amount that has not been recovered. This means that there probably was and still is a lot of ill-gotten treasure, stored and hidden in parts of Austria and Switzerland.

As the Allied advance pushed on against the German army and the Allies closed in on the German capital, Nazi officials decided to move the remaining contents of the Reichsbank to Oberbayern in southern Bavaria. There, in the mountains, the Nazis hoped to hold out and try to regroup. At least nine tons of gold were sent to Oberbayern along with bags of foreign currency and coins. This treasure, including 730 gold bars, was thought to be hidden around Walchensee. At the end of the war the U.S. military were able to find and account for $11 million of that final hoard. However, over $3 million was never found. Some small portion of it might have been smuggled out of the country by escaping Nazi officials, but what happened to the rest of the missing gold?

The link to Switzerland became an interesting one because following the work in Nigeria, Mike was on a commercial diving job in the North Sea where one of the dive team members was a Swiss National. There are many hours that pass where divers wait around during operations for some form of activity. If a diver is down working the others are on the surface waiting, as there may be a requirement to send down tools or an under water camera or even to recover the working divers. During these periods of time divers stand about and talk, discussing various topics. It was during one of these discussions that Mike's Swiss colleague raised the question of searching for underwater treasure. This was considered to be a very hit and miss business with no guarantee of finding anything. When the subject was raised Mike immediately thought of sunken wrecks at sea and the complexities of obtaining information, searching for, and recovering the treasure.

However, Mike's Swiss colleague spoke of treasure or loot that had been dumped not in the sea, but in lakes in Switzerland. He went on to explain that the Nazis had aledgedly, during the World War II removed valuables from within Germany. They were taken covertly across the border into Switzerland and deposited in lakes for safe storage.

If it had been in Austria it would have been more appropriate, as it had been well known for a long time that the Nazis had used the lakes to hide treasures looted by them during their rampage through Europe. The objective being that their loot would remain safe until they could get back and recover it. At the time Mike had never thought about Switzerland being a place to look for such things, as the country had been neutral during the Second World War. Of course it is now known that gold and art treasures were removed from Nazi Germany, taken into Switzerland and deposited into bank vaults for future use.

Mike's colleague had researched this subject over a period of time, locating newspaper articles and any other sources of information that he could obtain. Remember, in the mid 1970s there was no Internet to search, computers were a luxury, and mobile phones were almost the size of a public telephone box. It was not a question that a trip to a Swiss library would immediately provide an answer to. Direct questions about looted Nazi treasure would be unwise so it was a case of identifying, as best he could, that looted treasure was submerged in lakes in Switzerland. It's a well-known fact now, that there were Swiss Nationals and others in the country who were sympathetic to the Nazi cause. This enabled assistance to be given to those who wanted to hide the appropriated treasures, for a fee of course. In the 1970s it was not public knowledge.

The discussions held in the 1970s, in the middle of the North Sea, focused on how much loot was submerged in the lakes and what it would consist of. Gold bars in bullion form and jewellery would be the easiest to hide underwater. Mike's colleague told him that, having researched the subject over many years, he was able to say, and show through items of evidence, that in the period after the war there had been mysterious goings on at some of the lakes closest to the German border. It was not unknown for divers or frogmen to be observed going under water and recovering boxes. Mike had not begun researching the life of Crabb at this time and so no connection was made to what was being discussed.

It was all fascinating stuff and would no doubt make a very good film plot, but the conversation towards the end of a two week trip got more interesting when Mike's colleague asked if he would join him in a search for any treasure that might remain in the lakes. When confronted with this, there were some very obvious questions that had to be asked. The only evidence they had were vague locations and the conspiracy theories that were in the newspapers. But what about the authorities? For example, would they go to the Swiss Government and say they wanted to dive in lakes to look for Nazi treasure? The alternative was not to tell anybody and do it covertly. If they did it covertly and the authorities found out, how would they view the situation? The big question was what to do with any treasure that might be found. Assuming they did come across a box and manage to recover it and it was filled with gold that had come out of European countries, who owned it? It was known that the gold teeth and other items of personal jewellery had been melted down to form gold bullion blocks and marked with a Nazi stamp. It brought home the fact that there was a moral background to this venture as well as a legal one. They concluded that it would be an adventure and if they did find something there would obviously be lot of interest in such a story and any recovered valuables would be handed over to the Authorities. In the meantime, secrecy was the word.

Mike's colleague went back to Switzerland, where he spent the next two weeks gathering as much information as he could. It had to be done very carefully because too many enquiries might cause somebody to start asking questions. When they met up a few weeks later there was more research material; there were quite detailed maps of lake areas and he had managed to take photographs of a lake where loot might be located.

It was identified that at one lake in particular the local authorities had put a 'No Camping' sign to stop visitors from camping there. It had been a well-known site for setting up tents and spending some time in this very beautiful and tranquil surrounding of the Swiss mountains. However, there had been a decided push to try and stop members of the public frequenting the area. Most important was that the lake in question was close to the German border.

The lake, having been identified, would have required access by a road or a track for a vehicle in 1944/5. In all probability, it would have been a military type vehicle or possibly a horse and cart. It would have been used to carry the containers so it they could be taken to the water's edge and then dumped into the water. Putting such a heavy weight into the water would not have been a major concern. An inflated inner tube from a lorry tyre could be tied to a box to enable it to be floated out before puncturing the tube, allowing the box to sink. Getting a box of loot into a lake would have been done covertly because the last thing they wanted was the population of a village standing on the banks of the lake watching the nefarious activities going on.

Mike and his colleague would need to be able to go to this lake and set themselves up with diving equipment. They needed to be able to get there covertly, going at night so that they could access the water. If they did find anything they would need to be able to get a vehicle close to the edge of the lake so as to drag it out. Working at night would immediately reduce the posibility of being spotted by anybody, but it would not totally eliminate the risk. They would need somewhere to fill their breathing air cylinders. They had decided that, wherever the location was, they would not be able to use a boat as that would be difficult to handle and easily detected. One report and the local police would be round rather quickly to find out what was going on.

By the mid 1970s roads and tracks in Switzerland could have changed from those of 1945, so they looked at an older map of the area. It identified tracks and roadways with access to various parts of the lake. The whole project was a bit hit and miss, so they would search by setting up an underwater grid so they knew the area searched. They could then spread the search out to a wider area.

They identified from snippets in the newspapers one area as being a good location. A more recent article was about people being by the water, setting up tents and the police arriving and moving them on for no apparent reason. They identified a campsite where they could set up tents well clear of the lake. They would drive to and from the lake on a daily basis. Once everything was in place they just had to set a date for the dives to take place.

Mike's colleague returned from Switzerland concerned that all was not right. He produced some newspaper cuttings. The story was dramatic; four people had arrived at the lake and set up a tented camp, and for all intents and purposes were four tourists holidaying in Switzerland. They had a car, which was parked close to the tents, and their diving equipment, including spare cylinders containing compressed air for underwater diving. It was in the exact location that had been identified for Mike and his colleague to undertake their first search.

The focus of the story was that the four people had arrived at the lake and set up camp. Locals in the area had seen them. However, it was noticed that the people seemed to have disappeared. Because nobody was seen at the camp the alarm was raised and the police were called. The police found two tents, clothes, diving equipment, food and a car, but there were no individuals to be seen anywhere. There was no information as to the identification of the missing people. They could have been Swiss nationals or people that had travelled into Switzerland on holiday to dive in the lake.

The police searched the area, but apparently nobody did an underwater search for any bodies. The four were not in their diving suits, which were neoprene fabric wet suits, as they were still by the tents. It was concluded that these people hadn't disappeared whilst diving, but it was not known if they disappeared while swimming. It was a bizarre story because they just suddenly vanished. All efforts to try and locate these people drew a blank and over the space of a couple of weeks nothing had been found.

This stopped Mike's planned venture. Clearly something strange had happened and with four people on the missing list, the police would obviously be monitoring the area. Local people may be looking at the water's edge to see if they could find or spot any bodies. Meanwhile the tents, equipment and vehicle were removed from the location.

They monitored the situation over a couple of months and when the press interest diminished Mike's colleague went back to the area to have a look round. They assumed at this stage that the four divers had gone to the lake location for the same purpose and that they were searching for something underwater. As with all things in life the job came to an end and his colleague disappeared off. Mike went to another job. They did not keep in touch. Some years were to pass before Switzerland, looted treasure and diving was to raise its head again.

3

The Real 'James Bond'

I view this able and energetic man with some detachment. He is loyal to his own career but only incidentally to anything or anyone else.

Hugh Dalton 1887-1962

Our hero's family line is provided in a brief profile and shows that, in 1878 William James Crabb was the owner of a corn merchants at 210 Kingsland Road where he moved into the house with his wife Lavinia, their children Lavinia, Arthur and Hugh, and two servants. Just six years later William Crabb died at the age of 46. Lavinia would pass away 5 years later, aged 51. He left the children when they were 16, 14 and 7 years of age. Both are buried in Stoke Newington's Abney Park Cemetery. It's not known who raised the young Hugh Crabb following his parents' deaths in the 1880s or what became of the family business, or whether there was any significant inheritance passed on to the children. However, what is known is that when Hugh eventually married Beatrice Goodall in 1906, his occupation was described as 'traveller'. Hugh was eventually listed as missing or killed in action in World War One.

Lionel Kenneth Philip Crabb was born on the 28 January 1909 at 4 Greyswood Street in Streatham, South West London. He was only five years old when his father was killed, and his mother never re-married.

His playmates in his younger years were his cousins and he used to go on holidays to Eastbourne, where they stayed at the *Grand Hotel*. He told his fiancée Pat Rose that the best part of those holidays was when the man in the lift let him control it, and he spent a lot of time going up and down. He went to Brighton College but did not get on very well, and he referred to himself as the 'black sheep of the family' in so far as he was more of an adventurer, whilst his cousins followed the more orthodox professions. He made friends easily, and would talk about them to his other friends, but he rarely talked about himself. His main ambition was to go to sea, and at the age of thirteen he joined the training ship *Conway*. When he reached the age of sixteen he was apprenticed as a Merchant Navy cadet. However, Crabb did not like the formality of exams and when the vessel he was sailing on was plying between Buenos Aires and New York, he jumped ship in the USA. He was next heard of working at a petrol station in Windygap, Pennsylvania. He wrote to his mother during this period but never explained how he got there; but then there are a number of things about Crabb that are not very clear.

When Crabb returned to England in the 1930s he worked at an art studio with two friends in one of the little streets between the Strand and the River Thames. He was not an artist himself but knew the fine details of the subject and confined his talents to that of selling. To this end he grew a beard and became a renowned salesman, known as the *Admiral*. It was his job to interest prospective clients in the studios work, and to that end he was a great success.

Although Crabb was good at the job, he became bored and told his companions that he had itchy feet and needed to travel. He decided that he wanted to go to Singapore, and a short while after he departed for adventures in the Far East. He remained away for some time, and learned some of the language before returning to England. There is little information about his life after his return, as he did not speak about it, and many of those with whom he was associated have long since died, but what is known is that he found himself back in the world of art and the social scene of London.

It was in 1936 that Crabb departed England for his second visit to the Far East. This was a period of deviation from his artistic activities, although the family he lived with ran a curiosity shop. They provided him with a teacher so that he could work on the language, both by speaking and writing. He wrote to his mother on the subject:

"I am lucky, such friends are not easy to make among the Chinese. I think the secret is trying to be polite…The old man is very pleased with my progress in writing…I am quite proud of my Chinese hand, and would give a good deal to become one of the few Englishmen able to write after the manner of an educated Chinese".

While protected by the Chinese family, he engaged in active espionage for Chiang Kai-Shek, supplying important intelligence about Soviet controlled activities in the region. To this end he had made contact with a strong anti-Soviet expatriate enclave who were very active in China. The outcome was that the Russians became very interested in Crabb, but before any action could be taken against him, he returned to London to take his place yet again in the world of art. One person whom he met during his travels in China was the renowned artist Sir Francis Rose, who was to feature in Crabb's life up to the time of his disappearance, and was even implicated in those events.

When Crabb returned from the Far East he resided at the Cavendish Hotel in St. Jermyn Street, which was owned and run by Rosa Lewis. As the *Admiral,* he occupied a room, and returned to the art circle that would make use of his talents. The Hon. Daphne Fielding, who was a popular British author in the early 20th century, produced a series of popular books about high society including, the *Duchess of Jermyn Street: Rosa Lewis* the story of Rosa at the Cavendish.

She wrote of Crabb:

"Rosa Lewis would claim the effects of her debtors but there were occasions when they themselves were pressed bodily into service in the hotel, not that it was any great hardship, for they still remained in the family. Commander Crabb went to the Cavendish to celebrate on a small legacy. Being exceedingly popular

as well as very generous, he found all too soon that he had spent every penny of his inheritance, and was still left with a heavy bill to pay. In order to discharge this debt, he worked in the hotel for some time as an extra porter."

A valuable contribution to the life of Crabb came from Robin Bryans (Robert Harbinson Bryans), a writer was who born on 24 April 1928, and died on 11 June 2005, aged 77. Bryans described himself as being dramatically involved in sensational and sometimes scandalous events among Britain's political aristocracy from the 1940s until the 1960s. As a distant member of the Royal family he was a very real thorn in the side of the establishment, because he exposed the nefarious activities of the wealthy and privileged. His books *The Dust Has Never Settled (1992)*, *Let the Petals Fall* (1993) and *Checkmate* (1994) were made available to us, which, with personal interviews and letters, provide an insight into Crabb's secret life.

It took almost a year of continuous effort to have our first meeting with Bryans. Letter followed letter carrying requests for a meeting and a growing list of questions. Then he agreed to meet with us and help where possible. The link to Bryans began when our colleague Murray was part of a controversial TV programme, *After Dark*. It was where a group of those in the know sat and discussed murky subjects of spies and spying. During the programme Murray managed to direct the conversation to the subject of Crabb and posed a searching question to Bryans. However, before the topic could be discussed the programme went to an unplanned commercial break. During the break it was made very clear by the programme's 'people' that Crabb could not be discussed, although everything else was apparently fair game. When the programme returned to air, the subject of Crabb was gone. Before they departed the studio Murray managed to speak to Bryans. It was evident that he had first hand knowledge of Crabb and the murky events that surrounded him.

We arrived at the appointed time at Bryans house in Ealing, London, and were met by a large, well-spoken man. He wore carpet slippers, a velvet jacket and appeared to be an eccentric within a suitable setting. In the living rom, he sat on one side of the room and we on the other side. The hallway and living room were a veritable art gallery, with the walls adorned by original paintings. He began to explain that he had published under the Honeyford Press imprint, which was his own publishing company, as no mainstream publisher would take on his political books. He told us of the attempts that had been made on his life by the Establishment, who wanted him silenced. They could not prosecute him through the courts because of what he might say. So in time honoured tradition, they used other methods. They failed to dispose of him, but only just.

He turned to the subject of Crabb and probed to find out what we knew. It soon became clear that we knew very little of his life outside of the Navy and his diving exploits. We had put Crabb in a little 'box', as of a frogman who was a war hero, an adventurer who had disappeared on some unexplained mission. Bryans sat impassive, observing us before introducing a plethora of names of people with whom Crabb associated. They were names we had never heard of. However, it became very evident, very quickly that they apparently all had several things in common; links to high society, homosexuality, smuggling of art and spying for the Soviet Union.

Robin Bryans described Crabb as a small, insignificant man when younger, which was in contrast to the tall, lean, angelic faced men he associated with. While he did not have the looks and social background, he had a good nature and humour. He was always ready to help anybody he considered a friend. The problem was that those who employed his services played on his good nature and used him. Bryans said because of this, he developed a chip on his shoulder, perhaps because they had plenty of money and he didn't. But things changed immediately after the war when Crabb returned a hero. He had been awarded the George Medal and an OBE for his underwater activities. Bryans said that people were keen to hear of his daring exploits. While he was a good storyteller, he never told anybody why the King had given him the George Medal and subsequently, the OBE. But the war was over and it was not long before everybody wanted to get on with life and forget about it; that is everybody apart from Crabb, whose war had been a successful adventure. As time went by Bryans said, people humoured him and listened because Crabb was a good storyteller, however, once you had heard the story a few times, interest wore very thin.

We asked Bryans if he knew why Crabb carried out the dive under the Soviet warship. He smiled and reiterated that we really did not know anything about Crabb. He was right and we did not want to force the issue; we were there to learn. It became apparent from what we were told that there were people in high places who were involved and implicated. Was Mountbatten one of them was a question we ventured. Without hesitation the response came back, "of course, but you would never be allowed to prove it." In his own words, Bryans albeit a renegade, had first hand knowledge. However, because of what he knew and could prove, the establishment would never take action and put him in the high court. We were not in that position, and would certainly be expendable. Throughout our meeting he told us that we had a long way to go, but in many respects we were on the right track. He did warn us to be very careful because 'they' would not allow us to publish the truth. We continued to push the name of Mountbatten. Bryans gave us details about the man, which are recounted elsewhere in the book, and it was confirmed that Crabb told him on many occasions that he reported to 'M', who of course was Mountbatten. The question as to whether he would have sent Crabb to the Soviet Union was given an evasive answer; "Certainly, if it suited his purpose". Well did he send Crabb? Bryans again smiled; it was the height of the Cold War and Crabb associated with known Communists and Russians whilst serving in the Royal Navy. He said that Crabb was an adventurer, a storyteller. He would have done whatever he was bid by his master and indeed he did.

In his book *Checkmate,* he tells us that Lord Chancellor Hailsham, frequently sent police to warn him about criminal libel, but publicly declared; "all law is a gigantic confidence trick." However, "Too much would come out," said Lord Shackleton, Labour's Leader in the House of Lords, if the establishment put Bryans on trial. It is claimed that Bryans had been through a maze of intrigue of the murderous underworld of Anthony Blunt, the Soviet spy and Surveyor of the Queen's Pictures, and other purveyors of stolen art, such as the alledged criminal Princess Dil de Rohan. Bryans was put in prison for his politics and several times left for dead after murder attempts.

How reliable was the information that we were being told? One source of support was in *Mask of Treachery*, where the author John Costello reveals that what Bryans told him appeared to be gossip, but it did contain some hard facts. In the book he states:

"Bizarre though some of Harbinson's [Bryans] theories may be, those that could be checked mesh with established record. When I made enquiries, I discovered that many of Harbinson's more exotic assertions about the degree of homosexuality in the Palace network were discreetly confirmed by reputable authorities who knew of matters from their official positions or personal contacts."

We considered Bryans to be a reliable witness to events, as he had nothing to gain from us. Costello also checked his stories out. Without doubt, the Establishment will throw tons of mud, particularly as Bryans is no longer alive to defend himself.

Bryans revealed to us in interview that among the mystery and intrigue that surrounded Crabb's pre and postwar life were four individuals, one male and three female. The male was the artist Sir Frances Rose, a fourth baronet whom he met in the Far East. Rose had returned to Europe. He was an eyewitness to the events that had placed Hitler as head of the Third Reich, through to his love affair with Ernst Rohm, head of Hitler's SA. After the murder of Rohm and the turmoil of pending war, he fled to England.

Sir Francis Rose was to write in his book *Saying Life:*

"My old friend Lionel Crabb (later known as Buster) whose precarious career from merchant seaman cadet to companion-guardian to a hasty-minded friend on a world tour was now assisting Freddy Mayor in his gallery. His help in arranging my exhibition in the Cork Street gallery was invaluable to me, and I grew very fond of him, largely because he was outspoken and courageous about his own life which had been an utter failure, and he could be relied on."

Of the women in Crabb's life, the one who had the most influence in the smuggling of art and blackmail was Princess Carlos de Rohn, more commonly known as Dil. She, in turn, was the long-term lover of the Russian ballerina Catherine Devilliers, who, under her adopted name, Katusha, was a drinking partner of Crabbs. Bryans told us that Crabb adored Katusha and spent a lot of time with her. The fourth member of the circle was the Russian Baroness, Moura Budberg, who was a socialite in the London scene and allegedly a Russian spy.

As Crabb's circle of friends and contacts grew he was approached by the proprietors of one of London's famous picture galleries and was offered a job. Crabb accepted, and continued in business as the *Admiral*, where clients took to his old fashioned charming manner. The proprietors, Tom Harris and Anthony Blunt (Blunt was many years away from being exposed as a Soviet spy) are recalled as saying that sales increased as clients asked to deal with the *Admiral*.

When Blunt was granted immunity from prosecution, he had insisted that the immunity cover all crimes he had committed in addition to his treason. Desperate to ensure the success of the cover-up, MI5 granted his demand. Bryans stated:

"Blunt is almost certain to have admitted that one of his crimes was involvement in a child sex ring based at the Kincora Boys' Home in Northern Ireland. The origins of this child abuse ring dated back to his days at Cambridge where he had become involved sexually with a group of upper class paedophiles

from Northern Ireland. In the years after Cambridge, Blunt maintained his contacts and occasionally travelled to Ireland for long weekends spent abusing young boys at parties attended by some well-known names from British and Irish ruling circles."

He added: *"Mountbatten was a visitor."*

The question that must be asked is what did Crabb have in common with these people who floated among the rich, the ruthless, the arrogant, the spies and the homosexuals? Bryans explained that it was art in the form of paintings and jewels, as well as the lifestyles of those involved. Some say he was bisexual at a time when homosexuality was illegal. It is well known that he had a rubber fetish that would have made him welcome by other 'eccentrics'. However, Crabb did not make a fortune; Robin Bryans explained that he was used in what could be described as a smuggling enterprise. He liked the adventure and, prior to the war he had the ability to circulate among the artistic world, selling paintings and helping with collections, but he was used by the unscrupulous, and there appeared to be many of them. In a letter to the authors Bryans explained, "Long before the Second World War and subsequent British currency controls, Rose and Crabb immersed themselves in the smuggling of stolen goods".

Those involved in Crabb's life were the parts of a jigsaw and each played a part. Princess Carlos de Rohn was born in the Dilkusha Palace, Lucknow, India, the daughter of a British major and his American wife. Her mother was a rigid American Quaker and an oil heiress who christened her Dilkusha Wrench. The family travelled to England some three months after she was born, which raised an interesting point in that her birth was not registered at Somerset House and, so as far as the UK authorities were concerned, she was never born. Her early life was eventful and when she was five years old her father kidnapped her from his estranged wife. This placed her in the public eye, where she was to remain throughout her life. Bryans explains in *The Dust Has Never Settled,* that following the 1929 Wall

Street crash she became obsessed with money, or more appropriately the fear of not having any, which would have restricted her ability to buy whisky and stolen pictures.

After a short-lived marriage of convenience to a homosexual Prince called Carlos De Rohn, she left him to become a designer at Catherine Devilliers' ballet school in Berlin. Apart from being a brilliant dress designer she was a very adept businesswoman who never lost an opportunity to make money and keep herself and her lover Devilliers (Katusha) in drink. Bryans says that the numerous letters he received from de Rohn were signed Dil and that was the name she was known by. Devilliers was simply called Katusha, adopting a Russian name after having fled the Russian Revolution. This was a time when the World War II was looming, so they both departed Berlin and set themselves up in London, living at Selwyn House, which was one of the places that was to feature in events surrounding Crabb.

The Second World War was to intervene and change dramatically the course of Crabb's life, causing him to move from being a first rate art salesman to a Naval hero. Whilst Crabb departed to play his role in the war, de Rohn became head of the Swiss desk at Brendan Bracken's Ministry of Information. That was a great opportunity for de Rohn because, as Bryans points out, she sat in the middle of the spider's web waiting for flies to catch. She was hired to compose black propaganda for German consumption but the Germans were not the only targets and the information that she was privy to was to be of great value in the future for blackmail and the smuggling of treasures. This is a link to Switzerland, Nazi Germany and those on all sides who used the war for their own ends, and generally some form of financial reward.

Bryans tells us that when in London, de Rohn lived with Katusha, and enjoyed the companionship of Baroness Moura Budberg who also had a vested interest in de Rohns information. Budberg had the talents to play a very clever game in managing to keep close friends with the anti-Bolshevik White Russians in London and Paris, while maintaining the closest links with some of the regular Bolshevik leadership. She continued to visit the USSR at regular intervals, and had a Soviet passport; a most useful asset for playing the spying game. Profit was an additional bonus.

She had been imprisoned in the Kremlin until she was allowed to leave Russia and settle in London and, as *The Times* obituary in 1974 states:

"For nearly four decades she was in the centre of London's intellectual, artistic and social life."

Budberg was the third and youngest daughter of Count Fgnary Platonovich Zakrevski, an aristocrat of Czarist Russia. Budberg acquired her title following her second brief marriage to Baron Budberg. After being cleared of spying, she fled to become the mistress of the Russian writer Maxim Gorky. She moved to London in the early 1930s and quickly established intellectual connections, which included H G Wells, the filmmaker Alexander Korda, for whom she worked, and George Bernard Shaw. Her social circle extended to Duff Cooper, the War Minister, through to Anthony Eden, the Foreign Secretary.

An article by Neil Tweedie and Peter Day in the *Daily Telegraph* on 28 November 2002, states that MI5 was warned as early as 1951 that Anthony Blunt was a member of the Communist Party and friend of a suspected Soviet agent. The Security Service learned of Blunt's associations in an interview with Budberg while she was a suspected Soviet agent. Burgess had been a regular guest at Budberg's flat in Knightsbridge, central London, and she became a central figure in the panic surrounding the two spies' defection. MI5 officers were sent to find out what she knew. One reported:

"The most startling thing Moura told me was that Anthony Blunt, to whom Guy Burgess was most devoted, is a member of the Communist Party."

She was investigated by MI6 for nearly 25 years as a suspected international master spy. In 1951 there was an official protest about 'the vast resources employed in keeping her continuously under surveillance' when no evidence against her had ever been found. Bryans, in *Checkmate* and personal interview, described old Russian newssheets that showed a photograph of Budberg standing beside Stalin. Bryans told us that she continued to go back and forth to Moscow because the great London Hostess was a much more important spy to the Russians than Sir Anthony Blunt. Through the association between de Rohn, Katusha and Budberg it is evident that Crabb was in the thick of it, but did he know and to what extent? Or was it just one big adventure to him?

During the 1950s Dil spent the winter months in Spain, leaving her flat in Selwyn House to the care of Robin Bryans. Francis Rose also lived there and Bryans was an intermediary between them, particularly in respect to works of art, some of which, it is said, were stolen by de Rohn from Rose. De Rohn did not waste her time in Spain and in *Checkmate* there is a description of how she pursuaded rich Americans into purchasing good pictures from her never ending supply. It was after Crabb's disappearance and the police investigation that she eventually admitted that some of the paintings and drawings may have been Rose's originally, but she had taken them in lieu of rent for his room at Selwyn House, when he failed to pay up.

Bryans describes in *The Dust Has Never Settled* and in interview, that Francis Rose and Crabb were a well-known pair in London. When Rose went to Paris, Crabb looked after the flat, keeping the paintings under lock and key. When both Francis Rose and de Rohn were in Paris, Bryans used to go to the pub with Crabb, but he explained that he found Crabb, with his swordstick, increasingly hard to take. During this period, Stephen Ward, who was later implicated in the Profumo Spy Scandal, joined them on these outings. Bryans thought that there was nothing political in Ward's interest in Crabb, but like many others, was fascinated by the Commander's eccentric behaviour and his wartime adventure stories. Bryans says that when he read Rose's book *Saying Life* it was like listening to Crabb in the 1940s, entertaining the pub with stories of Rose's early life and their liking of Russia. He states in *The Petals Have Fallen* that he had reservations about some of Crabb and Rose's political claims, although he adds that he thought the claims were generally based upon some shades of the truth. Bryans sums up the situation by explaining that just as Second World War and the Cold War produced an underworld of spying for and against the British, American and Russian Governments, there was another underworld in smuggling works of art and jewels on a massive scale, which gave rich pickings for blackmailers.

Blunt was the Surveyor of the Queen's Paintings, as well as the Deputy Director of the Courtauld Institute of Art in Portman Square. His rooms at the Institute received a regular visitor in the form of Guy Burgess, prior to his defection, and the Institute was to be a focal point of the major spying operation. He also knew Rose and de Rohn because Selwyn House was owned by London University, where he was a senior member of the faculty. He knew that they were dangerous people determined to obtain money by any means, including blackmail. As an art historian, he was in the same circle and a devout Communist from his days at University. He had served in British Intelligence from 1939 to 1945, in which, during the latter years he dealt with the security aspects of exile groups in England. This had provided him with valuable details of British controlled agents operating in the Eastern Bloc, and those names were forwarded to Moscow. After his service on the inside, he continued to work for the Russians as a talent spotter, and one man who he knew from those pre-war days, and who had risen to become a leading exponent of underwater warfare, was his art friend and former employee, Commander Crabb. Through his Royal position, Blunt also had connections with Mountbatten.

In *Checkmate,* Bryans explains that when spy-book authors had interviewed him he had tried to get them to see who, in Anthony Blunt's world, was of importance to the Russians, and one in particular was Katusha. But he continued to explain that they dismissed her as merely the *"Russian Ballerina Katusha"* who lived with de Rohn. He explains that the Russians had enormous respect for her until her death in 1959 and while Katusha had the respect of the Russians, she had the companionship of Crabb. Bryans would join them at The Lamb public house in London where Crabb would put on an eccentric act by drinking to excess and, in Bryans words, sleeping in his frog suit between rubber sheets.

When we asked Bryans the significance of the link between Katusha and Crabb, he drew reference to his book *The Dust Has Never Settled* and explained that in 1956 the Communist leaders had allowed the Bolshoi ballet to pay tribute to Crabb's drinking partner Katusha. He further explained that although the whole Bolshoi Theatre Ballet company's tribute was a magnificent gesture, he could think of nobody more feted by the Russian Embassy in the years that he knew her. He made the observation that, while Blunt and Burgess hated and distrusted de Rohn, they loved Katusha and so the Russian link to Crabb was well established. They had valuable information about him, his private life and particularly his diving exploits. Did that make him a target for blackmail?

In the *Dust Has Never Settled*, Bryans explains:

> *"It did not displease Dil (de Rohn) to be called The Queen of Spies since she had been fully aware that in order to deceive German Intelligence, the departments agents had to put out Black Propaganda and a number of these agents were lawyers who sat as High Court Judges under Lord Chief Justice Parker. Black Propaganda in wartime could be blackmail in peacetime."*

Bryans told us that when Crabb disappeared, Special Branch descended upon Selwyn House and questioned Francis Rose; this sent de Rohn into a rage. They had both been under the eye of the police because of their trading in art treasures, and the last thing that de Rohn wanted was police investigation. As Bryans explains in *Checkmate,* it was little wonder the police could make neither head nor tail of what had been happening over the years at Selwyn House with de Rohn, Katusha, Budberg, Francis Rose and Crabb. Bryans said that Blunt had been concerned as to what Francis Rose and Crabb were scheming at Selwyn House.

In *The Petals Have Fallen*, Bryans explains that de Rohn robbed and blackmailed the rich and she knew too much for the authorities liking but they would never put her in court. If she had been put in the witness box the letters she had written to Bryans revealing who had received pictures would have been made public. He explained that it would have included members of the Royal family, Blunt and those in 'high society'. The authorities made a deal that if she left the UK, never to return, they would not prosecute. She departed for the USA without retribution or exposing those in *high places* who may not have endured the scandal.

4

Smuggling and Deception

Money couldn't buy friends but you got a better class of enemy
Spike Milligan 1918 – 2002

It is relevant that the world of art in the late 1930s seems to have had a number of recruits into the world of Intelligence, including Tom Harris, the art collector. He was born in 1908, to an English father and a Spanish mother, and brought up in an atmosphere that Bryans describes as, 'Redolent of the artistic and Bohemian world'. His father, Lionel Harris, founded the Spanish Art Gallery and brought to Britain many Spanish works of art. Thomas carried on the task, though his own inclinations were towards being artistic rather than a dealer. It is alleged that Harris and Blunt provided the art world with many fine and rare works of art, aided by Crabb, who had also supplied Blunt with fine Chinese art that he had smuggled to Britain by way of Pakistan.

After leaving the Slade School, Harris studied painting and sculpture at the British Academy in Rome. Then in 1930 he decided to become an art dealer. It was in Rome that he was first recruited into the Soviet Secret Service through an Italian underground Communist who was also an art dealer and a member of the pre-war Soviet apparatus in Switzerland. When Harris started art dealing seriously this involved much traveling in Spain. Some of this dealing was done on his own behalf, but much was done on behalf of the Soviet Government through secret channels in Paris, Brussels and Rome.

Harris's entry into British Intelligence after the outbreak of the Second World War was strange. He was brought into MI5, where his intimate knowledge of Spain and all the complex political ramifications in both the Franco administration and underground was considered invaluable. Before Harris joined MI5 he was, together with Philby, at the SOE training school near Hertford; Philby himself described Harris as, "Our outstanding personality...taken on, at Guy's (Burgess) suggestion as a sort of glorified housekeeper, largely because he and his wife were inspired cooks. The work was altogether unworthy of his untaught, but brilliantly intuitive mind."

Bryans explained that Harris's very close friendship with Philby, which extended over many years, began at that period, though they may have met before, in Spain. In any case the Russians had, by this time, realised that Harris was a shrewd and ruthless operator who had all the makings of a highly professional counter-espionage officer. Then, quite suddenly, he was brought into MI5. Bryans described him as a handsome, swashbuckling man, gregarious and charming, providing all the indications of considerable wealth, and an admirable, generous host. Harris's magnificent home in Chesterfield Gardens was almost a museum in itself. The Harris parties, even in the midst of wartime rationing, were noted for the quality of the liquor and the skilled and imaginative cooking. In MI5 the Harris party circle was known as the 'Chesterfield Gardens Mafia'. He was wealthy and entertained lavishly, providing a meeting place for members of the British security and secret intelligence services as well as those employed by the KGB and GRU. It could be described as a melting pot of east and west spying and smuggling agents.

Bryans expands the Soviet link by suggesting that Harris was another Soviet mole from the Cambridge ring. The most specific charge was made, according to Bryans, by a former member of a

Soviet network in Switzerland who says that Harris became an art dealer and that Spain was his target, especially his exploits during the civil war, when he bought Spanish Art. He was most active when Soviet *advisers* masterminded the systematic stripping of monasteries, churches and castles of their art treasures.

In January 1964, Harris was driving his wife along the Lluchmayor Road from Palma, Majorca, when the car skidded for several yards, knocked down a telephone pole, then went off the road and crashed into an almond tree. Mrs. Harris escaped with minor injuries, but he suffered a fractured skull that proved fatal. The accident puzzled everyone, both in Majorca and in London, though it was noted that this came about shortly after Philby's defection to Russia and the consequent interrogation of various other suspects in London. There was no question of Harris being drunk. Some thought there could have been foul play and that his car had been tampered with before he drove it. Richard Deacon recalls in *The Greatest Treason* that a telephone call was received by a top executive in MI5 suggesting that somebody should be sent to Majorca to investigate the whole affair and make sure nothing incriminating was left behind at the studio. But, as far as can be ascertained, no action was taken. The question that has never been answered is which side killed him?

The incident occurred prior to Blunt being questioned by MI5, and there is a strong suspicion that the car had been tampered with to eliminate him in case he was brought in for interrogation, which may have meant the downfall of others and particularly Blunt. The whole aspect of east and west dirty tricks was at its height at that period and that meant that the 'side' that carried out the deed is open to speculation. It is ironic that upon his death he had bequeathed a large collection of Goya prints to the British Museum.

Crabb had worked at Harris' Spanish Gallery in London, while Dil de Rohn manouvred in an attempt to get Harris to allow her to live in his house in Majorca when he was not there. This would provide her with a base from which to operate and help the funding of her lavish lifestyle. Bryans told us in interview that there were currency restrictions in place, which meant that money could not be moved freely out of the country without permission, and so illegal methods had to be adopted. That meant smuggling cash, paintings or other works of art to sell abroad. Bryans said that this process was also used to bring valuables into the country.

Another key player that Bryans identifies is Peter Wilson, who was, for many years, the head of Sotheby's, the world-renowned auction house. He was thought by many to be the fifth man in the Burgess-McLean spying operation. There is no evidence however, he did have his hands in what were 'complicated' art deals. Peter Watson, in his book *Sotheby's: The Inside Story*, claimed that Sotheby's was guilty of smuggling, fabricating documentation and rigging auctions and that Wilson was the perfect Sotheby's man, a penniless aristocrat at home in the highest circles yet capable of great ruthlessness, a man who made his own rules, above all a man with a passion for beautiful objects, a mercurial man with a great eye.

During a five-year investigation Peter Watson set out to prove that Sotheby's was involved in a web of illegal practices. These ranged from selling stolen antiquities to rigging auctions. He also highlights the fact that Wilson left the firm abruptly after Sir Anthony Blunt, the surveyor of the Queen's art collection, was revealed to have been a Soviet spy. So it was that Wilson, who was a member of MI5 during the Second World War, was also involved with Soviet spies. Robert Lacey, in his book *Sotheby's: Bidding for Class* describes Sotheby's Peter Wilson as a world-class auctioneer, business promoter, closet homosexual and rogue.

Mike thought no more about the Swiss connection until after the first meeting with Bryans. The main focus for Crabb's disappearance has always been a military type operation under the Russian cruiser. Nobody had focused very much on his past, or his other life in the world of art and smuggling. However, that's where Bryans wanted us to explore, if we wanted to really know what happened to Crabb.

Each time we raised a question with him he would actually draw us back and say that the key to Crabb's disappearance was in art, jewellery and gold. He made numerous references during our meetings to Peter Wilson of Sotheby's, and smuggling activities at the time. Whenever we refocused back on Mountbatten's connection as being the person who sent him on the dive he would just sit there and say:

"Yes, that's who sent him on the dive, but you are not listening, you have to look at the wider picture".

He would then pause and smile at us before going on to explain:

"Remember what I told you. Dil de Rohn was head of the Swiss desk in the war. She was in contact with the Nazis prior to the war, she associated with Sir Francis Rose who had been the lover of Earnst Romm, head of Hitler's S.A prior to the war. It was about smuggling and blackmail and Crabbie was in the middle".

There was a connection and a link to Switzerland and the Nazis. Intertwined into that was Crabb, because he could be used to locate loot then smuggle it into the UK. We never at any stage during our discussions talked about loot being submerged in lakes in Switzerland and Mike didn't immediately make the connection about his exploits of the 1970s.

From what Bryans told us, a lot of valuable items travelled from Europe into the UK to be disposed of through the various 'outlets', including Blunt. Knowles told us that when he was with Crabb in London he would obtain money from Blunt in exchange for packages. These exchanges were often done in a taxi outside the Courtauld Institute and Knowles never knew for certain what those packages contained, but suspected that it involved art or jewels.

Bryans explained that de Rohn would move any item of value from anywhere, and a valuable asset was that part of her job on the Swiss desk was looking at propaganda and people who had connections with Nazi Germany who should not have had such connections. This enabled her to have a large 'black book of who is who' in order to use blackmail as well as the knowledge of where items of value were located.

Bryan's said that Crabb's role was not that of an international spy, but that of an international smuggler, who was used by the spying fraternity and those of devious character. He told us that many people in higher society were the recipients of some of the treasures that found their way back into the UK at that time, and he actually stated, and does so in his books, that one of them was Queen Mary. We can only go by his allegations as we have no first hand knowledge, but Bryans was able to say from personal experience what happened at that time.

He made it very clear that if we found substansive evidence of the prominent people and families in the UK who benefited from these looted treasures, "they would just have you killed, it's as simple as that".

He explained that they are powerful and influential people. Of course, the next question was, who are these people and would he give us any names? He declined to do so, on the basis that he did not want it on his conscience that he had given us information about these people, as the consequences would be quite horrific.

What he did say was that Blunt had considerable power and influence within the Royal Family, the art world and of course with the Soviet Union, although at this particular time of the Crabb story, Blunt was not yet exposed as a Soviet spy. He stated that Mountbatten played with his Navy, but he was not happy with Britain and the way his family had been treated and so he protected the interests of the Blunt gang of spies. For clarity we asked if Mountbatten would expose them if he knew they were Soviet spies. He said no, because he was part and parcel of what it was all about and they were all in it together. We responded that it was a very strong and damaging statement. He replied, "The truth is the truth".

So we have this mysterious situation where you have a melting pot of treasure that had been stolen from people subjected to the Holocaust and the savage rape of numerous countries in a World War. Their valuable assets were then spirited away by unscrupulous Nazis to be hidden for future activities. Then there was the little group in London that Bryans was a part of and included Crabb, de Rohn and Francis Rose. However, whilst de Rohn and Rose were there purely for financial gain, it appears that Crabb was there for the adventure. After Crabb's disappearance, their activities became the focus of police investigations leaving de Rohn and Rose panicking in case their illegal exploits were uncovered. Bryans was quite adamant that Crabb was not a crook or a gangster, but he was an adventurer, and in his opinion had not really grasped the enormity of the overall scheming that was going on.

We asked Bryans if he thought Crabb had gone to the Soviet Union and he said that at this period of time Kim Philby was the focus of the security services, and Blunt was also under the spotlight. He then told us that, from his personal knowledge, Mountbatten had sent Crabb on the last dive as part of a plan that involved the Soviets and may have involved Philby or Blunt. With Crabb gone the smuggling gang dissolved, leaving Blunt and Mountbatten safe from exposure of their spying and illegal activities with looted treasure.

We gave this some thought during these discussions and imagined Crabb's delight to be part of an adventure to go to Switzerland and then covertly dive in lakes and recover boxes of Nazi loot. It may not have been restricted to Switzerland; it could have been to Austria as well. Remember he could go under the auspices of Mountbatten's umbrella to undertake such operations. We know beyond doubt that Crabb travelled undertaking covert operations on behalf of Mountbatten. What we don't know is where he went to do these operations. And so it is quite plausible and feasible that people in Austria and Switzerland were part of the operations.

Would Crabb have realised the implications of where such valuables had come from? Probably, but then the people that were engaged with him were very plausible serious criminal minds and could have given him any story of recovering the treasure and passing it back to its rightful owners. Crabb was devoted to the Royal Family and would have no problems with somebody like Blunt who was now looking after the Royal art collection. He may not have seen it as a dangerous and difficult situation but thought it part of his duty to the country and Royalty in particular. The fact that he was being exploited would probably not have occurred to him. De Rohn would have concocted some elaborate story that would have convinced him that everything was OK. She was a past master at that, she had spent six years dealing with all the intricacies of what was going on in Switzerland during the Second World War, particularly the latter parts when it was alleged that loot was being recovered from lakes or banks in Switzerland.

5

Crabb's War

The first step in having a successful war is getting people to fight it.

Fran Lebowitz 1946

For much of the details describing Crabb's wartime exploits we must acknowledge the huge debt owed to Marshall Pugh, his official biographer, who began writing his book before Crabb's disappearance (*Commander Crabb*). There is also a well documented account of the wartime activities in Sydney Knowles' book *A Diver in the Dark*. Frank Goldsworthy, who had served with Crabb in the war, also provided an insight. With this in mind, the activities of Crabb in the war are only briefly covered in this book.

When the war started in 1939 the Navy still did not want Crabb, and he accepted a position in the Merchant Navy, as a gunner, and in 1940 he wrote to his mother explaining that he did not know what to do, as he still wanted to go into the Navy, and even accepted that he would be 'lower deck'. In the autumn of 1940 he decided to try again for the Navy, and this time he was successful, and entered as a gunner. He considered his life uneventful, and in 1941 he was commissioned, despite the fact that they found that he had a problem with one eye. Fearing a mundane job, he volunteered for 'special duties' and attended an interview from which he was accepted. Thinking that the real adventure would now begin, he was appointed the Drainage and Passive defence officer of the coastal forces base at Dover. He felt let down, as he would see less action than he had as a gunner on a merchant ship. He was at a low ebb when he met up with a friend who was sympathetic to his problem and suggested mine disposal. It was a risky job, but offered more action than drainage. From that conversation, Crabb converted from drains to mines and bombs and, after training, was posted to Gibraltar.

It was in 1942 that Lieutenant Lionel Crabb RNVR (Special Branch) took up the duties of principal mine and bomb disposal officer in Gibraltar. His superior officer was commander Ralph Hancock, who was in command of minesweeping and extended defences. During the meeting when Crabb was briefed on his duties, he was informed of the exploits of the Italian underwater attacks against the ships berthed in the Gibraltar area. He was told of the work undertaken by the Naval underwater working party, whose role was to search the undersides of ships and recover any mines or warheads they found. Hancock explained that when the divers found a device, they would remove it and bring it to the surface where it would become Crabb's responsibility to dispose of it. Crabb reflected on the huge task of searching the undersides of ships in deep water, in all weathers and during day or night, never knowing when a mine might explode.

There must, he decided, be a large and highly trained underwater party for such a task, and ventured to ask Hancock how many divers were available. "Two", was the astonishing reply, "they are not professional divers, they are not mine disposal people and they have no proper diving gear". Even though he was not a strong swimmer, Crabb decided it was his duty to learn to dive himself in order that he could do his assigned job more effectively. He introduced himself to the two divers, Lieutenant Bailey and Leading Seaman Bell, and soon discovered what 'no proper diving gear' meant. Instead of the protective rubber suits used by the Italians, all they had were swimming trunks and overalls; instead of flippers, they wore plimsols; and instead of proper diving masks and breathing apparatus, they had 'scrounged' Davis Submarine Escape Apparatus (DSEA) designed to help submariners escape a sunken submarine. With some trepidation, Crabb ventured into the water for his first dive, tethered by a rope held by Bailey in case he got into difficulty. After this, Bailey escorted him on an inspection of a ship's hull, and then the two men celebrated Crabb's 'graduation' with a drink.

Leading the enemy was Lioria Visintini, the most idolised man in the Italian underwater assault group. On the 19 September 1941, his plan was to force his way under the defensive anti-submarine steel net at Gibraltar's harbour entrance. Aboard his chariot he carried compressed air cutters and lifting gear, but he was lucky for the net was lowered to allow a destroyer to pass and he was able to slip through in its wake. He left his chariot's warhead beneath a tanker, forced his way under the net he had passed earlier and got away. Visintini made the Spanish coast and joined his equally successful companions. A cloud of smoke inside the harbour at Gibraltar announced that his charge had broken the back of the Naval tanker *Denbydale*. Soon after there were similar explosions in the bay below the 10,900-ton cargo ship *Durham* and the 2,444-ton storage tanker *Fiona Shell*.

The Royal Navy at Gibraltar were not idle after the attack. At irregular intervals, searchlights swept the harbour approaches, combined with harbour and bay controls. Around the entrance gate, small explosive charges, sufficient to kill or stun a person underwater, were thrown into the water every few minutes of the night. The most significant move of all was the creation of the Gibraltar Naval Diving Party, whose members were to show no less devotion, endurance and courage than their Italian adversaries. This was to expose one member of the party to newspaper headlines, long after the World War II was finished, and would also enable him to forge strong links with his former 'enemies'.

With Gibraltar being used as a key port in support of the Allied war effort in North Africa, merchant ships moored in the bay and were valuable targets for the Italians. The Royal Navy had endured the assaults by the Italian 'human torpedoes' and provided defences against them. In order that the underwater war could continue against the allied shipping, the Italians had already made moves to develop a covert method of underwater attack by using the Gamma Brigade. These were underwater swimmers, or limpeteers, trained to swim to enemy ships carrying special mines. Italy had also developed rubber suits that kept the swimmer dry and warm and they had fins to aid swimming. They also had oxygen closed circuit breathing apparatus. The Gamma limpeteer assault group was tasked with attacking the British at Gibraltar.

The background to the Italian covert operations began in Spain, which was neutral. Commander Pierleoni, an Italian Naval officer, was sent to Spain to direct sabotage activities under cover of a consular appointment in Barcelona. He spent the winter of 1941-42 building up a sabotage organisation in Spain. Every seaport consulate had a radio station reporting allied shipping movements to the Embassy in Madrid. At Algeciras and La Linea roof top observatories kept up a constant watch on ships and aircraft at Gibraltar.

When there was a large number of allied ships moving in and out of the area the Italians decided to launch underwater attacks, and a team of twelve Gamma swimmers were ordered to Spain. Six were carried by submarine and infiltrated ashore. The other six were signed onto a merchant ship as seamen and when it docked at Barcelona they deserted and, through the effective network that was in place, were taken to a safe house on the coast, overlooking the bay and their targets. At the house plans were made for attacks against the ships that lay close to them. The British were looking for 'human torpedo' attacks and directed their defences out to sea. The Gamma group was to sneak in through the unsuspecting and relatively undefended rear. The team had an unsurpassed view of the ships and each swimmer could identify a target, so that on the night of the operation, the twelve men dressed in their rubber suits fitted the underwater breathing equipment and placed the fins on their feet. In the water they towed the mines, which were fitted with a rubber ring. The ring kept the mine afloat during the swim and when placed under the ship, the swimmer could inflate it so that it held the mine fast against the ship. Under cover of darkness the swimmers made good progress and reached their targets which included the merchant ships *Meta*, *Shuma*, *Baron*, *Douglas* and the *Empire Snipe*. Each swimmer dived down and fitted a mine to a ship, before surfacing and beginning the long swim back to Spain and relative safety. From the confines of the safe house the swimmers were able to observe the results of the operation.

Meanwhile Visintini, seeking new ways of attacking the ships in Gibraltar, came up with the idea of making a human torpedo base inside the *Olterra*, one of two Italian tankers detained in British contraband control anchorage in Gibraltar bay when Italy entered the war. A few minutes before the declaration of war, both ships' captains received secret radio signals to scuttle their vessels, and both ships were later towed to Algeciras harbour. In 1942, the *Olterra* was lying at a lonely breakwater berth just inside the harbour entrance.

Under Visintini's direction, the Italians cut a 25-foot-long section of the steel bulkhead separating the bow compartment from a small cargo hold, and hinged it like a coffee stall front. Then, telling the Spanish 'neutrality' guard that they must clean the trimming tanks, they pumped out the forward tanks till the bows rose high out of the water. Early one morning, while the brandy-soaked security guard was sound asleep in the galley, a four-foot door was cut in the side of the ship, opening into the bow compartment six feet below the normal water line. It was hinged to open inwards and so neatly done that only a diver could have detected it. When the ship resumed her normal trim, the bow compartment was flooded but the hold was still dry. The plan was to sling human torpedoes on pulleys in the bow compartment. When night came for an attack, they could be lowered into the water, pass out of the ship through the door in the side, do their job and return to the secret base. The next part of the plan was to secretly bring through Spain the human torpedoes and the 500lb warheads disguised as parts needed for an engine overhaul. This done, the team was ready for the next attack.

On the night of 7 December 1942, Visintini stood on the bridge of the ship with his team and pointed out the silhouettes of two battleships and two aircraft carriers of Force H inside Gibraltar harbour, three miles away. They left the safety of the *Olterra* and began their attack. It took them several hours to reach the harbour approaches, and all the time they could hear through the water the thud of small charges exploding by the harbour gate. They had to gamble on getting through between charges. Visintini and his companion, Petty Officer Magro, paid with their lives; killed by the explosive charges dropped at the gate, their bodies were found inside the harbour two weeks later. Two other members of the team were captured and one drowned, so that night the Italians lost five men and gained nothing. Visintini and Magro were buried at sea with naval honours. Crabb managed to find two Italian flags and a priest to officiate. There was one wreath, which was thrown on the sea by Crabb and Bailey, the British officers whose task it had been on that night to search the ships' bottoms after the attack, knowing that at any moment a warhead explosion within half a mile might kill or maim them. It was a generous gesture, much misunderstood and criticised by others at Gibraltar.

Sydney Knowles provided an insight into one of the Gamma swimmers, Giari Vargo. He volunteered for special service and went to La Spezia to be trained as a frogman. He became a non commissioned officer in the Gamma Brigade and was one of the first of twelve members of the Brigade to be clandestinely infiltrated into Spain. They were to take the war to the Allies in Gibraltar and even in Spanish ports.

Their covert attacks were successful largely due to the fact that the Royal Navy expected attacks from submarines at sea, although it was known that the Germans were able to operate in Spain with little harassment. Britain did not have frogmen and so there was no counter to the threat, apart from dropping depth charges or other explosive charges, which is not effective if you do not know where the enemy is or where he is coming from.

One controversial operation undertaken by Crabb at Gibraltar involved the Liberator aircraft that was carrying General Sikorski to England from the Middle East, which crashed into the water beyond the runway of Gibraltar. Kim Philby (long before being identified as a Soviet Spy) was head of the Iberian desk of the UK Secret Intelligence Service and it is alleged that he was part of the plot by the Soviets to assassinate Sikorski. For Crabb it was a race against time and the tide to locate the wreckage and recover the bodies, secret documents and microfilms that were being carried. Crabb dived around the clock until everybody was accounted for and every scrap of paper and film was recovered. This was a high profile task and this was the work that earned him the George Medal. Those who knew Crabb said that, whilst he relished in telling stories of his underwater exploits, he never discussed the Sikorski operation even after the war.

The underwater war continued, with the Italians attacking and Crabb's team defending. But it was becoming more difficult for the attackers and they were subjected to greater losses, often without even gaining access to a target. Eventually Gibraltar was considered too well defended and the attacks ceased. For Crabb it was the end of one era and the beginning of another.

Lieutenant Crabb was promoted to Lieutenant Commander in the summer of 1944, and ordered to select one of his divers and proceed to Italy. He chose Sydney Knowles, who had joined the Gibraltar team in 1943, and they departed the now quieter Gibraltar to join the Joint Services Intelligence Collecting Unit, which was based in Florence. The mines that Crabb and his team had been disarming were produced there and he soon became an authority on the mines as well as warheads and operations of the Italian Tenth Light Flotilla. Crabb had waged his war against this unit and was now carrying that fight into their homeland.

In Florence, Crabb and Knowles teamed up with Lieutenant Tony Marsloe, an American of Italian descent who was a member of the US Navy Reserve. He was a trained intelligence officer and spoke Italian. One of their first tasks was to interrogate a former Italian Naval officer from the Tenth Flotilla who had joined the partisans to fight the Germans after Italy's surrender. He provided details of a new type of mine that would cause the divers a great deal of trouble when they tried to disarm or remove them. He also stated that pro-German members of the Tenth Flotilla had regrouped and would continue their underwater attacks against captured ports and the Allied ships in them. This was news to British Naval Headquarters, who decided to pull Crabb (and his team) away from the Intelligence Collecting Unit and give him the job of supervising anti-sabotage diving operations in the whole Allied-controlled northern part of Italy.

Crabb and Knowles moved to Leghorn (Livorno) where another Italian, Ventiorini, who became a stalwart member of the team, joined them for diving operations. Command of all anti-sabotage diving in northern Italy was a monumental risk, but Crabb was fortunate when other members of the Tenth Flotilla joined them. Those who joined him found an understanding leader, for he allowed his prisoners considerable freedom, often against the wishes of his superiors. After two months in hospital with jaundice, Crabb rejoined his team in March 1945, and immediately Tony Marsloe discovered from the partisans that the Republicans of the Tenth Flotilla had set up a base for training Italian and German frogmen in the use of human torpedoes on the small island of La Vignole. It was no longer operational, but was guarded by two sergeants who refused to surrender to the Communist-led partisans for fear that their valuable equipment would ultimately fall into Russian hands. Crabb and Marsloe were, however, able to secure the base and the services of the two sergeants. Crabb learned from these men that the partisans had a very important prisoner in the form of Commander Angelo Belloni, who had designed much of the Italian diving equipment used during the war. In fact it was he who had persuaded Mussolini to form the Tenth Flotilla. Crabb negotiated to have him released, and Belloni joined the growing underwater work group. Belloni had two daughters, Minella and Paola, and the latter joined them to help with secretarial work. Knowles recalls that Paola's sister Minella ended up marrying their number two, Marsloe.

"We all thought that Crabb and Paola would marry, it was like that, and they were close. It was strange, I've never known why they didn't marry, one of the things that never happened, but I believe that they met again after the war, in England, and Crabbie went to Italy. He had little time for women." Knowles continues: "I don't mean anything by that. It was just that there were not many divers, and we were kept very busy."

Nevertheless, it may well have been his relationship with Paola that encouraged him to change his religion, for he became devoted to Italy and its people and a devout convert to the Catholic faith.

Many of the stories about Crabb were never told and Knowles revealed one that occurred during the war. He explained that Commander Crabb did a quick survey using oxygen re-breathing apparatus before Knowles, dressed in 'standard dress' (heavy deep-sea diving gear), submerged below the surface, equipped to work, as opposed to Crabb in the light equipment. They were working on a sunken mine sweeper that was lying at an awkward angle and Knowles found it difficult to move about the wreck. Through his face port Knowles saw Crabb swimming towards him towing a dead sailor, the head almost decapitated; a heavy steel door had slammed across his neck whilst he was trying to escape. Inside the vessel Knowles found nine bodies, which floated or lay in grotesque positions amongst the debris of bunks, tables, mattresses and kit bags. There had been knocking heard from those trapped but they were too late to rescue them. Knowles picked up the body of one young sailor and passed the corpse up the ladder to Crabb. In this way they recovered all of the bodies before locating the ship's log and secret papers. Knowles continued to check the vessel and opened the door of the galley, where he found the body of the cook. He reached out to lift it up, when the body slowly turned to face him, erect and with one hand reaching out to the face port of his helmet. He recalled the white-clad figure of the cook, his arms undulating, following him through the murky gloom. In that moment he panicked and tried to escape, but he was dressed in heavy equipment. He could not go far as his air hose and lifeline had become fouled. The corpse continued to move towards him until he pushed it away and watched it sink slowly to the deck. Knowles cursed himself for his out of character actions.

Crabb, as the principal diving officer in the area of northern Italy, was next ordered to secure Venice from mines and to open the port to Allied shipping. He was faced with the largest mine clearing task of his career. His command included Tony Marsloe as his number two, Angelo Belloni in charge of equipment, a doctor and other divers. They were very successful, even devising measures against magnetic mines, which could be set off by the presence of their metal air tanks, as described in Marshall Pugh's biography, *Commander Crabb*.

With the war ended, Crabb personally accepted the surrender of one of the Tenth Flotilla's leaders, Lieutenant Eugenio Wolk, who had continued to fight the Allies, both working with and training the Germans. Now he was to lead many men of his former unit in searching for those German mines. Technically he was a prisoner, but he was a prisoner who went home to his wife and family in the evening. He often stated that his men never carried arms and that the limpet mines were too small to endanger the crews of the ships. "Only our own lives were in danger," was his argument, forgetting the British Naval divers who had made it their business to seek and remove the charges. Yet when the day came for him to be judged for his anti-Allied work, after the armistice, one letter saved him his liberty and his civil rights; it came from Lieutenant Commander Crabb.

It was Wolk who arranged the introduction of Crabb to Maria Visintini, the widow of the diver Crabb had buried at sea off Gibraltar.

Crabb and Wolk called upon Maria Visintini, who wanted to hear how her husband had died and been buried. The young woman he met was blonde and attractive, and was dressed in mourning black for her husband. Although she said little, Maria had a profound effect on Crabb and, as she spoke some English and had secretarial experience, he considered offering her a job. Wolk was not over-enthusiastic about the idea but, a few days later, Crabb was told that Maria Visintini had come to see him. She had written a letter, which Wolk asked Crabb to read before he saw her. In it she expressed her appreciation for his concern and her desire to work for him. One of the most poignant passages in her letter read:

"Now everything is dead and it is very strange that I'm speaking so just with you. May I think to be rightly understood by you? Life goes on. One must go on with life trying to be plucky and honest. Heart is a secret precious thing that can be seen by nobody. I need working. My husband's spirit from his heaven of peace sees in my heart and he can't but approve me. (This for your peace of mind.) My pride and his was, is to show how much Italian people can value. This is my strength and my consolation. (And this is the promise for my well to do work.) Now I'm very grateful for you to give me the possibility of work among you rather than other where and so I've come to hear your conditions."

Crabb read the letter several times before inviting her into the office and asking her to become his secretary. She accepted, and turned out to be very efficient.

In December 1945 Crabb was ordered to Naples with his diving equipment, where he was briefed on a new job, helping overcome the terrorist bomb problem in Palestine where militant Jews were trying to expel the British in order to establish their own homeland. British ships and police launches were prime targets, and teams of frogmen made limpet mine attacks against them. Crabb's task therefore was to go to Palestine and establish an underwater bomb and mine disposal working party. He had only just arrived in the country when he was awarded the OBE for his work in Italy. The task of the team was that of searching the undersides of ships as they had done so many times before in Gibraltar and Italy. It was not until the spring of 1947 that Crabb was finally ordered home, and a year later he walked out of a demobilisation centre in Portsmouth with a cardboard box, which held a grey chalk-stripe flannel suit, and moved back into his circle of pre-war friends.

In the ensuing years between the end of the war and his disappearance, Crabb spent time in the Navy and as a civilian. Most wartime Royal Naval Volunteer Reserve (RNVR) officers, once demobbed, remained civilians. However, Crabb was not like any of the others because, not only was he brought back into the Navy but he was promoted. All of the circumstances were unusual. As a Reserve Officer he was not entitled to a pension and his service in the Royal Navy was presumed to have ended in March 1955. However, the Navy Lists of 1955 and 1956, published and printed by HMSO, enter: 'Commander (Sp.Br) L.K.P. Crabb, RNVR, GM, OBE, *HMS Vernon*'. This indicates that through the 1955—56 period, Crabb was still actually a serving officer in the Royal Navy. Officers who had served with him during and after the war recall seeing him wearing the uniform of a Commander on *HMS Vernon* during 1955. However, one fellow officer stands by the fact that Crabb left the Navy in 1955, and Knowles also says that as far as he knows, Crabb left the Navy in 1955. However, Knowles agrees that he was involved with secret service type people, so probably had some connection with the Navy. It was all very unclear.

Crabb's work in Portsmouth was so secret that fellow officers would see him come and go, but did not know to whom he reported or what he actually did. He was on the mess list of *HMS Vernon,* but would baby-sit for fellow officers rather than attend the Mess dinners, which he disliked. He had always had a dislike for formality and displayed this with an idiosyncratic variation in his uniform. At that period, Naval officers had a coloured stripe between the rank stripes, depending upon their particular qualification. Crabb had pale blue between his Commander's stripes and, as far as is known, no other officer used this colour for it had no official designation.

Cdr. A.J.C. Dean wrote to the authors on 14 April 1986 and explained:

"Unlike all resident officers in HMS Vernon he had his own caravan parked in the base in which he lived but was still a member of the officers mess and used it for victualling (taking meals) only. This led me to believe that he was attached to Vernon for special duties and not necessarily bourne on the books. Whilst he may well have been receiving naval pay as a Commander RNVR this does not follow that he could live well on his income especially as his mess bills would have been heavy. Most peacetime officers relied on a private income to supplement their living expenses. When I last saw him I really do not think he was fit enough to take on a swim of this magnitude. Even if a boat was used (and I doubt this) the tides are very strong in this area and he was never a good swimmer anyway. If he surfaced and was seen, I doubt if guards would have killed him. Much more likely is that he was picked up exhausted and interrogated. I cannot see him serving in the Soviet Navy but he may have been useful as an advisor. I do not think the body buried in Milton Cemetery in Portsmouth is Buster Crabb. It smacks to me of a plant as it was unidentifiable and very convenient to cover the possibility outlined above."

Formality replaced informality in the 1950s which was a period of great change for divers (frogmen) in the Navy. There were structured training courses, standardisation of diving equipment, formal annual fitness medicals and they abided by formal orders and procedures. It was actually in 1950 that a Home Station Clearance Diving Team was set up with other Clearance Diving Teams established soon after, to support the Mediterranean Fleet and the Far East Fleet. In 1951, clearance diving training moved to *HMS Vernon* and a new Clearance Diving School was established, combining the training of clearance divers with that of 'deep' divers. The latter used the heavy standard diving equipment that did not have the flexibility of the free swimmer. This school also took on the new task of training Ships' Divers so that every ship had a properly equipped air diving capability under its own Diving Officer to conduct ship's bottom searches and undertake simple underwater engineering tasks. The Clearance Diving (CD) Branch was officially formed under an Admiralty Fleet Order on 7 March 1952, although a training nucleus had been set up some two years earlier to take advantage of the few remaining men with wartime experience. These officers and ratings had, in the main, qualified as Shallow Water Divers trained to use the Sladen 'Clammy Death' diving dress and oxygen breathing apparatus. This was a change that Crabb did not like or accept. This was the new world and Crabb was a member of the old world. That said, he did continue to participate in military underwater activities however, nothing about Crabb's circumstances was normal.

6

The Ordzhonikidze Mystery

Many journalists have fallen for the conspiracy theory of Government. I do assure you that they would produce more accurate work if they adhered to the cock-up theory.

Bernard Ingham 1932

Returning to the question as to whether Crabb did in fact leave the Navy in 1955, we know that the 'official' version is that he did, but the Navy List tells us that he did not. Whatever the truth, it is known that the mysterious claim of a return to *'civilian'* life in 1955 was centred on Maitland Pendock. He was a long-standing friend who owned a company called Elmbourne Ltd, which had its office in Seymour Place, London. Pendock was a London advertising consultant, a jolly middle-aged man with a round Pickwickian face. It is alleged that he was a spy and that his business was a cover for spying activities. He and Crabb had been friends for over 20 years, and Pendock had employed Crabb to sell a new type of build-it-yourself furniture, mostly to the new espresso coffee bars. Crabb maintained a strong friendship with Pat Rose and she states that they were engaged. She recalled visiting Pendock's office on a number of occasions and getting to know him fairly well, although she did not particularly like him. On some of the visits she was introduced to other people, and remembered meeting

Anthony Blunt, who also appeared to be a close friend of Pendock. Burgess, Maclean and Philby were all associated with Pendock, which suggests that the furniture business, while providing a genuine face, was a front for spies and informants. Mike had a discussion with a former police officer who recalled a raid on a property in London about 1956. The shop sold furniture but the rooms above the shop were the centre of the search. The police officers were not given any information as to why the raid was carried out other than it was a matter of security. He thought that some of those attending who were not recognised as police officers were in fact from the security service.

Crabb, in the social circle of nobility and titles, was certainly the underdog and even his hero status seemed to mean little. To counter this he had another social circle of friends with Pat Rose, Marshal Pugh, the Naggs Head publican, Len Cole and Knowles, Crabb's right hand man throughout the war and even in the post war years.

All of these people looked up to Crabb and none more so than Knowles. Robin Bryans acknowledged that Crabb welcomed Knowles's presence as it gave him a position of authority. However, the place where Crabb was in his element, was underwater and in the Royal Navy. He had achieved the impossible at the time and progressed to the rank of Commander, where he had authority and the respect of his peers. He had become a hero in the war and in the Navy, a status that was understood and respected. The problem for Crabb had come when he reached the end of his active service life, and civilian life in either of the social circles did not offer a rosy future.

When Knowles left the Navy, he entered into a partnership in the purchase of two trucks, of which he drove one, on long distance haulage. Seeking his fortune as a civilian, he was still an adventurer at heart and thus maintained contact with Crabb, both eager to get into the water at any opportunity. On the face of it, it appears that the Navy had dramatically curtailed Crabb's underwater exploits. However, evidence shows that he found himself working when required on adhoc underwater jobs for the Admiralty, MI6 and the CIA. He still yearned for the adventure of being a full time diver, for he was, in his own words, a *diverholic*. Prior to his disappearence Marshal Pugh was writing Crabb's autobiography. One man who was to be valuable in this task was Knowles and he was to become a frequent visitor to London, having obtained a contract for transporting large rolls of paper from the north of England. On these visits he would stay at Pugh's house, where, joined by Crabb, they would talk about their war experiences and Pugh would make copious notes.

It was during those talks and story telling that Knowles recalls how other visitors often popped in for a chat, and one he remembers very well was Crabb's posh art friend, Anthony Blunt. They would talk about the values of communism, which confused Knowles. He raised the subject with Crabb, who brushed the matter off, saying that they had left wing views but were harmless. Blunt also told Crabb that his services in diving would be treated much differently in the Soviet Union and that the Russians would make use of his experiences. It was, according to Knowles, probably part of what was to be an effective plot by the KGB and GRU to obtain Crabb's services. Apart from the meetings with Pugh, Crabb was very much a man about town and partook in activities of a more formal nature called *last suppers*. It became apparent to Knowles that those who attended were in his words a 'bunch of commies'. Apart from being Communists many were gay and Knowles felt out of place. Often they spoke above him, but Crabb always insisted that he attend, and they, for their part, accepted him. He told us:

"We were like two adventuring buccaneers and they loved to hear stories of our diving exploits and to that end Crabb was a very good story teller."

The unofficial leader of the aptly called *last suppers* was Anthony Blunt, known as the QM or Queen Mother who, as a prominent founder member of the *Apostles,* guided the small groups in conversation. Knowles was introduced to a wide variety of people from the British

Security Services, the CIA and the West German Secret Service. He was perplexed to see these people from the West's intelligence services talking freely about their work and ongoing operations with dedicated Communists, many of whom were to be exposed as KGB or GRU agents. However, what shocked him more than anything was that Crabb was actively mixing with them. At this point Knowles said that he knew that Crabb was a spy, but what he did not know was, on whose side. He assumed he was working in some capacity for the British. He further stated that the two diving operations on the *Sverdlov* and the *Ordzhonikidze* (described below) involved those attending the *last suppers*.

Knowles told us that those present at the *Sverdlov* briefings were Mathew Smith and Blunt. He went on to explain that Blunt just sat in on the discussions but did not have an input into the operation. He could best be described as a recruiter and it was becoming evident that his target was Crabb and that Knowles would simply follow the leader. Blunt was, as far as Knowles was concerned, something to do with the security service; his treachery had not been uncovered at that time. Whilst he was educated and well spoken, according to Knowles, he had strange ideas about how good it was in the Soviet Union.

After the *Sverdlov* operation, all of those who attended the *'last suppers'* spoke to Crabb, with Knowles in the background, and congratulated them on a successful operation, which in the future was to further fuel his suspicion that the dive was a practice for something of far greater significance.

Knowles wrote to us:

"To Crabbie civilian life was alien. He missed his diving and with drink, he was suicidal. What an easy target for Blunt and Co with all their promises. I never dreamt that I would be stronger than him…They scared me! Only God knows the hours of arguments when I tried to dissuade him."

He continued to explain:

"I suspected after a while that Crabb was a spy but I didn't know which bloody side he was on".

Knowles states that the *last suppers* were held about once a month, at different locations in London; although he did not attend regularly, when in London he would accompany Crabb. A large house, said to be on the left hand side of Tite Street, down near the river, was one place that featured regularly. Other locations included a houseboat; a house in Mayfair; Marshall Pugh's house and a number of other flats in and around the centre of London. Knowles recalls that there was no security of any sort and people came and went as they pleased. Many were homosexual and clearly did not hide the fact, and to his disgust he found himself on numerous occasions at the end of sexual advances by those of the gay community.

Knowles named Americans present at the meeting as Falk and Bedicheck, who according to him were not, as far as he knew, involved with the CIA, although they knew Smith very well. After the *Ordzhonikidze* operation where Crabb disappeared, Smith departed both the Security Service and the UK, to live in the USA. It is alleged that the residents of the USA made their visits to London frequently and extended their travel into Europe. As members of the Communist Party of the USA they would have made use of the valuable information that passed between the guests. Knowles alleges that the only woman participant of the *last suppers* was Lillian Hellman. He told us that she was American, a Communist, and had social contacts at a high level in the USA. Knowles did not know much about her background other than she had travelled to the Soviet Union during the war and was a frequent visitor in the post war period during what was the anti-Communist era, and was a visitor to Blunt's gatherings. She was an accomplished writer and regular broadcaster, who is alleged to have lived in Rome when not in London. An interesting twist follows in that a woman who had completed a radio broadcast and lived in Rome had approached Pat Rose. Was it she, an alleged member of the *last suppers,* who had spoken to Rose and then written to her stating that Crabb was alive and in Russia?

Another frequent visitor to the *last suppers* was a man named Ellis, who Knowles described to us and could have been Colonel Charles Howard Ellis, a senior MI6 officer. He had been in close liaison with the Russians during his service and had actually married a White Russian. In 1951 he came under suspicion for being a spy and was carefully shielded by Philby, but an internal political battle between MI5 and MI6 ensued, the result of which meant that Ellis could not be questioned. In 1953 he took early retirement on the grounds of suffering from heart trouble and travelled to Australia, where he immediately joined the Australian Secret Intelligence Service. It is ironic that the Australians did not contact either MI5 or MI6 to enquire about their new man. After two months he resigned from his post and returned to the UK and was employed part time by MI6, weeding out files held by the department and disposing of those he deemed not to be of value. He was employed in this role during the critical period of 1955-56 and the Russians wanted somebody in place with access to the files. Who gave him the job and how much damage was done is unclear. The strength of the answer lies in bringing the man already under suspicion back to London after two months in the Australian secret service, to a post in MI6 archives. It was also at this time that the third man debate had been raised in the House of Commons, denouncing Philby as a spy, of which he was cleared and was actually taken back into MI6, albeit unofficially at the Beirut Station.

Crabb's strange lifestyle continued. It is claimed that he received mysterious letters in plain envelopes that would be delivered by typists from a Government department. There is little doubt that he was frequently on secret missions. One mission was to the Canal Zone (Suez Canal), and upon his return he was taken directly to report to Lord Mountbatten, who was playing in a polo match. Such was the life of those in the murky, dirty world of secret operations.

It was in October 1955 that Knowles was contacted by Crabb and asked if he would like to join him for a small diving job in Portsmouth. Crabb said that it would be an easy task and that they would get a fair fee. Knowles accepted the offer and met Crabb in London as well as Mathew Smith who, according to Knowles, was organising a mission to look under the soviet cruiser *Sverdlov*. The claim was that the cruiser had displayed a good turn of speed, could enter port very quickly and seemed to be very manoeuverable. It is said that the British and Americans both wanted to know what made the vessel so versatile, but because the ship was in British waters an investigation could not involve the Royal Navy. It had to be a private job.

Crabb and Knowles had diving equipment of Italian origin from their wartime exploits. They travelled to Portsmouth with Smith during the hours of darkness. Knowles said they dressed in two-piece diving suits, donned their breathing sets and entered the water. On their heads they wore skullcaps with black veils attached. The latter was a net that hung down over the head and face allowing them to see but broke up the silhouettes of their heads when on the surface. They reached the stern of the cruiser and dived down to the propellers and rudder. They found nothing out of place or unusual. They then moved to the bilge keel, where Crabb signalled Knowles to remain where he was while he went forward. A short while latter he returned and signalled for Knowles to follow him forward. The two men moved to the bow, where Knowles found himself on the edge of a large circular opening in the bottom of the hull. He waited on the edge whilst Crabb went up inside and examined a propeller. It was evident that the propeller could be lowered and directed to give thrust to the bow and aid the ship's manoeuvering. After the inspection both men moved away from the ship to swim back to their rendezvous and report to Smith.

Knowles told us:

"I was told that the Sverdlov *job was an MI6 and CIA operation, and the Royal Navy were not involved in any way."*

To further place the operation as MI6 and CIA, there was, according to Knowles, the introduction of an individual called Taylor, whom he describes as an MI6 electronics whiz kid. He was developing a small device to attach to a ship, which sent out a signal that could be picked up by a submarine and allowed the target ship to be followed at a distance. Taylor did not go to Portsmouth, and Knowles was told that the *blip stick*, as Crabb named it, did not work. Knowles's description of Taylor possibly points to John Taylor of the Special Investigation Unit of the Post Office at Dollis Hill. Knowles states that he was a boffin who was providing a technical piece of equipment for what appeared to be a Western secret service operation.

Knowels explained:

"I don't think Taylor was one of them, but it was such a bloody mix up, you didn't know whose side anybody was on." He continued: *"HMS Vernon was not used by us, although, at the time we went on the Sverdlov job, Crabb was a regular visitor there. We did not use Naval equipment nor did Naval personnel brief us. We kept clear of any Naval establishments and personnel, and went directly to a house at Eastney."*

The man who owned the house had equipment to charge up their Italian oxygen bottles, which had a different connecting thread to those of the Royal Navy. Knowles never knew the name of the man, only that he was a keen diver and had equipment that he used in the newly formed British Sub Aqua Club. Knowles thought it ironic yet again that the man gave a clear indication that he was a Communist. The house was small and cramped but provided a place to rest until they were ready to undertake the *Sverdlov* dive. It was on the final brief between them that Knowles had more reservations about Crabb and Smith.

Crabb told Knowles that if the Russians caught them they would request political asylum.

Knowles explained:

"It was as if we were going to the vessel to be picked up, but of course in the event nothing happened and we made the swim in and out again without any problems."

But the principle question that remained in knowles mind was why was it so easy, and what were they really doing? Upon reflection he said that it was as if the *Sverdlov* job was a practice run for something bigger, as he knew that the Navy would look under the ship, and submarines had gathered information about the propeller signatures, so apart from the bow thruster there was nothing new to be gained.

Knowles told us:

"There was little to nothing of value, but we were diving again and the wartime adrenaline was flowing."

When the job was completed the three men departed Portsmouth and travelled back to London by car. The man at Eastney was never to be seen again. Knowles assumed that the information of the bow thruster would be passed through to MI6 by Smith. On the question of money Knowles told us that they were paid a total of three thousand pounds. Two thousand pounds went to Crabb, and Knowles received one thousand. They had to go and see the paymaster, Murray Michaljohn who paid out in cash and did not require them to sign a receipt, which is most unusual. Knowles did not question the vast sum of money involved. He told us:

"It was an awful lot of money in those days and if they were to pay out like that, then I looked forward to more."

The cruiser *Sverdlov* was on a visit to take part in the Spithead review and was moved to be anchored at sea, in clear water. We have been told by several official sources that a naval clearance diving team then carried out an official covert underwater survey of the hull. The team was dropped off to drift with the current using closed circuit breathing apparatus so as to remain undetected. After completing the survey they were picked up well clear of the cruiser. This operation was a separate operation from the one carried out by Crabb and Knowles, and could have been undertaken to confirm Crabb's findings and obtain more details.

The *Sverdlov* class cruisers were large and fast, displacing some 19,200 tons, and having a maximum speed of 34.5 knots. Their overall length of 689 feet (207 metres) and a beam of 70 feet (21 metres) served as a platform for a considerable array of weapons. The main armament comprised twelve six-inch (152.4mm) guns, mounted in four tripple turrets. Secondary armament was in the form of twelve 3.9inch (101.6 mm) guns, mounted in six twin mounts. Anti aircraft firepower came from thirty-two 37mm guns. As with ship design of that period, additional weapons consisted of 21-inch (533.4mm) torpedo tubes and between 140 and 240 mines. The complement was some 1,050 officers and men. The area of the hull that was underwater, while not measured, was considerable, especially in terms of a diver inspecting it.

The *Ordzhonikidze* was built in Leningrad and launched on 17 September 1950, to be commissioned on 30 June 1952. The cruiser took part in numerous naval exercises and visited foreign ports including Portsmouth, Copenhagen and went twice to Helsinki. In February 1960, Soviet leader Nikita Khrushchev paid a visit to President Sukarno of Indonesia and signed an agreement for the Soviets to supply ships, planes, helicopters, tanks, and other armaments. The most expensive part of the deal was the cruiser *Ordzhonikidze*. On 11 January 1961, the Soviet Government issued a special resolution for the ship's tropicalisation which involved a large-scale modernisation that would make the cruiser suitable for service in tropical climatic conditions. However, Indonesia could not afford such a large project and, as a result, the modernisation was confined to the installation of more powerful diesel generators to power additional ventilators. On

14 February 1961, the *Ordzhonikidze* went to Sevastopol and on 5 April 1962, it began to run sea trials at which time the ship's Indonesian crew of naval officers were on board the cruiser. On 5 August 1962, the *Ordzhonikidze* arrived in Surabaya, after which it was transferred to Indonesia in a formal ceremony and renamed *Irian*.

However, by 1964 the cruiser had actually lost its operating efficiency, and it was decided to send the *Irian* to Vladivostok for repairs. Soviet sailors and repairmen were shocked to see the state of neglect on the ship and the large amount of minor repairs. Such repairs are usually carried out by the crew, but nothing had been done and it was down to the Soviet Union to fulfil all the points of the repair contract. In 1965, Suharto, who was not interested in the Navy, replaced Sukarno as President and the cruiser remained moored at Surabaya. It was made into a prison and later in 1970, the abandoned *Irian* was washed onto a sandbank, and its hull soon became filled with water. In 1972 the flagship of the Indonesian Navy began to be scrapped.

Peter Wright describes in *Spy Catcher* how MI6 carried out an operation against the *Ordzhonikidze* whilst in a Soviet port. They used one of the X craft midget submarines that MI6 kept at Stokes Bay. A naval frogman had attempted to enter the harbour, but security was too tight and the mission was aborted. By 1955 the Soviets were well aware of the potential vulnerability of their ports and harbours and would have taken appropriate measures to defend them. There is also the question of where MI6 found the crew, because by 1955 all the wartime expertise with the craft had been dispersed back to civilian life. There were people like Crabb and Knowles willing and able to undertake covert operations, but running a submarine is different to partaking in an underwater swim. We have been told that Crabb was the diver on this operation.

The X craft midget submarines were 14.4 metres (48 feet) long and had a maximum diameter of some 1.68 metres (5 ft 6 in). This meant the four men in the crew were unable to stand up straight, unless they were on the small side. The boat was divided into four compartments. The forward one contained the battery that supplied power for the ballast pumps and the auxiliary machinery and powered the craft when it was submerged, and it was in this compartment that the divers' equipment was stored.

The second section was called the 'wet and dry' compartment. It was an escape chamber based on those designed and fitted in the latest submarines. Although quite small, one man in diving equipment could leave and enter. The door of the compartment was sealed closed, and the diver opened a valve allowing water to enter. Once full of water, the outer hatch was opened and the diver could go outside. On re-entering the submarine, the diver would seal the outside door then blow out the water until the compartment was dry. The inside door could then be opened, and the diver would be back inside the submarine. The use of this compartment did not alter the trim of the boat, nor did it allow water into the remainder of the compartments.

The third compartment was the main one and housed all of the controls for operating the submarine. Dozens of levers, wheels and gauges were crammed into the restricted space. The two periscopes were housed in this area, one giving a general wide field of view, the other narrow angled for attack. Also set in this over-crowded area were the air purifiers and cooking equipment, where the most basic of food and drinks could be made. The fourth and final compartment was the home of the gyrocompass, the high-pressure compressor and a further mass of pipes, gauges, levers and valves.

These small craft could remain submerged for 36 hours on battery power, and when cruising the crew operated in two shifts, two men at the controls and two men resting, changing round every four hours. On the run-in for attack, all four men would man their stations, one of them dressed in the diving equipment. To ensure a reasonable endurance, the X craft was towed to the operational area by a large submarine or surface vessel. As all those involved in Second World War operations found, there were major hazards with the towing aspect and as a consequence the Navy, at the end of the war, did not continue the use of the craft.

Further evaluation of the midget submarines, situation is explained by Paul Kemp in *Underwater Warriors,* in that, in 1945 Britain possessed the largest midget submarine 'fleet', with five X20-series craft, six XT-series training craft and ten XE-series craft. The drastic reduction of the Royal Navy in the immediate post-war period saw this fleet reduced to four XE-Craft which were employed until *1953,* when they were sold for breaking up. The four XEs had shown themselves so useful that in September 1951 four replacement boats were ordered, known as the *X51* class.

Kemp explains that most of the activities of the *X51* series are still covered by the provisions of the Official Secrets Act, but there are a number of references to an operation conducted in 1955 when an X-Craft was involved in an attempt to measure the diameter of the propellers of the new Soviet cruiser *Ordzhonikidze,* the design of which was of inordinate interest to naval intelligence. The information thus gained could be used to identify targets using the newly established bottom-arrays of the Sound Surveillance System (SOSUS). The details of this unusual operation are still shrouded in secrecy, but at least one X-Craft was sent to Kronstadt in order to release a diver to measure the cruiser's propellers. However, the diver found the harbour defences too tough to penetrate and the operation was aborted. One *X51* class submarine commander, commenting on this rumour, wrote:

"To take (i.e. tow) an X-Craft to Kronstadt covertly, through the narrow and shallow entrance to the Baltic, would be tricky to say the least. Moreover, the tow would be extremely lengthy. The risks for a very, very iffy peacetime / Cold War operation would, in my view, have been unacceptable."

Another X- Craft commander commented:

"...Midget submarine exercises and evaluations tended to be frankly hairy,

happily hairy, but hairy nonetheless. The sort of training they were bound to
undertake in order to maintain a realistic wartime efficiency in peacetime was
liable to attract the kind of publicity that Naval officers concerned with PR
have always tried to avoid."

The value the Royal Navy placed on such vessels is shown by the fact that the British X-Craft unit was disbanded in 1958.

The interesting points here are that the *Sverdlov* visited Portsmouth in 1955 and the *Ordzhonikidze,* in April 1956. Both these events would be planned well in advance and the mini-subs could have been used on both these occasions saving the risky, long underwater swim that frogmen endured to get to their targets. We know from an interview with Simon Pendock, the son of Crabb's friend Maitland Pendock, a former Royal Marine Special Boat Squadron frogman, that in the 1950s Crabb was operating with mini-subs. He knew this for a fact because he worked with him.

Stan Currie-Davis, a former Naval diving officer and friend of Crabb, said that he was part of an operation that was tasked with investigating the underside of the *Ordzhonikidze* when it visited Sweden prior to its visit to Britain. That operation involved the US Navy and Royal Navy working with the Swedish Government. He described a scene of military people sneaking about in the dock at night with a variety of equipment, including diving equipment. Their objective was to obtain information about the ship, including its hull and anything that may have been of interest. The British and Americans knew all about the underneath of the cruiser, so why was the Portsmouth operation organized? The simple truth is that it had nothing to do with the inspection of the ship's hull or propulsion system, and that is why there was a cover up that has been so effective for all these years.

Crabb telephoned Knowles and told him that there was a very important job and he needed Knowles to be part of the dive team; he could not discuss the details but it involved the Soviet cruiser the *Ordzhonikidze.* Knowles originally told us that he declined because of personal problems at home. He later told us that he would have followed Crabb anywhere, as indeed he had done during the war. It had become apparent to Knowles that Crabb had changed and was obsessed and angry about being discarded by the Navy. He sought a place where he could use his underwater knowledge and skills. Knowles was aware that one place could be the Soviet Union but whether as a spy or defector was a matter of speculation. Sydney told us:

"I had a terrible scene with Crabbie and I accused him of going 'home' to which he replied that he was just a diverholic and millions would benefit from his action, but I did not understand that statement."

Pat Rose, in interview, described how Crabb asked her to travel to Portsmouth with him. She had agreed to marry him but had to wait for the ring until he returned from Portsmouth. She knew he was going to do a job and not wanting him to go, did at first decline to travel with him. He was quite insistent and she asked why he was so adamant, because he normally travelled alone when going on a jaunt. She said that things were not normal but did not know what was wrong. She explained:

"I had never seen him uptight and it troubled me".

She eventually decided to go with him and they boarded a train at Victoria, bound for Portsmouth. They found an empty compartment and Crabb moved into a corner and sat looking out of the window. Out of character, he almost ignored Rose and seemed deep in thought. After a while of silence Rose challenged him to say what was wrong. He relented enough to tell her that he was going to try out some new equipment. Rose told us:

"That was wrong because Crabbie was always testing something or other and when he was going to dive he was always excited. This time something troubled him."

Rose was not satisfied with that and told him that if he did not tell her what was wrong she was going to call off the engagement. That caused him to open up a little and he told her he was going to look under the Russian cruiser. She said he was mad because the Russians would be on the lookout for anybody doing that. He replied that he had a special job to do and she asked if Knowles was going on the job. When told that he was not, she demanded to know why. He did not answer but said that it was a very important job and that it was top secret, then he sat in silence and smoked a cigarette. He took out his wallet and removed the photographs he had of her, one taken in the South of France with her brother and sister-in-law and the one of her sitting beside a swimming pool. After studying them he put them back in his wallet and sat in silence. When discussing the situation with Rose she said that he told her not to worry and that he would be back in London the next day or the day after. She was to conclude that his strange attitude towards her throughout the day was caused by the discomfort of lying to her.

When they arrived in Portsmouth she told him to take her to the Queen's Hotel for tea. He told her that he was not staying at the Queen's and did not know what the arrangement was, but he had to meet Smith to be briefed on the operation. They waited at Portsmouth station for the London train. Rose boarded the train and left Crabb on the platform. Having said their goodbyes, she watched him walk through the barriers, to disappear from her life. As Rose recalled the events of long ago she said that things were not right.

Knowles told us:

"He did not tell her (Rose) why I refused to go. I asked her if she suspected anything and she just said that he had changed. I am sure she knew but could not face the embarrassment."

Prior to the *Ordzhonikidze* operation, Crabb wrote to Petty Officer David Bell, a former member of the Gibraltar team, which was very strange because he never wrote letters, apart from those to his mother. Frank Goldsworthy, the reporter with the *Daily Express,* told us that

Crabb did not like paperwork and treated it with distain. During the war he used to pin his operational report to a wooden door with a bayonet. He also wrote to the publisher, which was considered by Marshall Pugh, his biographer, to be completely out of character. They had difficulty in getting him to make alterations to the manuscript. He also wrote to his mother and instructed her to tear the letter up after she had read it. We do not know the contents of the letter, but it is said that she told others that it was not like her Lionel and she was very worried.

It was the day before the Russian ships were due to berth, when it is said that Crabb and Smith went to the office of Chief Constable Arthur West. They explained that they were working for the secret service (MI5) and that their mission was to examine the bottom of the *Ordzhonikidze*. West was to learn later that the ship had already been examined in the Baltic (Sweden). West checked the story offered by Crabb and Smith and it was confirmed by MI5 that they were on an underwater operation, which is in contradiction to other evidence. However, it is not known whom West spoke to, bearing in mind that MI5 was already a nest of Soviet spies. They were provided with an office in the Central Police Station, fitted with a scrambler phone and assigned Supt. Lamport to look after them. They decided to stay at a hotel convenient to the docks but not one that would draw attention to them. It was the Sally Port Hotel.

The manuscript given to the authors by Goldsworthy provided some of the background to events at Portsmouth. With poetic licence he described a black saloon car which brought the next stage of the Crabb mystery to the cobbled High Street of Portsmouth on the evening of Tuesday the 17 April 1956; Budget Day. The car ran slowly along the filled-up tramlines and pulled in, past the Sally Port Hotel. A waitress preparing dinner tables in the bow-windowed dining room saw two men get out. The Sally Port Hotel, a four-storied, 200-year-old building, is double fronted and was painted in cream and blue with gilt lettering. It is the centre of the old town of Portsmouth, famous in

Britain's naval history, near the ancient and historic Sally Port from which Admiral Horatio Nelson sailed and beside which Admiral Anson lived.

The two men entered and approached the hotelier, 53-year-old Mr.. Edward Richman, who, wearing a white coat, was seated in the square paned reception and was very busy. It was about 8pm and the twenty-room hotel was full except for two top rooms, numbers 17 and 20. Most of the guests were businessmen connected with shipbuilding and a couple were Admiralty inspectors. When one of the two men asked about accommodation, Richman told them that there were two attic rooms, but was busy and unable to take them to the rooms, so he gave them the keys and told them to go and have a look. The keys were handed to the taller of the two men. This is the man who signed the register as Smith. He took the smaller of the two rooms, number 17, and a single, to allow his companion, Crabb, to take the larger, more comfortable number 20. Crabb's room had a double bed and sloping walls typical of an attic in an old building. The square window overlooked Vosper's shipyard, part of the dockyard and harbour. In the centre of the view was the South Railway jetty, the berth to be occupied by the Russian cruiser carrying Bulganin and Khrushchev on a goodwill visit, framed with a forest of cranes and masts, with stretches of harbour water with ferry boats, sails and smoke, all of which was, of course, most convenient.

Witnesses detailed the movements of both Crabb and his companion Smith. It was recorded that having arrived at the Sally Port Hotel on Tuesday the 17 April at 8pm neither took dinner at the hotel, but Crabb appeared in the Porthole Bar of the Sally Port at about 8:30 where he drank two whiskies. At 9pm Crabb left the hotel but returned about 9:30pm, expecting to see Smith in the bar. He went to Smith's room to see if he wanted a drink, but about 9:45pm Crabb returned alone, smiled and said that his companion had gone to bed. When asked about morning tea Crabb replied that he would be out early, so they should not bother about a call, tea or papers. He told them not to bother with number 17 either and said that they would both be out early. He accepted, from Richman, front door keys for himself and Smith, in case they were late. So, after a nightcap of whiskey and water, Crabb left the bar about 10:30pm, presumably to go to bed. Nobody remembered seeing him again that night.

The brass barometer in the Sally Port Hotel was set at Fair, on Wednesday the 18 April and it was a mild spring morning. The hotel life awoke at about 7am but nobody saw either Crabb or Smith, as they were out early. High tides for this day were at 4:32am and 5:26pm. It was about 8:30 when Crabb returned to the hotel and ordered breakfast of eggs and bacon and read a newspaper. The waitress remembered that he looked out through the net curtains up and down the High Street as if expecting somebody, and then he suddenly rose and walked out of the hotel.

Sightseers crowded around the dock area of Portsmouth to watch the arrival of the Soviet warships. The principal ship, the cruiser *Ordzhonikidze*, moved into the harbour faster than would normally be expected from a ship of her size, as had her sister ship *Sverdlov* before, and displayed the ability to stop and manoeuver rapidly over a short distance. Following the cruiser were two destroyers, the *Smotryashci* and the *Sovershenny*. The *Ordzhonikidze* moved alongside at the South Railway jetty at Portsmouth Royal Naval Dockyard with her bows faced up-river, stern towards the sea. Once the cruiser was moored the two Soviet destroyers moved alongside the cruiser and also moored. Interest in the ships was twofold; first, they were part of the 'new' Soviet Navy and second, and probably of more interest, was the fact that the cruiser carried the Soviet Union's most powerful people, Premier Khrushchev and Marshall Bulganin.

Commander Crabb would have observed the ships entering the harbour and berthing in the dockyard confines. The shape and size of the cruiser would have been familiar to him from his exploration of the *Sverdlov* the year before. Later that day Crabb returned to the hotel and made a telephone call. He then proceeded to the bar and had a drink before having dinner. When he had finished he left the hotel, and walked towards Portsmouth centre and the railway station. It was before 9 o'clock that he arrived in Havant, and went to the Bear's Head Hotel, where he met an old friend, Lieutenant Commander John Crawford, RN and his wife Daphne. This encounter had been arranged by telephone beforehand and they chatted fairly generally over a drink or two. Crawford stated:

"I can remember no mention of frogmen or diving. We did not leave the Bear's Head until about 10 o'clock, when we dropped him off at Havant railway station, for his return to Portsmouth."

Also at the Bear's Head was a Petty Officer Loffty Gordon, who by coincidence ran a diving store at Vernon. He greeted Crabb as if they had not met for some time. Nobody saw or heard Crabb return to the Sally Port Hotel that night, and nobody had seen Smith leave or return. So the last friends to have seen Crabb before his disappearance were the Crawfords, and that was on the night of the 18 April 1956.

By 7am the following morning, the time of the earliest staff activity at the Sally Port Hotel, Crabb had already let himself out of the front door. Smith must also have left early, for not one of the staff caught sight of him. High tide on that day was at 5:54am and 6:53pm. Breakfast was laid for Crabb at a single table near the window and the waitress ticked off the guests at breakfast by the numbers of their rooms. When she cleared the tables, only two numbers were left unused, 17 and 20. Crabb, number 20, never came back. It was mid-morning, around 11:30am, when Smith appeared at the reception desk alone. He asked for both bills, stating that they were leaving. The total bill for two nights' bed and breakfast, and one extra dinner, was £3 16s (£3.80), which was paid in cash. Having retrieved belongings from both rooms he hurried out, carrying two bags.

Smith's part of the operation was completed. Crabb had been taken aboard the Russian cruiser. Smith departed from Portsmouth.

Having denied all knowledge of any underwater operation, the Admiralty later returned Crabb's clothes to his mother. Smith's cheque from the London meeting and the photographs Crabb had looked at on the train with Pat Rose were not with them. The swordstick, Crabb's talisman, was also missing. All investigations by the media and Crabb's family to find it drew blanks. Nobody knew at that time where it was.

The diving equipment Crabb used was of Italian manufacture, and was part of his obsession for everything Italian. One of the major differences was in the underwater diving suit. The Navy used a one-piece flexible rubber suit with seals at the neck and wrists to keep water out. Entry into the suit was through the neck, which was made of a very strong elastic rubber, which enabled it to be pulled open and allow the diver to get in. At the neck the rubber fitted onto a metal ring, where a clamp held suit and hood in place, while the hood itself fitted closely round the head, making a watertight seal at both the face and neck. Thin rubber cuffs fitted against the diver's wrists to form a seal, which meant that a diver in his undergarments should, providing the suit had no leaks, keep warm and dry.

The Pirelli or Heinke dry suit, which Crabb wore, differed in a number of ways from the Naval issue. This suit was a two-piece flexible rubber garment, with the lower part having built-in, reinforced feet. The top part of the suit overlapped the bottom and was loose-fitting. This allowed the two parts to be folded together to make a joint. A rubber band was put on to cover the joint, to hold the two parts together and ensure a watertight seal. This suit also had a rubber seal at the wrists, but the neck did not require a separate seal, for a thin flexible rubber collar fitted against the neck, making it watertight. This suit could be worn with or without a hood, but if a hood was worn, it would be loose-fitting and used for protection and insulation.

The breathing equipment used by Crabb and the naval divers also differed. The Royal Navy's Clearance Divers Breathing Apparatus (CDBA) was a relatively small and compact set that used the closed-circuit principle; the breathing gas is recycled within the system, rather than the expired gas being discharged into the water, as is the case with compressed air diving equipment. Combat swimmers used this type of system because it was compact and gave off no tell tale bubbles to give them away. It had one disadvantage in that when used with pure oxygen, it restricted the operational depth to ten metres (33 feet). This is because oxygen becomes toxic when used below this depth. There is a built-in safety margin, but this is only disregarded under extreme emergency. Royal Naval divers also used a mixed gas that allowed them to dive deeper.

The CDBA comprised a vest, which fitted over the head to rest on the shoulders. At the front, in line with the chest, was a flexible bag, the counter lung. In the centre of the bag was a round canister containing Protosorb, comprising soda-lime granules which absorb the carbon dioxide produced when the diver breathes out. A flexible concertina hose connected the Protosorb canister to the bottom of the full-face mask, and had, on the inside, a mouthpiece through which the diver breathed. The facemask had a round glass faceplate inserted into a soft rubber molding which fitted the full extent of the face, sealing onto the rubber hood. It was held in place by adjustable rubber straps.

The counter lung was supplied with oxygen from a small oxygen bottle set under the bag, which the diver opened and closed to fill it. If the bag should be overfilled, a relief valve discharged masses of minute bubbles, which dispersed so as not to show on the surface. When the bag was breathed down, it was refilled the same way. To balance the diver when in the water, ball weights were carried in a small pouch on the upper part of the back of the vest. The diver could release these in an emergency. Because of this method of ballasting, the diver did not require a weight belt.

The Italian system worked on the same breathing principle. It differed in so far as it was small and more compact than the Royal Navy's and was a firm favorite with Commander Crabb, who had used it in Italy. No full-face mask was worn, only a small half mask, similar to those in use today by recreational SCUBA divers. It did not have any built-in weight system, so when wearing a dry suit the diver had to wear a separate weight belt. The breathing tube travelled from the protosorb canister directly to the mouthpiece, which meant that it fitted directly into the diver's mouth.

The Royal Navy greatly preferred their own system, reasoning that, if a diver passed out whilst underwater, the mouthpiece of the CDBA would remain in his mouth, and the mask would prevent drowning. The fact that the mouthpiece could not easily be accidentally knocked out of the diver's mouth was also a safeguard when moving about in black water conditions. With the Italian system it was also possible for small amounts of water to seep past the mouth and down the hose to mix with the protosorb, causing a 'cocktail' that was harmful to the diver. However, Crabb had used the Italian system in every conceivable situation and would hear nothing said against it.

Crabb entered the water and swam to the ship. He did not return. There were no special anti-diver clamps or other devices awaiting him. Crabb simply surfaced and remained long enough to ensure that he was seen, whereupon the Russian divers went into action. Royal Naval observers saw a skirmish in the water and he was taken aboard the cruiser. If Crabb really had been looking under the cruiser, and had an equipment failure, he would have surfaced close to the hull, which would have afforded him some shelter from observation and there were suitable places amid the mooring pontoons where he could have gone. If in real difficulties, he was experienced enough to have ditched his weight belt, and used the breathing bag as a buoyancy aid to make his escape. Contemporary newspaper articles stated that the Russians reported observing a diver face up on the surface; where he remained, and there was no question of panic, arm waiving or other gestures. They reported that after a while he went below the surface again. If he had managed to surface and remain there for a period of time then buoyancy kept him there and would have continued to do so. If he went down then was it under control. In short, below the surface Russian divers would have had little to no hope of finding him if he did not want to be found.

As Sydney Knowles explained:

"Look how many hours police divers spend searching for a body in a pond, and we are talking about the vast expanse of Portsmouth harbour". He continued: *"I have wept a hundred times over the years when I have thought of Crabb's action. As a friend he hurt me so much because he betrayed me."*

What of Soviet Security? The best defence against any form of underwater investigation would have been to have a ship's ASDIC operating. Sonar emits a sound wave that would drastically affect a diver, and he would have to abort his dive. It is still the most effective measure used today, apart from turning the ships propellers, which in the *Ordzhonikidze's* case would have been impractical with three warships berthed together. In fact, cruisers were generally not fitted with ASDIC but relied on smaller anti submarine warships to use underwater detection systems and weapons to deal with any submarine targets.

During their stay, the Soviet ships were under constant observation by naval personnel at *HMS Vernon* and other establishments, who maintained detailed logs of events. Contrary to the Admiralty reports, there were no underwater experiments at Stokes Bay. It is claimed by one source that a naval diving team was moved to a new location during the period of the Crabb dive. We have examined the official log books for *HMS Vernon* for the time which show that earlier in the year divers from the school had carried out underwater searches for lost bodies. One of these was the body of a boy, which had been found after two days. In another case they searched for a body lost in a plane crash, all of which showed that the Navy were active in searching for lost bodies.

The *HMS Vernon* logbook shows that staff returned to base at 8:45am on the 19 April 1956, having gone on leave on the 3 April. This means that when Crabb went into the water at Portsmouth the diving staff were still officially on leave leaving only a minimum number of divers on call. The records show that they assembled at *HMS Vernon* after Crabb had disappeared. The official logbook is interesting in that entries were made until the 29 April, after which the pages are blank. By the 29 April it was public knowledge that Crabb was missing. Entries on or after the 19 April do not record any underwater searches being made or any record of the Crabb operation. A second logbook identified those undertaking diver training at Vernon. For the period covering Crabb's disappearance the pages are numbered in red pencil and after page 10 there had been a page 11, but it had been torn out. What became page 11 had originally been numbered 12. The two, had been rubbed out and replaced with a one. The two although faint, could still clearly be seen. There is no explanation for the removal of the page and entries stop soon after, leaving two thirds of the book with blank pages. Why was the original page 11 removed?

The naval watch on the morning of the 18 April is alleged to have comprised a Lieutenant and a Petty Officer, who, according to author Bernard Hutton, witnessed and recorded the following events. They observed Russian divers enter the water and remain near the cruiser. They then saw another diver on the surface, alone, between the cruiser and one of the destroyers. They watched the Russian divers move towards the lone diver. There was a 'skirmish' and all of the divers disappeared under the water near the cruiser. This action is said to have taken place at the stern of the ships. The naval watch continued to observe the Russian vessels but saw nothing more of the divers. Details of the events were recorded in the duty logbook and all the information was passed immediately to the Admiralty. Other witnesses came forward and made statements about the incident. Former Petty Officer Fleetway, whose observations made the national press, was aboard *HMS Starling*, moored barely 100 yards away from the *Ordzhonikidze* on the morning of Crabb's dive. He was struck by the unusual activity going on around the cruiser. The last thing Fleetway saw was three frogmen surface and make for one of the small boats. Two of the trio pushed the other into it. The other frogmen clustered round. The boat headed for the climbing ladder.

Lt Commander Stan Currie-Davis who was a diving officer at Portland at the time of the operation told us that many qualified diving personnel were, before the Crabb story made the newspapers, either given overseas postings or moved out of the Portsmouth area. This was a precaution so that when the press arrived in Portsmouth, those who might be questioned were out of the way. The authorities quizzed all officers who knew Crabb and were aware that he had been in Portsmouth. They were trying to find out if he had said anything about what he was up to. Those who remained at *HMS Vernon* were told not to speak about the Crabb incident to anybody, loss of pensions or worse were the order of the day.

In a twist to the whole story, there was, among official documents that have been released, a secret memo that identified two remarkable Statutory Declarations being made by a Lieutenant Commander G. Franklin RN. Both were made on 19 June 1956 to a Notary Public, which proclaimed that he was involved in assisting Crabb with not one but two dives. Franklin states that he was a good friend of Crabb, having first met him in 1949. Both had worked together on underwater operations. It is interesting that from all the communications with Knowles and other divers none had ever mentioned Franklin.

He claims that on Tuesday the 17 April 1956 Crabb, telephoned the Franklin and asked for a meeting that evening in a public house. They met and Crabb asked Franklin, who was an expert diver, if he would be prepared to assist him in an entirely unofficial dive and to do it in a private capacity. Crabb provided no details about the nature of the dive but he did state that the he was not to tell the authorities.

He agreed and on the afternoon 18 April he helped Crabb put on and adjust his equipment then assisted him into the water from the small boat. This happened in the Portsmouth area. Crabb was said to have been underwater for about half an hour. When he surfaced Franklin assisted Crabb back into the boat. He identifies that the exact location was from a boat mored in the Boat pound, immediately south of the Southern Railway Jetty in Portsmouth dockyard. Crabb wanted to make a second dive and it was agreed to do it the following morning.

Franklin accompanied Crabb on the morning of the 19 April 1956. There is no mention of Smith, who it is known accompanied Crabb. This occurred in the Portsmouth area just before 7:00am. Crabb was satisfied that his equipment was fitted and working correctly and that the weather was said to be fine with a calm sea and a slight ebb tide running. Under his two piece Heinke diving suit he wore a cotton vest, bathing trunks, rayon combinations, stockinet combinations and socks. On his head he had a little woolly balaclava with a bathing cap on top. Franklin states that Crabb had sufficient oxygen for a dive of about two hours. When Crabb went below the surface all of the conditions for a dive were good, but he did not return and was never seen by him again. When Crabb did not return, Franklin reported the incident to the Navy. Franklin concludes by explaining that the diving equipment was such that had there been a technical or physical failure and Crabb became unconscious then, as long as the equipment remained in place the body would not have come to the surface.

Such an activity on the part of Franklin would be an infringement of Navy Regulations, for which there would have been serious consequences such as Court Marshall, dismissal from the service, loss of pension and in this case a possible 'fatal accident' for any of the following:

1. Assisting Crabb (civilian according to the Navy) on an entirely unofficial dive in a military dockyard;
2. Breach of a directive from the Prime Minister;
3. A dive that involved a spying operation against a Soviet vessel on a goodwill visit to the UK;
4. Undertaking a mercenary operation in a private capacity whilst still serving in the Royal Navy;

5. Not informing his superiors about the proposed venture; Partaking in a diving operation that could have involved the defection of Philby, a Soviet spy.

The critical aspect of the story is that a serving naval officer has assisted a civilian with an unauthorised spying operation and, having got away with it, agrees to assist on a second dive. The second dive is claimed to have occurred the following morning about 7:00am. Again he claims to have helped Crabb get into his diving equipment. But again, there is no mention of Smith, who we know had stayed with Crabb at the Sally Port hotel the previous evening. Smith is identified in the widest number of documents and witness statements. Smith was the controlling element of the Crabb operation and was the link with the local police. It was Smith who returned the Sally Port hotel and recovered Crabb's belongings.

One of the most unbelievable aspects of Franklin's statement is that the first covert spying dive took place in the afternoon, in broad daylight. They were then operational the following day at 7:00am, diving from a boat in the southern boat pound. Based upon this evidence, secrecy apparently did not matter and could be considered to have been a joke. Both dives would have broken every rule of covet diving operations, and diving in daylight would have not provided any benefit over diving at night. The dockyard and its surrounds would have people walking or working and the security would have been at its highest with the Russian warships in port. But we are asked to believe that these two men in their boat carried out a spying operation and were not observed. It also means that they were not seen either coming or going with their equipment or getting out of and into the boat. It must also be remembered that, according to the Navy, Crabb was a civilian and would not have been given access to dockyard facilities. That is unless he had personal authorisation from 'M'. When Crabb did not return and Franklin could not locate him, he was reported missing. Why would he report the incident to the Navy? After all Crabb was a civilian, or so the Admiralty tells us.

Then there are two bizarre stories emanating from the Russians. The first was reported in *The Sunday Times* on the 9 June 1996, under the headline 'Russian spy 'solves' 40 year riddle of Britain's vanishing frogman'. It ran a story that said that Crabb's secret mission was to spy on equipment fitted to the ship's hull. The article revealed a far more bizarre story, which was unearthed by Yigal Serna, an Israeli journalist who tracked down Joseph Zverkin, former head of Soviet Naval intelligence, living in Haifa. He states that:

"Crabb was discovered when he was swimming next to the ship by a watchman, who was at a height of 20 metres."

The article does not say how they knew it was Crabb, as a diver wearing a mask with his head barely out of the water, is unrecognisable. Zverkin continues:

"An order was given to inspect the water and two people on the deck were equipped with a small calibre sniper gun. One was an ordinary seaman, and the other an officer, who was an exceptional shot. The Lieutenant shot the frogman in the head and killed him, leaving the body to sink. All the stories about him being caught by us or that he was a Russian spy are not true."

From this story we are asked to believe that a diver swimming close to the Soviet warships was shot! The ships were berthed at the most prominent position in Portsmouth Naval dockyard at the height of the Cold War, and this was a peace mission being undertaken by the principal enemy; the leaders of the Soviet Union, a nuclear-armed super power. It was in early morning daylight and there were people about, both military and civilian. The Gosport ferries were busy transporting boatloads of people across the river to and from work, passing close to the berth and the warships that were the object of interest to those people. The vessels were under constant observation by naval intelligence, and naval personnel patrolled the jetty where the vessels were berthed. Amidst this scene, we are asked to believe that a Russian naval officer went onto the deck of the warship and shot a diver in the water.

Following the absurd notion that Crabb was shot by a Soviet sniper an even more absurd story emanated from Russia. In it Eduard Koltsov, a retired Russian Navy frogman, now aged 74, claims that he cut Crabb's throat in Portsmouth harbour when he caught him placing a mine on the hull of a the cruiser *Ordzhonikidze*.

His story is that, at the age of 23 he was a member of a group of combat frogmen known as 'Barracuda' when he was ordered to investigate suspicious activity around the cruiser *Ordzhonikidze*. He claims that after he entered the water he made out the shape of a frogman in the water, who was doing something at the starboard side of the ship, next to the ship's ammunition stores. Has he not considered that it would have been a very poor design of a warship to have an ammunition store close to the hull of the ship, a very vulnerable location. When he got closer he saw that he was fixing a mine to the ship. The task of fitting a limpet mine is simple. The frogman swims to the ship and offers the mine up to the hull then 'clunk', the mine is attached. The frogman then makes good his escape in case there are enemy frogmen on guard.

Koltsov claims he then produced a knife and attacked the frogman. We draw reference to the photograph of the Soviet frogmen and point out that their equipment was cumbersome and not conducive to underwater hand-to-hand fighting. However, he claims to have grabbed his feet and dragged him down before cutting his breathing hose then slashing his throat. He then allowed the body to float away with the tide. For his bravery he was secretly awarded the Red Star medal.

It is relevant to examine the reality of grabbing a frogman's legs and then cutting or stabbing that person underwater. It is not a straight forward action because water restricts movement. Crabb would have been well aware of the possibility of Soviet frogmen around the ship. If Crabb had been grabbed he would not have waited to be killed, he would have fought back, after all he was an old hand, having fought the Italians underwater for years. The prospect of grabbing both legs is almost impossible, as a frogman has to keep his legs moving because the finning action keeps him in place. So if he had been grabbed it would have been one leg, and his first instinct would have been to kick the attacker. This is effective and would cause the attacker some concern. Once attacked and free of a grasp, a few leg movements and he would have disappeared in the gloom of the surrounding water.

Although Mike has never attempted to cut the throat of another frogman underwater he would venture to say that it is almost impossible. It is well known that frogmen's knives at that time were generally heavy duty and not very sharp. Most knives used under water have serrated edges to be used for a sawing action as opposed to cutting. This means that cutting the breathing hose would be very difficult because if sufficient pressure was applied it would have pulled the mouthpiece out of his mouth. It would be much easier to crabb hold of Crabb, remove his mouthpiece and let him drown. Much easier and less messy than attempting to cut his throat, which would have required the attacker to get behind Crabb, pull his head back and draw a very sharp knife across his throat. We have already identified that the ship was not fitted with any special devices, there were no mines, special traps, head damaging ASDIC, moving propellers, electrocution, shootings or throat cutting. No, Kolstov has been watching too many *James Bond* movies.

The most important factor is that they would never have killed an intruder. Capture yes, then to be exposed and bring embarrassment on the Government. Equally important, they did not know who it was. Think of the consequences at the height of the Cold War. No, Crabb was not shot and did not have his throat cut in Portsmouth harbour. He was sent on an operation organised by British pro-Soviet agents that alledgedly and involved 'M', Mountbatten. These Soviet stories support the position that perhaps the Russians do not want the real story of what happened to Crabb to be revealed either.

7

The Official Response

No Government ought to be without censors: and where the press is free, no one ever will.

Thomas Jefferson 1743-1826

The Admiralty never announced the disappearance of Commander Crabb to the world; they only admitted it ten days later when the first newspaper enquiry was received. In those ten days, a private drama was played out between the Admiralty and Crabb's relatives and friends, which had probably never had its equal in peacetime. Maitland Pendock, Crabb's business associate was a little worried when he had not heard from Crabb by Thursday night and he became quite anxious when Friday passed without Crabb returning. On Saturday Pendock telephoned the Sally Port Hotel to enquire after Crabb, and was told that he had left on Thursday. Knowing that Crabb had many friends and colleagues in *HMS Vernon* and the Portsmouth area, he then phoned the Navy base. The duty officer at the gate stated that he had not seen Commander Crabb and told Pendock to hold while he made enquiries. These drew a blank, as he had not been seen in the wardroom or by any of the officers in the Portsmouth area.

That Saturday evening, casting around for possible explanations, Pendock phoned Commander Crawford. Crawford and his wife

Daphne had not seen Crabb since Wednesday night, and said that he had failed to keep a date with them on Friday evening. Pendock explained that he had no knowledge of Crabb's whereabouts. Now Crawford was worried and he told Pendock that he would make enquiries at *HMS Vernon*. It was arranged that Pendock should call back the next day. Pendock phoned on the Sunday and Crawford explained that he had not been able to discover anything and said that he was going to the Admiralty to try and sort things out. It seemed significant that Crawford never reported the result of his enquiries at the Admiralty and that he was not available during the next few days.

On the morning of Saturday the 21 April 1956, Detective Superintendent Stanley Lamport, Chief of Portsmouth CID, called at the Sally Port Hotel and spoke to Edward Richman. He asked to look at the hotel register, and removed four pages, neatly and with care. These pages covered the first weeks in April 1956. Richman raised an objection and said that hotel registers must not, according to the regulations, be tampered with. Superintendent Lamport told him that he was acting on orders from a much higher authority. He signed the next page as a form of receipt, to satisfy the proprietor. Before leaving, the police officer told Richman that the matter was very serious and that he should tell his staff not to talk to anybody about it, especially the press, as the Official Secrets Act covered it.

It is interesting to note the frequent use at that time of the Official Secrets Act by the police and secret service agencies, to silence potential witnesses. Many of those confronted were civilians going about their lawful business but fear of the security services and the Act in the 1950s cascaded to all levels of society and the mere use of the words would ensure silence.

Marshall Pugh relates that a meeting to finalise details for the Portsmouth job was held at Pendock's business, when Smith bought two tables for £4 18s. The sectioned tables were to be taken away in a private car, and because the buyer was a friend of Crabb a cheque was accepted. It was signed by Mathew Smith and drawn on the South

Kensington branch of Lloyds Bank, but it was dated 1955 instead of 1956. Crabb is alleged to have said to Pendock:

"All right, give me the cheque. I shall be seeing him when I go to Portsmouth."

The cheque was never seen again, but after Crabb disappeared a woman with a foreign accent, giving the name of Anderson, called at Pendock's furniture office. She asked to see one of the principals and was shown into an inner office, where she said she had come to settle the Smith account. She paid the bill with four one-pound notes, a ten-shilling note and eight shillings. The incident was said to have been noticed by a reporter, who followed the woman. She dodged through the busy hallway of the Cumberland Hotel, jumped on a bus and got off at the next stop, stood waiting in a queue, then suddenly slipped away in the crowd. She has never been identified.

Following publication of *Frogman Spy,* we received a letter from a doctor in the USA who wrote that when he was at Harvard University there was a vivacious and beautiful young lady who upon graduation in the early 1950s went to London. Whilst in London she married an Englishman by the name of Smith. A few years later she returned to the USA with her husband. The reason for their return was never confirmed but he said that the Smiths left England rather abruptly because he had been involved with the disappearance of Commander Crabb and thereafter was considered *persona non grata* in England. Was this the woman who went to Pendocks premises and paid for the furniture prior to their departure from England?

Having known Crabb for many years, even before he employed him as a furniture salesman, Pendock had been the first to hear of the intended Portsmouth trip. A month earlier, Crabb is reported to have said:

"I'll be doing another job for the Admiralty at Portsmouth in mid-April and will need a couple of days off."

As he had already talked of having dived under the Russian cruiser *Sverdlov* the previous October, it was quite clearly understood that he would be doing something similar this time. Crabb is reported to have continued to say with a dirty chuckle, in his gravely voice: "I'll be having a look at the Russians' bottoms."

It is claimed that he stopped Pendock in the street, pointed to a building about 50 yards (45 metres) away and said: "That will be as far as I shall have to swim at Portsmouth."

When Crabb did not return to London, Pendock became worried, but more so when he received a telephone call to say that an Admiralty representative would be calling at 5:00pm. Why would an Admiralty representative be involved? After all, it is claimed that Crabb was a civilian and not in the Navy. Captain Richard Ivan Alexander Sarell, DSO, a senior Admiralty officer, whose appointment on the staff of the Deputy Chief of Naval Staff forms a link with the Cabinet Office through the Ministry of Defence, arrived at Pendock's Seymour Place salesroom at the appointed time. He was in civilian clothes, and declined Pendock's suggestion that they should talk over a drink in a neighbouring hotel. He thought it best if they walked and talked but changed his mind and suggested that it would be better if they talked at his flat, and they went to a bachelor flat in Dorset House, Gloucester Place. There, the Captain, obviously ill at ease, asked if Commander Crabb had told him why he was going to Portsmouth. Pendock was obviously placed in a difficult position and replied that he did not. The captain poured out a whisky and then told Pendock that he was sorry to have to report that Crabb had failed to surface after diving to test some new equipment. He continued to add that they should keep it to themselves. As if to clarify the situation he thought that they should give him a day or two, as a fishing boat may have picked him up. At this point Pendock was confused and concerned, but what could he do? He reflected that he had many journalist friends and Crabb was news. He was a brave man whose passing deserved notice. The naval concern was that the Russian leaders were still in Britain. What would be the effect of news that a frogman was lost near Portsmouth, and what would happen if the truth came out?

Then a curious fact emerged: the Admiralty apparently did not know the address of Crabb's next of kin. The Captain asked where his wife lived, and Pendcok explained that Crabb had no wife, as his marriage had been dissolved 18 months previously. He also told the officer about Crabb's fiancée, but said that his mother would be his next of kin; he knew that she lived in Oxfordshire and said that if he had a map of the area he might be able to remember it. Sarell wrote down an Admiralty extension number and gave it to Pendock with the request that if he could remember anything to telephone him. He added that if he was not available there were a couple of junior officer's who would take a message. Sarell certainly stressed to Pendock that Crabb's disappearance should not be talked about, so Pendock explained that Crabb's biographer Marshall Pugh would need to be told. Sarell agreed, but asked that he should be the one to tell him. Pugh told Frank Goldsworthy that he did meet the Captain at the Dorset House flat, and he also came back impressed with the necessity of making no hurried move to release the news, saying, "Crabbie would not want to embarrass the Navy."

Remember, Crabb was not in the Navy if we believe the official version of events. It was not until the following Friday that Pendock remembered that the Oxfordshire village where Crabb's mother lived was Towersey, near Thame. He phoned the Admiralty extension number and was told that the Captain was not available, but that he spent most of his time at the Ministry of Defence. Pendock was given another number, which he phoned, only to be told that the Captain was in conference, so he left a message. Pendock's call was returned later, and Sarell told him that he was going to drive down to see Crabb's mother and break the news to her. He remarked that he hated the prospect, and also stated that it had been decided that the news of Crabb's death could now be released. Pendock did not immediately connect the fact that Bulganin and Khrushchev had departed, smiling broadly and waving cheerily from the bridge of the *Ordzhonikidze*, which had lain for nine days alongside the jetty at Portsmouth. Captain Sarell later told Pendock that he had seen Crabb's mother and now intended to go down to Kent to see his former wife. Both women were to later describe the visit of the Naval officer in civilian clothes. He was obviously ill at ease and unable to give a clear account of what might have happened, but said there might be hope if Crabb had been picked up by a fishing boat or a foreign vessel. Sarell asked Pendock if he would call on the housekeeper where Crabb had his flat and say that he would not be returning. He also asked him to pay any outstanding bills and forward the receipts to the Admiralty who would reimburse him. He could offer no adequate explanation to be given to the housekeeper and Pendock refused to do it.

Frank Goldsworthy, in interview, raised the fact that a naval officer, a Captain, was involved in the quest for information and the cover up process, was incredible. The Admiralty claimed not to be involved and knew nothing of the unauthorised operation, but played a significant part in the post-incident events. The Admiralty involvement was not restricted to Captain Sarell; the entire information office was thrown into the front line.

During office hours, the staff of the Chief of Naval Information dealt with newspaper enquiries to the Admiralty. Unlike some Ministries, the Admiralty neither kept a late team of information officers nor made the telephone number of the stand-by man available to reporters. Instead, after 6pm and on Sundays, press calls were switched to the duty commander who was provided with 'briefs' to cover subjects that were likely to arise out of office hours. He would be in touch with operational matters but occasional enquiries normally handled by the civilian side of the Admiralty were referred to the resident clerk. One anonymous civil servant (in fact it was an overnight duty shared in rotation by several responsible men) was to play a vital part in the Crabb story on the evening of Sunday 29 April. Bernard Hall of the *Daily Express* made the first call to the Admiralty where the duty commander referred him to the resident clerk. When the phone rang in the Clerk's office he was able to refer to a typewritten brief prepared some days before by senior officers who knew that press enquiries would have to be dealt with sooner or later.

The media moved into action and sought out everybody who could add something to the story. One newspaper reporter claimed to have spoken to the officer on 'duty watch' with the Petty Officer when Crabb was seen by them to be captured in the water. He told him that they saw Crabb in the water; they saw the Russian divers and the ensuing struggle. They made their report but they could not go on record officially for the Official Secrets Act precluded them from doing so. If Crabb had disappeared on an espionage mission that would embarrass Britain and possibly endanger peace with Russia, this would have been the moment to produce a convincing lie; it was also the opportune time for the Admiralty to disclaim any involvement with a man who was reputedly a civilian. As it was, the brief merely contained details that, it was hoped, would play down the affair. He had no communiqué to issue as such, just points of information he was authorised to give.

It was agreed that the story would follow the line that Commander Crabb was missing, presumed drowned, having failed to surface after a dive whilst experimenting with secret equipment. While the Admiralty might consider that the answer given was complete, reporters continued to dig and search. The questions and answers flowed in the following sequence:

"What sort of equipment?" "Sorry, no information can be given about that." "Well, where did it happen?" "In the Portsmouth area," "The Portsmouth area is a big place! - whereabouts?" "Just in the Portsmouth area." "Well, when did it happen?" "Oh, a week or so ago." The Clerk would say no more.

It took no great leap of the imagination for a journalist to remember that in Portsmouth, where this George Medallist frogman hero had been lost, a Russian cruiser and two Russian destroyers had previously been berthed.

It was some time later when the resident clerk, after having taken other advice, agreed that he had also been authorised to say that the tests had been undertaken in Stokes Bay. This was the weak link in the story given out and it was the key statement that encouraged those seeking a story to delve deeper. If the original statement had been made with a little more conviction, with some mention of rescue attempts and the tidal currents that swept the bay, it might have satisfied the curiosity of the newspaper men. However, if newsmen are denied information from one source for no apparent reason, they have a habit of looking elsewhere for it.

Commander of the Soviet ships, Rear Admiral V. F. Kotov, reported to the chief of staff of Portsmouth Naval Base, Rear Admiral Philip Burnett, that: "At about 7:30 am on 19 April, sailors on watch aboard the Soviet ships had observed a frogman floating on the surface between the ships. The frogman stayed on the surface for a short time before submerging out of sight."

Burnett knew about the ban on any intelligence-gathering involvement against the Soviet ships but stated that he knew nothing about any covert underwater operations, nor could he give any indication about the identity of the frogman.

That same evening the subject was raised again. Jamie Thomas, the First Lord of the Admiralty, was at a dinner with the Soviet officials from the ships when he was asked: "What was that frogman doing off our bows this morning?"

There was no warning of the pending and embarrassing question and Thomas was taken aback. He could only reply that he knew nothing about any frogman, or his identity. He stated that whoever it was, was there without authorisation and was certainly not a member of the Royal Navy. The Soviets were gloating in the very evident embarrassment the incident was causing and made best use of it. They would not be doing this if they had killed Crabb as described above.

The following day saw the first of several high-level secret meetings begin in Whitehall, with the purpose of organising a cover-up. Help came from an unexpected quarter when a row between the guests of honour, Bulganin and Khrushchev, and the two Labour Party leaders, Hugh Gaitskell and George Brown, erupted at a dinner organised by the Labour Party Executive Committee. This was well covered by the media, and provided a welcome distraction for Government ministers and the senior officers of the Royal Navy. But by Sunday 29 April, ten days after Crabb's disappearance, friends of the Commander were asking very leading questions. The authorities had not expected the reaction to be so great, nor that many of those enquiring would be involved with Fleet Street: Crabb's reputation as a loner without many friends was beginning to backfire.

Eventually the Admiralty issued a statement to the effect that Commander Lionel Crabb was missing presumed dead, having failed to return from a test dive, connected with trials of certain underwater apparatus in Stokes Bay. This statement was pure fabrication on the part of the Admiralty, who were trying to delay the media linking Crabb's disappearance with the visit of the Soviet ships. It soon became apparent that the statement was simply an attempt to save embarrassment in Westminster and Whitehall. The media reported the statement but were not satisfied and began their own investigations into the affair, and it was not long before they were to see through the cover-up. The Russian leaders, now back in the Soviet Union, saw the possibility of making political capital out of the debacle and on 4 May issued the following note to the British Authorities, as quoted in full in Hansard on the 30 May:

"The Embassy of the Union of Soviet Socialists Republics in Great Britain presents its compliments to the Foreign Office and has the honour to state as follows:

Warships at Portsmouth at 7:30 hours on 19 April, three sailors of the Soviet vessels discovered a diver swimming between the Soviet destroyers at their moorings at the South Railway jetty. The diver, dressed in black light-diving suit with flippers on his feet, was on the surface of the water for the space of one or two minutes and then dived again under the destroyer Smortyashchie."

Rear Admiral Burnett had categorically denied to Rear Admiral V.F. Kotov, the possibility of the appearance of a diver alongside the Soviet vessels and declared that: "At the time no diving operations of any kind were being carried out."

However, the British press of 30 April 1956, reported that British Naval authorities were actually carrying out a secret diving investigation in the vicinity of the anchored Soviet vessels at Portsmouth. Moreover, the carrying out of these investigations appears to have caused the fatality of a British diver. It is sufficient to quote the *Daily Sketch* in reporting the loss of Crabb:

"He went into the water for the last time at Stokes Bay, Portsmouth, on secret investigatory work near to the anchorage of the Soviet cruiser Ordzhonikidze. Attaching as it does, important significance to such an unusual occurrence as the Soviet warships visiting the British Naval base at Portsmouth, the Embassy would be grateful to the British Foreign Office to receive an explanation on the question. London, 4 May, 1956."

Prime Minister Sir Anthony Eden was obviously faced with the embarrassment that a covert operation had taken place against his direct orders. He could have divulged more information to his closest Ministers, if not Parliament in general, but he chose not to do so. Was he faced with the facts that Commander Crabb had been sent on a dangerous mission, but had been double-crossed by members of the British security service who had allegiance to the Soviet Union? In the Parliamentary debates, which were noisy and prolonged, one former Labour Minister who knew most about security, Mr. Herbert Morrison, removed himself from the scene and took no part in the harassment of the Prime Minister. Did he have some knowledge of what had happened, but feel that the matter should be left? He would have been unable to state such, for the Opposition was out for blood.

Mr. Gaitskell, for the Opposition, told the Prime Minister that his speech was totally unsatisfactory and asked whether he was:

"Aware that, while all of us would wish to protect public security, the suspicion must inevitably arise that his refusal to make a statement on this subject is not so much in the interest of public security as to hide a very grave blunder which had occurred?"

To this the Prime Minister replied that the House and the country could draw their own conclusions from what he had said. He added that he had anxiously weighed every consideration, but these were decisions that only a Prime Minister could take and he was convinced that the decision he had taken was, "The right and only one".

This again highlights the fact that the Crabb operation was far more significant than a frogman having a look under a Russian ship. At the time, this in itself would certainly have been embarrassing, but not sufficiently so to explain the constant questioning and barracking that the Prime Minister received on the matter. The subject would not go away and the Opposition delivered questions from every angle. The next demand came from Mr. 'Manny' Shinwell, who wanted to know against whom the disciplinary action was being taken and for what reason. Sir Anthony was reluctant to answer, but there were fierce demands for a reply. He rose to the box, clasped it determinedly and said: "I have nothing to add to the answer I have given."

While there was to be no change from the Prime Minister, there were changes in the security services. The disciplinary procedure started at the top and the chief of MI6, Major General Sir John 'Sinbad' Sinclair was retired early, to be replaced by the man who was serving as the Director General of MI5, Sir Dick White. Roger Hollis was promoted.

Papers released by the Public Records Office reveal that blame for the Crabb affair went down to the Director of Naval Intelligence, Admiral Sir John Inglis. He was the scapegoat for the 'dirty deeds'. The report of Sir Edward Bridges, a former Cabinet Secretary, into how the operation was authorised and carried out has been withheld on grounds of national security. This is because it is alledged that it was was not Inglis, but Mountbatten who was actually to blame.

We now know that the permanent secretary at the Foreign Office, responsible for MI6, was told what had happened on 23 April 1956. He did not tell the Foreign Secretary, Selwyn Lloyd, or his Minister of State, Anthony Nutting. Sir John Lang, the permanent secretary at the Admiralty, was not told until the following Friday, and also said nothing. The two permanent secretaries only told their political masters what had really happened on 3 May. It was left to Viscount Cilcennin, the First Lord of the Admiralty, to brief the Prime Minister. The Prime Minister wrote to Lord Cilcennin, one of his closest advisers:

> *"From what I hear, there is a tendency among senior naval officers to talk as though the Royal Navy has been unfairly treated over this affair. They resent, I am told, any suggestion that the Admiralty was closely concerned. I hope you will take steps to correct this."*

Three things emerge quite clearly:

> *"It was the Naval Intelligence Department (NID) who asked that this information about Russian warships should be obtained.*
>
> *It was the NID who asked that efforts should be made to obtain it while the Russian warships were in Portsmouth.*
>
> *The NID knew of my direction that nothing of this kind should be done on this occasion."*

Sir John Inglis was censured, but he kept his job, and the two permanent secretaries were told they were guilty of an error of judgment in not informing ministers.

The Crabb controversy continued to rage unabated in the House of Commons, where the Opposition still demanded more answers than those so far given. However, on the 14 May, after a heated and turbulent debate, MPs approved by 316 votes to 229 to the veil of secrecy which the Prime Minister had deemed necessary to draw over the Commander Crabb affair. Sir Anthony's ten-minute speech never once mentioned the frogman by name and provided no further insight into the subject. It ended with a final declaration:

"In this business I do not rest only on the national interest...there is also in this business a very important international interest, and I confess that all I care for is the outcome of our discussion with the Soviet leader, should this in truth prove to be, as I have said, the beginning of a beginning. I intend to safeguard that possibility at all costs. I believe that is also in the mind of the Soviet leaders, and it is for that reason that I deplore this debate and will say no more."

Mr. Hugh Gaitskell for the Opposition, who having opened the debate, had also earlier raised the matter of the pages of the hotel register which had been removed in a manner no more legal than was threatening the staff with the Official Secrets Act. The question was asked: "Can the Prime Minister tell us under what authority these officers acted?" The question remained unanswered.

The Prime Minister was deeply impressed by the report of the operation, which was sufficiently serious that he did not discuss it with any of his Cabinet Ministers and carried the responsibility alone.

In the Soviet Union, Crabb's capture was apparently being celebrated with a gold watch being presented to Admiral Kotov, who had brought Bulganin and Khrushchev to Portsmouth. This happened at the end of May 1956 and Western observers were certain that it was a reward for the smooth diving operation that had enabled Crabb to be captured and taken aboard the cruiser. Marshall Zhukov, Soviet Minister of Defence presented the watch to Kotov as well as a watch to Captain G.F. Stephonov, commander of the *Ordzhonikidze* for his part in the operation. The official reason for the rewards was as recognition of the two commanders who distinguished themselves during their stay in England. The Russians had initially encouraged the fiasco that had developed within the House of Commons and in the media. When evidence began to emerge to the effect that Crabb had been captured and taken as a prisoner to the Soviet Union they became perturbed and issued statements to the effect that the British were 'rattling skeletons in the cupboard' in an attempt to cover up a security scandal. They went on to declare that Commander Crabb had 'perished' whilst engaged in underwater espionage against the Soviet cruiser. That was a very damaging statement to make, for the vast majority of people did not know what had happened to Commander Crabb, and those who did were not saying. While the debate raged at a political level there were other chinks in the armour that spurred on the question as to what really happened. Doubts were increased when information became known both at home and abroad.

When Sydney Knowles heard the details of Crabb's disappearance he was outraged that no proper search had been made for his friend. If Crabb was reported missing, surely somebody, either military or civilian, should have carried out some form of search, but nothing happened. Knowles decided that, if the authorities were unconcerned, he was not, and so he set out for Portsmouth to search for Commander Crabb. Portsmouth Harbour is a very large expanse of water and Knowles watched the movement of the tides and currents. He found an area of water where the current washed up anything moving with the tide, and decided that if Crabb's body was anywhere it could be in the quiet area. He prepared his equipment and made a dive. Swimming amongst the mud and flotsam of Portsmouth harbour he made a thorough search, but found nothing. Knowles prepared to make another dive but was approached by a serving officer, who told him not to dive again, because Crabb's body was not there. He said that he knew a lot about the secret operation but could not elaborate for fear of the Official Secrets Act. Knowles knew the officer and realised that he was not being fobbed off, and he knew that Crabb would not be found by diving, so he abandoned his attempts and returned home. Knowles wrote to us:

"I knew I would not find Crabbie's body but I prayed I might. It helped the cover story. This dive was for the Daily Mirror and given the 'thumbs up' by Col Malcolm."

Much has been made of what Crabb was looking for when he went under the ship. Following the earlier *Sverdlov* mission, there could have been no reason to risk another operation on a sister ship. Moreover, only six years after the incident, in 1962, the *Ordzhonikidze* was transferred to the Indonesian Navy, where she was renamed the *Kri Irian*. This would hardly have happened if she had really been one of the most modern warships in the world. The main issue in the debate has been about the way the ship could manoeuvre, and that is said to be why Crabb was deployed on the operation, but again that issue is countered by the fact that any superior capabilities that the vessel displayed would have been noticed by Captain Northey of the Royal Navy, who, the media reported, travelled from the Soviet Union to Portsmouth with the Russian party. He had every door open to him, and saw everything there was to see. He was allowed to mix with the officers and crew. So there was no need for underwater spies, but then Crabb was not spying against the ship.

The Admiralty maintained its account of the Stokes Bay incident and this drew much attention to the fact that there must be a 'cover-up', which was going wrong. If Crabb were indeed on active Naval service in Stokes Bay on the 19 April 1956, experimenting with a new secret mine, he would have embarked on his mission from *HMS Vernon* or another Naval establishment and would have been taken to the starting point in some Naval craft, since Stokes Bay is more than three miles from Portsmouth harbour. Moreover, if he was carrying out a top-secret underwater experiment with a new type of mine, why did Sir Anthony tell a thoroughly aroused House of Commons that:

"It would not be in the public interest to disclose the circumstances in which Commander Crabb is presumed to have met his death"? To which he added: "I

think it necessary, in the special circumstances of this case, to make it clear that what was done was done without the authority or the knowledge of Her Majesty's Ministers. Appropriate disciplinary steps are being taken."

Apart from the reports that were raised throughout the ensuing years, Parliament had not heard the last of the matter.

Frogman held in Moscow Gaol declared the headline in the *Daily Telegraph* dated 30 June 1956.

"Cdr. Crabb, the missing British frogman, is in Moscow's Lefortowo prison awaiting trial for espionage", according to a report in the West German newspaper *Bild Zeitung*. It quoted a French left wing politician recently returned from the Soviet capital as saying that Crabb was taken to Moscow after being arrested by Soviet frogmen in Portsmouth harbour on April 19.

The *Daily Herald*, dated 30 June 1956 also quoted Bild Zeitung as saying a Russian officer told a French politician at a Moscow banquet:

"We have got Crabb, he is our legitimate prisoner. He is at the moment in solitary confinement in the Lefortowo prison in Moscow. He has been given the number 147. Officially, he has no name."

Sunday Dispach, 27 May 1956 stated:

"It is expected that a special death certificate will be issued for Lionel Crabb, the frogman who disappeared in Portsmouth Harbour without trace during the visit of the Russian warships. This certificate will avoid the necessity of having to go to court to get him officially pronounced dead. The Government wants to hear no more about Crabb's activities. They fear that a court inquiry or a body-less inquest might mean the disclosure of certain facts which they want kept quiet."

Even if the hearing was in secret, many people would have to be let into the secret of how Crabb met his death and it is thought that the fewer people who knew the better. This did not happen; fourteen months after Crabb went missing, a body was found by fishermen near Chichester and began what has been the greatest spying cover-up of the Cold War.

One person who played a part in the changing story of what happened to Crabb was Bernard Hutton. He was a Czechoslovakian emigré who had established himself as a reporter within a London newspaper group. He was credited with having good underground contacts in Russia and Eastern Europe. It is through these secret organisations that he obtained the evidence that Crabb was in Russia, and had the new name of Korablov.

We have been asked on more than one occasion whether we believe in the secret reports that were supposed to have been smuggled out of the Soviet Union and forwarded to him. We have to answer that we don't know. In his books, *The Fake Defector*, *Commander Crabb is Alive* and *Frogman Extraordinary*, Hutton recounts conversations that quite frankly he could not have any record of. On the other hand much of what he wrote has a ring of truth about it.

We in turn, asked others for their views of Hutton's work and met with replies which ranged from 'pure fabrication' or as one commentator stated: "He would ask a question, and if the answer was not what he wanted he would ask the question a different way, until he had the answer he wanted. He was clever like that." What cannot be argued with is the fact that Hutton wrote a number of books depicting Crabb in Russia, but there have been none countering these allegations. In fact, as will be seen later in the book, he had some powerful and credible support. Until his death Hutton claimed to have continued to receive information from his contacts in the Eastern bloc.

Amongst those who took up the 'truth about Crabb' challenge was Commander J.S. Kerans, DSO, RN (Retd), who had been on HMS Amethyst when she withstood the bombardment by the Chinese and escaped from the Yangtse River. As Member of Parliament for Hartlepool, he made a very bold statement in 1960:

"I am convinced that Commander Lionel Crabb is alive and in Russian hands and the Government must re-open this case."

Kerans tabled a question in the House of Commons asking the then Foreign Secretary, Mr. Selwyn Lloyd, to start new enquiries into the case of the British frogman, Commander Crabb, who had vanished while diving near the Soviet ships. Kerans based his evidence upon the research undertaken by Bernard Hutton. Kerans discussed the details of his report with Naval friends, who had experience of espionage work. As a result he stated: "I do not believe Hutton's research is a fabrication." But Kerans, as others before him, received no satisfaction from the Crabb affair.

In 1964, Marcus Lipton, Labour Member for Brixton, submitted new evidence to Mr. Harold Wilson, the then Prime Minister. The information he placed before him was based on statements made by a high-ranking official who was linked with British and American intelligence. This official had helped to investigate the Crabb mystery. The statements revealed that British intelligence had received reports seven years previously, indicating that Crabb was in Russia. Lipton supported the report by saying: "I know the name of the British official who disclosed this information and to whom he disclosed it. I also know when and where the conversations took place. There is at least a circumstantial case for another look at the affair."

Wilson studied the report and would have consulted the appropriate authorities to seek advice on the matter. From the facts presented to him he decided, as had his predecessors, not to make any statement. It is a point of note that, although Labour Members of Parliament had made demands for the truth at the time of the incident, then, eight years after the event when they were in power, they would not reveal the facts. Wilson wrote to Lipton, "I have read the 25 enclosures, but I am afraid I do not think they provide the grounds for re-opening this case."

Lipton told the Press: "I am sorry speculation about this mystery is to be allowed to continue. I am convinced that one day the whole truth will come out."

In 1966 an Italian film team travelled to Portsmouth, to make a documentary about Crabb. The director, Carlo Tuzzii, was working for the Italian television company RAI. Tuzzii searched out everybody who had something to say and the interviews were recorded on film. As the team progressed, the British secret service became aware, and, because Tuzzii was asking questions about Crabb, the team was arrested, and the film was confiscated. Officers from London, who had the task of processing the film, directed the secret service operation. After being held for five hours, the team was released, with the head of the secret service team stating that it was all a misunderstanding. When Tuzzii watched the film he could not believe it, because some of it was missing. He raised the matter with the British authorities, but, as would be expected, they denied all knowledge. On the 30 September 1966 the film was shown in Italy, and in December of that year a copy of the film was, after a request, sent to East Berlin. We were able to obtain a copy from the East German archives following the reunification of Germany.

In 1968 a Russian merchant Navy officer, based in Leningrad, made it known to Bernard Hutton through the underground that he was a close friend of Crabb/Korablov. He explained that he was part of the network that had passed information from Crabb to Pat Rose. During Hutton's investigations to find out if the officer, Captain R. Myelkov, was indeed a friend of Crabb's he explained that they had met whilst on leave in Moscow. The friendship developed over a period of time. Myelkov knew that Crabb had been with the East German Volksmarine and that he had been posted back to Sevastopol after the underground had provided the West's media with details of his work. Myelkov then offered to provide irrefutable evidence that he was indeed in contact with Crabb, that Crabb was Korablov and that he was alive and in Russia. Hutton was asked to convey this message to

Sydney Knowles, which he did. Knowles first reaction was astonishment, but then he became certain it provided strong evidence that Crabb was alive.

During a meeting I asked Knowles about the content of the message. He explained that he had never discussed it with anybody before, even his wife. He then told me that it provided strong evidence in the case, so he told me the story, which involved an incident when they had finished a diving operation in Italy and were showering. Knowles said that it was a normal process to share the facility but on this occasion Crabb grabbed hold of Knowles's penis. Knowles was stunned and it is a story that certainly would not be common knowledge. Knowles states that the information could only have come from Crabb himself in a desperate bid to make contact with his friends, and let them know he was alive.

With the message delivered, it was agreed that the next time Myelkov was in the West he would meet Knowles and Hutton to talk about Crabb. On 8 May 1968 Myelkov, master of the 3,246-ton Russian ship *Kolpino,* which was berthed in London docks, prepared to defect. Before he could move to freedom he was found shot dead in his cabin, a shotgun lying near his body. The following day, the Coroner's Court at Southwark recorded a verdict of suicide. Myelkov was another link in the long chain of the Crabb affair who died at the hands of an unnamed organisation.

A number of writers have followed the Crabb story over the years and for the most part provided the public with an official view of what happened. One example is that of Chapman Pincher, who wrote that Smith was not a member of the CIA or American, but a Ted Davis, an MI6 officer, who suffered an untimely heart attack yet managed to continue to aid Crabb and raise the alarm when he failed to return from the dive. Pincher does not explain how he knew that Davis suffered the heart attack, nor how he managed to return to the Sally Port Hotel and climb the stairs to recover both his own and Crabb's belongings and make good his departure. Sydney Knowles's view of this statement is that it is rubbish, for he met Smith and thought that he was American. If the official versions are fabrications without foundation, then the Crabb affair is among the greatest cover up's in the history of the British Secret Service.

Amongst the volume of mail we received following the publication of *Frogman Spy,* one letter stated:

"Let me expand on the postscript. I recount an incident or two when I was around seven years old; These took place in the village that Rear Admiral Sir John Inglis lived. My father was his head farm manager and we had a cottage opposite the manor house.

"I recall one Sunday night, several black cars, possibly four or five Humber types, parked on the land by the side of the manor house, these cars were not there in the morning when I went to school. I think this was the same weekend that my dad asked us not to play on the farm.

I also remember a 'brown man' that is dressed in brown rather than with a brown complexion. You may think nothing of this but the village I was raised in is completely hidden, we rarely saw strangers because they would have had no reason to be there, this man was older than my father, who would have been 35 in 1956, but about the same build; short with stocky chest. He asked us about school, told us of his school days, then departed, towards the bungalow next to the manor house. Was this Lionel Crabb?"

8

Battle of the 'Crabb' Women

We are here to claim our right as women, not only to be free, but also to fight for freedom. That is our right as well as our duty.

Christabel Pankhurst 1911

The quest to find out what happed to Crabb began after his diappearence in 1956, but all attempts drew a blank. For example, when in May of that year Margaret Crabb attempted to find out about her former husband, she got no help from the Navy. She was told that there was more at stake in the inquiry and that it involved international questions. Her first approach was to the office of the Commander-in-Chief at Portsmouth, Admiral Sir George Creasy. His secretary told her that the admiral would not see her as he was in a conference. She was told to write to the Admiralty and make an appointment. When confronted by the media, the secretary stated that her talk with Mrs. Crabb was a private matter between the two of them. She did confirm that she did not consult with the admiral.

There began a 'battle' between the two 'Crabb' women for the title of next of kin and for the settlement of his estate. It became very evident that Beatrice Crabb, his mother, was his undisputed next of kin and the rightful inheritor of his estate. Margaret Crabb, his ex wife, who had divorced him on the grounds of cruelty, sought maintenance and, as we will see, sought money from the Admiralty. In examining this aspect of the story, other more revealing issues arise. The third woman in Crabb's life, Pat Rose, had no rights and did not enter this battle. She only wanted to know the truth of what had happened to her Crabb.

The following are extracts taken from letters released by the public Records Office:

The National Provincial Bank in Brompton Road, London, wrote to the Admiralty on 30 April 1956 saying that they had read of the death of their customer Commander Crabb and requested knowledge of his next of kin and sight of the death certificate.

Also dated 30 of April 1956 was a letter from Crabb's solicitors Tamplin, Joseph and Flux, requesting information as to his next of kin. During their dealings with the Commander there had never been occasion to identify such a person. They were aware that his marriage to Margaret Crabb was dissolved. They also sought information as to the particulars of any monies due in respect of his service under the Admiralty.

Then on the 1 May 1956 a letter arrived at the Admiralty from solicitors Piper, Padfield and Horniball, to say that they acted for Beatrice Crabb in the winding up of her son's estate. They also confirmed that Crabb's marriage to Margaret Crabb was dissolved. However, a hand written note on the bottom of the page states that a subsequent telephone call from the firm confirmed that they no longer acted for Beatrice Crabb.

It was the 7 May 1956 when the firm Tamplin, Joseph and Flux wrote to the Admiralty stating that they had not received a reply and to confirm that they were acting for Beatrice Crabb. They were, on her behalf, applying for a Grant of Administration of his estate. This meant that they were asking for a certificate stating that he was missing presumed killed so that they could progress matters. Importantly they were seeking to obtain information about any sum of money due to Crabb in respect of the last assignment upon which he was engaged, as it formed part of his estate.

This is of course most interesting because Crabb was not in the Royal Navy, or was he?

A letter dated 10 May 1956 was sent by Lewin of the Admiralty to the Chief Constable of the City Police, Portsmouth. It states that Crabb was undertaking diving operations in the Portsmouth area and had failed to return from the dive. His body was not recovered and he was presumed drowned. It goes on to say that a description was attached and asks that if a body answering the description was found that the Admiralty be notified immediately. The annexe gives Crabb's age as 46, height of 5 feet 7 inches, medium build, brown hair, brown eyes a prominent nose and tufts of hair on his cheekbones. He was believed to be wearing a two-piece Heinke suit, breathing apparatus Rosetern 5562, a service type facemask and service type swim fins.

In reality, the Admiralty had no idea what Crabb was wearing or what underwater breathing apparatus he used.

Messrs. Tamplin, Joseph and Flux wrote on the 10 May 1956 again asking for a certificate of presumption of death.

The Admiralty responded to Messrs. Tamplin, Joseph and Flux on the 11 May 1956 noting receipt of their letter and advising that they would be in communication regarding the points raised in the letter.

On the 12 May 1956 the Chief Constable wrote to the Admiralty acknowledging receipt of their letter and advising that Crabb's description had been circulated.

This was a bizarre piece of communication because when Crabb did not return, Smith reported to his masters in London that he had not returned from the dive. This raises the question as to who his masters were. Then Chief Inspector Lamport of the Portsmouth Police went to the Sally Port Hotel and removed pages from the register, and thereby the evidence that showed Crabb had been resident. He also threatened the owner, Edward Richman with the Official Secrets Act, which of course he had no authority to do. The police, from the Chief Constable down, would have been involved in the Crabb saga evolving around them.

Following Crabb's disappearence, Margaret Crabb, his estranged wife demanded to know what had happened and made a claim for maintenance. Margaret Crabb was married to him for just twelve months and provides an insight into his world. She refers to him as Ken and states she met him some twenty years previously when she worked as a commercial artist. It was at the Adelphi studio, where she was employed and he was the boss. They often went out together and there was even talk of an engagement, but that was not to be and they drifted apart. She married; which was only to last until after the Second World War, when she was divorced. She had a son, Michael from the marriage. It was a twist of fate that brought her back to Crabb, which occurred when she heard his voice on the radio one evening describing his adventure in diving for treasure in a sunken galleon in Tobermory. She recalled their past friendship and, being alone, had an urge to see him again.

On impulse she wrote him a letter but had second thoughts and decided not to post it. Something in her mind held her back, but a girlfriend persuaded her to send it and see what happened. At the post box there was still hesitation and her friend pushed her hand into the letterbox and the letter was on its way. Thinking that she would hear no more, she was surprised when Crabb arrived at the caravan where she was living with her young son. He brought flowers for her and presents for Michael. Memories flooded back and for both of them it was like the old days. A year later, in 1952, they were married. As far as she was concerned at that time things were normal and Crabb was the charming man she had always known. However, it was after the marriage that she found the real Crabb. It was then that she found out that he was deeply in debt, owing more than £2,000. She managed to pay off his more pressing debts, costing her some £300. She states that, at the time, he was working as a Civil Servant at the Naval Research establishment at Tedington, near London. Crabb hated his Civil Service job and wanted to rejoin the Navy. That wish was fulfilled shortly after the marriage and he became a diving officer at the

Underwater Countermeasures and Weapon Establishment (UCWE) near Portsmouth. With this new job came the need to move the caravan to the grounds of Leigh Park House.

It was whilst living in the caravan that Margaret Crabb encountered what she described as an extraordinary year. It ended with the marriage being dissolved with special permission only 12 months after the ceremony. She gave a vivid picture; that Ken Crabb, the famous diver, the George Medalist and man she loved and married, was closer to being a frog than a frogman. The obsession was that he had to have the feel of cold rubber touching him day and night, either awake or asleep. The first she became aware of this was after he had taken a shower and wrapped himself up afterwards, not in a towel but in a blue roll of rubber, like a sarong. This was to become a feature of their lives, because after every shower he would sit wearing the sarong for hours. She was to observe that the smell of the rubber and the damp, cold, frog-like feeling it gave him were his greatest satisfaction. She knew his obsession with diving but this was eccentric.

The problem got worse when she found him one day dressed in a complete frogman's suit, watching television. He sat there for hours, which for her was unnerving. She described him as sitting like a black frog. When she confronted him to explain why he did it, his explanation was that it reminded him of being under the sea, where he said he felt more at home. Watching television was not the only problem; he would go to bed in a frogman's suit because he claimed that it made him sleep more soundly.

When not in a rubber suit he would put rubber sheets on the bed with the same explanation; that it helped him to sleep. The most disconcerting aspect for Margaret was when she turned over in the night and touched the rubber sheets. She stated that the cold, damp, frog-like feeling gave her the shivers. A further revelation was that he had old raincoats and always wore one under his shirt even in the hottest weather. Her concern for Crabb grew and she became frightened of his obsession of becoming like a frog. When she attempted to discuss his strange activities he avoided the subject and would only reveal that she should wear rubber next to her skin and she would understand the feeling.

Another strange aspect of Crabb's behaviour was his collection of fancy walking sticks. She explained that he would spend half an hour every morning choosing one before he went out. His favourite was a swordstick which he would pull out of its scabbard and flourish before he left home. Apart from the obsession with rubber she also became concerned when he posted letters without stamps and then put the money in the letterbox. She also noted that he stopped using buses and only travelled in a private car or taxi. He seemed to be adopting the persona of a frog trying to cope with being a human, but not adapting very well.

Unable to take more of his strange behaviour, they parted and she was awarded £45 a month. He only paid for a short while before payments stopped, and Margaret took him to court. Crabb told the court that he received sums of between £60 and £100 but would not explain to the judge where the mysterious sums came from. It was a couple of weeks prior to his disappearance that the judge stated that if he did not pay up or reveal his sources of income he would go to prison for 28 days. Margaret Crabb thought that when she heard he had disappeared, it was a clever ploy to escape paying the maintenance. On reflection, she said that if they had not divorced she would be the widow of a Commander and not penniless with a child to raise.

A letter dated 15 May 1956 from solicitors representing Margaret Crabb outlined the case for their client. It stated that she married Crabb on the 15 March 1952 and that it was dissolved on the 29 November 1954 on the grounds of cruelty. On the 1 April 1955 an order was obtained that Crabb should pay maintenance during their joint lives of £45 per month, but to be reduced to the rate of one shilling in old money per annum. The latter provision was to keep alive the right to maintenance pending Crabb finding civilian employment after he retired from the Navy. No proof of civilian employment was ever forthcoming and Margaret Crabb did not receive any maintenance between February 1955 and the date of his disappearance. No application for maintenance could be made now, but as Crabb died on what was considered to be active service, it was deemed appropriate that the Admiralty should pay maintenance to her. She waited to see how much the Admiralty was prepared to pay.

Messrs. Tamplin, Joseph and Flux wrote on the 17 May 1956 that all they required was a Certificate of Presumption of Death to proceed to obtain a Grant of Letter for the next of kin, Beatrice Crabb, as there was no will.

They also asked if any light could be placed on the whereabouts of Crabb's wallet.

Messrs. Tamplin, Joseph and Flux received no reply and in a letter dated 31 May 1956 advised the Admiralty that they would have to take the matter to court. They pointed out that such a course of action would continue the publicity that surrounded the Crabb saga.

On the 1 June 1956 the Admiralty issued a Certificate of Death which states:

"This is to certify that Commander Lionel Kenneth Philip Crabb, OBE, GM, RNVR is presumed by the Admiralty for official purposes to have died in the nineteenth day of April 1956.

Signed Nigel J. Abercrombie, Under Secretary."

Why was the Admiralty involved? They claim he had left the Navy in 1955 and that the operation was nothing to do with them. Well, he had not left and their official involvement clearly supports this. This provided evidence to support the inference that 'M' (Mountbatten) was involved.

A letter from the Admiralty was sent on the 1 June 1956 with a certified statement of his death. They would send a letter with information about monies owed to Crabb and stated that the effects recovered in Portsmouth were sent to Beatrice Crabb and nothing was known about the wallet.

There is a note dated 30 June 1956 from the Treasury Solicitor, who had been consulted on the letter of 15 May from Margaret Crabb's solicitors, seeking maintenance. The advice is that the Admiralty was not authorised to pay maintenance and they ought to be prepared to do some stonewalling.

On 16 July 1956 a letter from Messrs. Tamplin, Joseph and Flux sought to know how much money was due to Beatrice Crabb as the next of kin. A hand written note, undated but referring to a letter from Messrs. Tamplin, Joseph and Flux dated 16 July 1956, provided sums of gross value £1205-9-9 (£1205.48 approx) and a net value of £374-19-11 (£374.99 approx).

A letter from the Admiralty confirmed on 18 July that Margaret his ex wife was not entitled to receive any money from them and they had no responsibility for her maintenance.

Then, on the 18 July 1956, W. R. Lewin, on behalf of the Admiralty wrote to Messrs. Tamplin, Joseph and Flux, acting for Beatrice Crabb to advise that a sum of money was to be paid to her. This again was evidence that Crabb was in the Navy, otherwise they would not have paid out any monies, after all, it had been made very clear at a high level that Crabb left the Navy in 1955.

It was in the letter dated 18 July that the Admiralty revealed that a box of kit belonging to Crabb was located at *HMS Vernon,* which was then dispatched to Beatrice Crabb. Among the belongings were three wallets.

Now there were three wallets; but clearly there was no wallet with the items returned to her from Crabb's stay at the Sally Port Hotel. One may well ask how Beatrice Crabb knew a wallet was missing. Pat Rose may well have provided the answer, because she travelled with him on the train to Portsmouth prior to the last operation. She told us, when researching *Frogman Spy*, that he was in a strange mood and acted as if he wasn't going to return but then made a brave face to say that he would see her in a couple of days. During that journey he took out his wallet and removed from it two photographs and looked at them. There was one of Rose standing with her brother and sister-in-law, both dressed in riding clothes, at their villa. The other photograph was of her wearing shorts and sitting next to a swimming pool with a dog. Crabb then put the wallet away with the photographs in it. When he did not return, Rose told us that she spoke to Beatrice Crabb and asked if the photographs were among his belongings. They were not. Now the official statement telling us that a wallet was missing was in the official papers held under the Official Secrets Act. The story does not end there because it is important to know what happened to the photographs.

When the media began to make enquiries into Crabb's disappearance Rose became embroiled in the events and she departed to stay with her brother James, and her sister-in-law, Naomi, in the south of France. It was whilst there that a family friend, Tony Kessler, a former Austrian cavalry officer, phoned them and asked to speak to Rose. He told her that he was looking at an East German newspaper and that it had two photographs of her in it. She thought he was joking. He described the first one, of her standing with her brother and sister-in-law; both dressed in riding clothes, at their villa. Rose was shocked. He then told her that the other photograph was of her wearing shorts and sitting next to a swimming pool. Rose could not believe it, and Kessler told her that he would bring the paper to show her. When he arrived with the newspaper the three members of the family examined the photographs, unbelieving, for they were certainly of them. The caption beside the photographs read:

"The beautiful blonde fiancée of Commander Crabb, the British frogman who disappeared when the Soviet warships visited Britain on a goodwill visit. She is also missing."

The text gave strong indications that Crabb had defected to Russia and that she had followed him. How had the East Germans got hold of the photographs? Rose had a set and the family had a set and these were still in their photograph album. Crabb had had a set which were the same ones he had in his wallet and had looked at on the train. It follows that they must have been the ones the East Germans used.

Rose told us that she received many messages over the years, reputedly coming from underground sources in the East and Russia. She explained that the first contact came when a man stated that Commander Crabb was alive and well and that she would see him in ten years time. She herself answered the phone and a man repeated the message that Commander Crabb was alive and well. She then demanded to know who the man was, and asked if it was some sort of horrible joke. The man told her that Crabb was being held at Lefortowo prison and that, if he worked for the Russians for ten years, he would be free to go wherever he wanted and that she would be re-united with him. Another caller telephoned and told her that Commander Crabb was alive. He was to remind her of a certain train journey to Portsmouth, when Crabb had studied the photographs he kept in his wallet. He also said that they were alone in the compartment. When Rose decided it was safe to return home she went to see Beatrice Crabb to ask about the photographs, but as we know, there were no photographs returned to her.

In another twist, in a letter dated 21 December 1956, the Admitalty decided to pay Margaret Crabb the sum of £50. This was to be paid from a small, private, charitable fund within the Admiralty. This was to be a single grant, and explained that, even though she may need help in the future, she would not receive any further assistance from them. She was directed to the office of the Officer Charities.

The Admiralty desperately wanted the story to go away but it would not and, from her home in Dover Margaret Crabb wrote to the Admiralty on 27 April 1957:

"Dear Sirs,

It is a year since you informed me that Commander Crabb, who was my

husband, was missing on trials in Portsmouth harbour. I was told that I should
be kept informed and that you would confirm his death if that had occurred. I
have not in fact been notified as to whether he is alive or dead and have received
no further communication from you. I urgently request that information now.
    Yours faithfully
    (Mrs.) Margaret E Crabb."

A newspaper cutting from the *Herald*, dated Monday 29 April 1957 raised the Crabb story, and Margaret Crabb was soon back in the headlines with a front page article entitled "No hero to me she tells gossips". She wrote the letter from a secluded cottage in Kent, where she wondered if he was still alive. People thought of her as the woman who divorced a hero, but she confided that he was not a hero to her. She had a court order for maintenance from him but had never seen a penny. A Naval Captain went to see her to say that he was missing. After several months of haggling, the Admiralty paid her £50 from a benevolent fund. Her view was that if they could say he was dead then they should pay her the maintenance. In the article she claimed that she was unable to get a job because she had divorced a hero. She was told by other naval personnel that he would never have dived into Portsmouth harbour as it was so dirty that he could not have seen or photographed anything. Most bizarre was the fact that she had a set of frogman's equipment in a cupboard which she claimed to have found on the beach at St Margaret's Bay in Kent. She said that she awoke one night hearing the noise of somebody walking around. She thought it was Crabb, but when she went to see who it was, she found her son creating a practical joke.

There was a confidential note from the Admiralty dated 3 May 1957 that stated:

"... We have already issued a certificate of presumption of death to the
solicitors acting for lieutenant Commander Crabb's mother, who is his next of
kin. The fact that we have done so seems to be known to the ex-wife, since it is

referred to in the press cutting. Moreover, the fact was mentioned in Parliament at the time... For these reasons, I should not myself see any reason why we should not inform Mrs. Crabb that her ex-husband is presumed by the Admiralty for official purposes to have died on the 15 day of April 1956... I notice, however, from the correspondence between Lewin and yourself, which is attached to the front... that there was some doubt in August last whether this was desirable. Moreover, in general I know that this matter, with which I have not dealt before is one of great delicacy... To the extent that our reluctance to inform the ex-wife of the presumption of death in August last was due to fear of embarrassing publicity arising from the contradiction between presumption of death by us and our statement that Crabb had been out of the Navy for over a year, it would seem in view of the press cutting that there is no need for further apprehension on this score. It is already open to the press to draw what inferences they like from this contradiction of which they are evidently aware."

This was followed by a hand written note which stated:

"Head of NL

I was not aware of any undertaking to tell Mrs. Crabb any further news of her former husband (as she suggests in her letter) perhaps it was done when DNI arranged for her to be notified that he had not returned from the dive.

7 May 1957"

On the 7 May 1957 a letter signed by one G. C. B. Dodds was sent to Margaret Crabb:

"Madam I am commanded by My Lords Commissioners of the Admiralty to inform you that Lieutenant Commander L.K.P. Crabb, OBE, GM, RNVR is presumed to have died on the 19 April 1956..."

While the two Crabb women communicated with the Admiralty, Rose began to ask questions and continued throughout the years to do so. In a letter dated 11 December 1980 she wrote to her MP:

"*Dear Mr. Flannery,*

Thank you for the copy of Defence Ministry letter of 28 November wherein the death of Crabb is accepted as being established. I have reason to disbelieve this:

Firstly, at the time the headless body turned up at Chichester, there were certain experts on the local tides who declared that a body lost in April 1956 would have been swept far out to sea by June 1957.

Secondly, a companion diver and close friend of Crabb, Sydney James Knowles BEM, has declared on a recording tape how, when asked to identify this body, he was unable to do so and, when recalled, was still certain it was not Crabb. Few men would have more detailed knowledge of each other's bodies than diving mates who were frequently together in a state of nakedness. Finally he was over-persuaded under some pressure to agree to the identification of this body as being Crabb's and was told that this came under the Official Secrets Act.

A few years later Knowles decided the truth must be told of his part in this affair; which was now praying on his mind and even affecting his health, so he made the recording referred to.

Thirdly, a Mr. Kenneth Elliot, who held a position for many years with the firm of Lucas, told me in London in 1968 that he had just returned from a trip to Russia for Messrs Lucas and that, when in Sebastopol, had observed some frogmen emerging from the sea and his guide/interpreter said 'Look, there is your famous Commander Crabb'.

Perhaps the above information, such as it is, may encourage you to pursue your enquiries into Crabb's present whereabouts (at least I hope so) and, if he is in Russia, to try to obtain his release.

Yours sincerely,
Mrs. Pat Rose"

The reply was typical of an MP's non-answer and moved her no further to finding the truth.

The fact remains; the truth has never been revealed by any Prime Minister. On 1 January 1987, many documents were made public for the first time under the 30-year rule and more information after 50 years, but nothing with any substance relating to the Crabb mystery. As far as the British authorities are concerned it is to remain buried for 100 years.

9

The Bodies

Truth is suppressed, not to protect the country from enemy agents but to protect the Government of the day against the people.

Roy Hattersley 1932

When Crabb did not return from the dive, his mother wrote to the Portsmouth coroner asking for an inquest to be held, even though there was no body. She explained that she understood that under some circumstances it is not necessary for there to be a body for an inquest to be opened.

She wrote:

"I believe the power of the common law of England through one of its most powerful exponents the coroner can still find out for me what Admiralty and other officials refuse to tell me."

Mr. Childs, the Portsmouth coroner, stated that under Section 18 of the Coroner's Amendment Act of 1926 [in force in 1956] it was possible to hold an inquest. It generally applies where fire, explosion or drowning is involved and, as a result, the body has been destroyed.

He replied:

"It depends on the coroner entirely and he would have to make a report to the Home Secretary recommending an inquest. If it gets that far, the inquest is always opened."

Crabb's mother was quoted in the *Daily Mail* on 8 May 1956 as saying:

"I want to know what happened to my son. No one else will tell me and an inquest will bring everything to light."

Little did she know that the inquest was to be at best a sham and did not answer one question, especially as to what happened to her son.

It is fair to presume that somebody wanted a body to be found so that the Crabb affair could be put to rest. So, 14 months after he disappeared, a body with only a rubber suit, some under-suit garments and a torso remaining was found by John Randal and two colleagues. It meant that positive identification was impossible. The body was, according to Hutton, deposited by the Soviets a concept supported by Sir Percy Sillitoe, the former Director of MI5.

Hutton alleges that after the Russians captured Crabb, the media speculation did not die down and so, as a precaution, they found a body similar in status to Crabb's, removed the head and both hands, and dressed it in Crabb's undergarments and rubber suit. To eliminate any other possibility of identification the body was placed under controlled conditions in the sea, and held by cables around the legs and thighs to decompose. Months later, because of developments in the media and reports of Crabb being in Russia, it was decided to deposit the body on a British beach, where it would be presumed to be that of Crabb. Hutton's information reasoned that the British Government would not deny that it was Crabb and that they would wish to act quickly in the matter of identification and disposal. He then claimed that the Russians decided to activate the plan and had the body removed from its original location in the sea. Three submarines moved down the English Channel on their way to the Indian Ocean, and Hutton describes, from evidence he claims to have obtained from a secret Soviet dossier, how one of the submarines towed a sealed container, inside which was the body. At a location where the currents seemed ideal to carry it to the coast, the body was released to float away. The submarines continued on their journey down the Channel. Three days later John Randall found the body. Hutton and the media raised the question of the submarines' passage, but the authorities never followed it up, either at the inquest or subsequently. However, one piece of evidence that supports Hutton's dossier is that Sir Percy Silitoe, former head of MI5, stated that an identical dossier was held by MI5. He confirmed the Soviet submarine theory.

However, there were also two other bodies in the mystery; one under the control of the MOD at a lake at Farnham which was being handled by the British security service, and one found by a fisherman, Harry Cole.

With regard to the Farnham body, evidence provided to Gary Murray by Captain Fred Holroyd, a former British Army intelligence officer, says that while he was on service in Zimbabwe (Rhodesia) in 1979 he spent some four hours crossing the bush in a Land Rover in the company of a senior British Government officer who was attached to MI5. During the journey the man told of an incident which occurred in 1956 whilst working for the intelligence service. He said he was ordered to go to a lake at Farnham, where people would be waiting for him. At the lake a member of the security service asked him if he knew Commander Crabb, to which he responded that he did, having worked with him on a number of occasions. He was then taken to the lakeside to be shown a whole corpse; a male in a Naval type diving suit, who had obviously been submerged in the water. Asked if the body was that of Commander Crabb, he responded that it was not. Thanked for his answer, he was allowed to return to London. Was that body of an unknown person submerged again to decompose sufficiently; to lose the hands and head and become unrecognisable before being deposited at sea to be found, identified and buried as Crabb?

Harry Cole of Emsworth, near Portsmouth, was out fishing in Chichester harbour in November 1956. It was dark and he was alone. As he drew a trawl with iron shoes through the water, he felt a tug on the equipment which suggested that he had caught something quite large in the net. He began the slow process of hauling the trawl to the boat and, as it reached the surface, saw a large object in it. Groping in the darkness, he grabbed hold of the thing and attempted to find out what it was. He realised that it was rubber and as he struggled with it he found, to his horror, that he was holding a human head. It had come away from the body. He let go of the head, which fell back into the water to sink out of sight. However he kept hold of a piece of rubber tubing, which had a mouthpiece that looked like a metal buckle, and part of a rubber belt, which was obviously part of a frogman's outfit. He then released the body from the trawl and let it sink into the murky waters. Cole took a compass bearing of his location and returned home. He reported the incident to the police on 7 February 1957, stating that he had found the body on or about 3 November 1956, but because of the tide movements and his delay in reporting the incident the police did not take any action. The reason for Cole's delay in reporting his find only emerged later.

Agent X had interviewed Cole and alleges that he was told that Cole had the body on the surface but could not drag it into the boat because it was far too heavy. Cole is alleged to have said that the body still had underwater breathing apparatus on it and he was able to draw a rather accurate sketch of that equipment. Agent X said that Cole was able to describe small pouches on the front and back of the vest which held round weights, and further stated that he kept the weights aboard the boat and used them as part of his fishing gear. This information is puzzling in two respects: first is the fact that Cole was able to describe and draw a sketch of very unfamiliar equipment. When the incident occurred it was dark and he was alone in the boat. While unable to get the body into the boat he seemingly, according to Agent X, managed to turn the body over to look at breathing equipment and it would appear that he must have held the body for some time, making a good examination before letting go. The most alarming aspect of Agent X's version of Cole's story, is that the underwater breathing equipment he examined and is reputed to have taken items from, was British Royal Navy issue. If he had removed the ball weights, the body would have been lighter and as a consequence may have floated rather than sunk below the surface. Further, equipment such as that used by the Royal Navy was generally not readily available to others outside the Navy. If Cole had located a body wearing such equipment the Royal Navy would certainly have visited Cole and investigated. There is no evidence that that ever occurred.

The equipment Crabb owned and always used, according to many witnesses, was Italian, and had no weight pouch and no ball weights. Divers using the Italian apparatus wore a separate weight belt. Sydney Knowles stands by the fact that Crabb rarely used any other equipment, and Gordon Gutteridge, Crabb's former diving boss, confirms this. There are numerous other Naval divers who state that Crabb had his own Italian breathing set and diving suit, and did not like to use the British equipment.

Vital questions remained and we sought to locate Harry Cole, bearing in mind that Agent X had told us that he was dead. We eventually located Cole and sought an interview, but because of the possible controversy of leading a witness, we asked Mike O'Meara, a friend of ours who was a former Naval clearance diver, to undertake the interview without our presence, so as to provide an independent statement. The brief to O'Meara was simple, get Cole to explain, as best as he could remember, what he found and what happened, without any prompting. The subsequent report was most interesting. Cole comes from a family of fishermen with some 400 years' fishing experience in the Emsworth area, and at the age of 67 he was still actively fishing when interviewed for *Frogman Spy*.

He recalled that he was trawling about 7:00pm on a dark and windy November evening outside Emsworth Harbour, near Chichester, on his boat, the *Raven*. The aft deck was well lit, a fact which had not been apparent earlier, and the boat was pitching and rolling in the choppy seas. Remember, Agent X said that Cole was able to examine the body so as to draw a detailed sketch. When he hauled in the twelve-foot beam trawl he saw a body, well tangled within the wing of the trawl board. In unfavorable weather conditions he struggled to free the body, which was dressed in a frogman's rubber suit and had breathing equipment. He gripped with both hands two concertina 'breathing tubes' which passed over either shoulder and around the back of the frogman's neck, to connect to a rubber bag. Unable to move the body, he reached down and felt a belt which was around the waist. He remembered feeling a squarish slab weight attached to it. Heaving on the belt, he realised that it was strong but could not say whether it was made of leather or rubberised canvas and he never felt any bottles or canisters. The body, particularly the face was covered with prawns, and the parts of the face visible were black, and so no identification was possible. The suit, apart from the prawns, was covered in a white/grey substance, which when scraped came away to reveal black underneath. He twisted the body in an attempt to get the body into the boat, and the head came away, to fall and sink below the water's surface. Unable to do anything with the body because of the weather, he let it go and allowed it to sink below the surface. He retained the only piece of evidence in the form of a corrugated rubber hose, with the mouthpiece, which he took ashore with him and put in the corner of his shed. Importantly, there were no weights recovered, ball or otherwise.

It was not until February 1957, when Cole reported another matter to the police that he told them about the body he had found. He gave details to a police inspector and a sergeant of West Sussex Police in Chichester. They did not log the details of his findings and loss of the body, and were visibly not interested. This is remarkable, as no action was taken, even though Cole possessed an item of underwater breathing apparatus, which at that time was not commonplace and could have been vital in the identification process. He was never visited by the police for further questioning, or by the Navy, or by anybody from the security services, all of which were well aware that a frogman had gone missing. Because of the lack of interest by the Chichester police, he reported it to his local Emsworth constable, an officer called Brown. The officer reassured Cole that he had done all that was required of him by informing the Chichester police. After John Randall recovered a body, Detective Superintendent Hoare visited Cole with regard to his earlier find. By now the vital physical evidence had been thrown away, and Cole was not asked to make a formal statement nor invited to attend the inquest. What is of interest is the statement made to the inquest, that the police officer had made enquiries from all police forces on the south coast about missing frogmen, yet the find by Harry Cole, an incident that the officer had personal knowledge of, was never mentioned.

Interest now centred on the unusual twin hose 'breathing set' which we wanted to identify, so Cole was shown a photograph of Naval issue Clearance Diving Breathing Apparatus (CDBA), which has ball weights and a single breathing hose. Harry examined the photograph carefully before stating that this was not the same equipment. He was positive. He stated that the breathing bag on the body he found was round the neck, not on the chest, as with the CDBA. He was then shown a photograph of Dunlop closed circuit equipment, That was of Second World War vintage and had twin hoses going from the mouth over the shoulder to attach to the breathing bag. He said that it was very similar to the equipment, which the body had been wearing, and he went on to explain that the breathing bag was higher up around the neck. We could not determine the origin of the equipment and so Sydney Knowles was called and asked to describe the Italian equipment, and while what Cole described could have been Italian apparatus, he could not be certain. From what we had been told he was certain that it was not British CDBA. The issue of the ball weights that had been reported by Agent X was raised with Cole, who categorically stated that there were no ball weights, he never saw or recovered any. The only item that was salvaged was the hose and mouthpiece.

The body found by Cole poses the question as to why the British authorities did absolutely nothing about the find, or take into possession the evidence, and why Cole was not taken to inspect the remains of the frogman that was recovered. As the examination of the events that surround the 'body' are revealed it becomes apparent that nobody was called on who could provide any positive evidence.

The body buried as Crabb's was that found when John Randall was out fishing in Chichester Harbour with two friends, Ted and Bill Gilby, on Sunday 9 June 1957. They spotted something floating in the water which they thought at first was an old tractor tyre, but not being certain, decided to recover it. With great difficulty they managed to haul it into the boat, where they found it to be a body, dressed in a black rubber suit. The suit had marine growth on it, indicating that it had been in the water for some time. The corpse had neither head nor hands. It was just 14 months since Commander Crabb disappeared in Portsmouth. They took the corpse to Pilsea Island and reported it to the Royal Air Force station at Thorney Island. Randall then returned to the boat to await the arrival of the police, who made arrangements for the body to be moved to Chichester mortuary.

Upon its arrival at the mortuary, a report states that an unusual situation occurred when, the mortuary keeper was told *not* to carry out his normal procedure of preparing the body for its post mortem examination. The body, when recovered, was kept in ice, while the mortuary was guarded and the mortuary keeper, Mr. Tracey White, was told by the police not to go near his own mortuary until further notice. It was a senior police officer that called on White at his home and told him that it was a matter of security. The Police Chief at Chichester said:

"This is not just an ordinary body, there are security, political and other reasons for precautions."

What could be the other reasons because this action was taken over the remains of a frogman who, for all intents and purposes was a civilian on 'a frolic of his own'. According, that is, to the Government, the authorities and spy writers who have followed the official line.

On 10 June 1957, it was Dr Donald Plimsoll King, a pathologist, who examined the remains of a male body clothed in a frogman's suit. A tight band around the middle of the suit left the upper torso as a collection of bones and fragments of flesh. The head and hands were missing, but the lower part of the body was well preserved and he found no recognisable scars or injuries, and so four features were submitted for use in possible identification:

1. Length of feet 8.74inches (22.2cms)
2. Moderate degree of bilateral hallux valgus (the big toe was turned out)
3. He was circumcised
4. The pubic hair was light brown in colour

Dr King was unable to establish cause of death because there was no easy means of identification available and so Dr King could only offer limited information for possible identification. The rubber diving suit was in good condition, apart from being covered in marine growth, except for a number of places around the legs, described by detective Superintendent Alan Hoare, in charge of the enquiry, as 'marks of rust', making it seem 'apparent that the body had been held by being caught on an underwater metal object'. Perhaps, the reader may conjecture that something had been attached to the body to hold it underwater. It was based on the Italian diving suits designed and manufactured by Heinke of London. As described earlier, these differed in design from the British suit, which was one-piece, by having two pieces joined in the middle. To keep the two parts of the suit together and maintain a seal, a rubber cummerbund was worn. Dr King stated that it was this band that had halted decomposition of the lower part of

Commander Crabb's medals –
now held at the Royal Naval museum at Portsmouth

The imposing Imperial Sanatorium at Karlovy Vary. Czech contacts told the
authors it was where Crabb spent his last years until he died in 1981

The Mayeruv Gloriet observation point overlooking the Imperial Sanatorium.
It is where the Czech's made contact with the authors.

The two photographs of Pat Rose which were published in an East German newspaper. Only three copies existed, one held by Pat, one held by her brother and the other by Crabb. His were never found after his disappearance.

The body being buried at Portsmouth. Evidence shows that it was not the body of Crabb. Beatrice Crabb, his mother attended the funeral but did not really believe that it was her son.

The type of equipment that was being worn by the frogman that fisherman Cole recovered.

A Royal Naval frogman in 1950's type of equipment. It was different to that worn by Crabb

Soviet underwater breathing equipment in the 1950's was much more cumbersome.

Mrs Margaret Crabb

The Sally Port hotel – Portsmouth where Crabb and Smith spent the night prior to the operation.

The authors examined old and new photographs of the grave and found that the headstone had been altered. The change was made in 1981 the year that the authors were told that Crabb died.

The nut taken from Garry's car engine. A police forensic test stated that it was a hairline crack. The photograph shows that the cut was the size of a small hacksaw.

Gary Murray, a TV researcher and private investigator played an active role in getting Frogman Spy published and then exposing a Government "spook".

Mike with Sydney after he fled from Spain following the attempt on his life.

A photograph produced by Bernard Hutton through his Soviet underground contacts. It is said to be that of commander Crabb, alias First Lt Lev Lvovich Korablov in the Soviet Navy.

A newspaper cutting showing a photograph said to be Crabb in the former East Germany. This picture was shown to a former base official who demanded to know who had taken it and sent it to the West.

Smith departed from Britain for the USA following Crabb's disappearance — he was traced back to the UK and photographed.

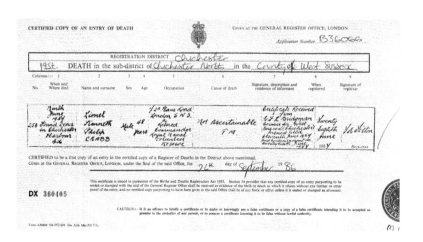

The death certificate claiming to record Crabb's death

The Soviet cruiser Ordzhonikidze was at the centre of Crabb's last operation. The 'super secret' warship was sold to the Indonesian Navy in 1962. Nothing was super and nothing was secret.

A member of Crabb's underwater party removing a mine. They had no rubber suits or fins for the feet, just small goggles and submarine escape breathing equipment.

A view of the remains of the body recovered in 1957 and said to be that of Crabb.

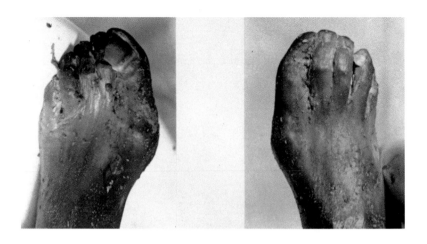

The feet of the body recovered in 1957 and said to be that of Crabb. Medical and witness evidence claims that these were not the feet of Crabb.

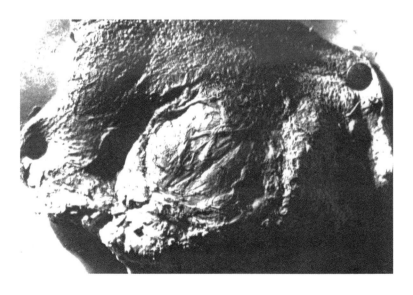

Sydney Knowles examination of the body identified that there should have been a scar which was not present. A piece of skin allegedly removed from the body was photographed at a police station. It was then claimed to identify the body of Crabb.

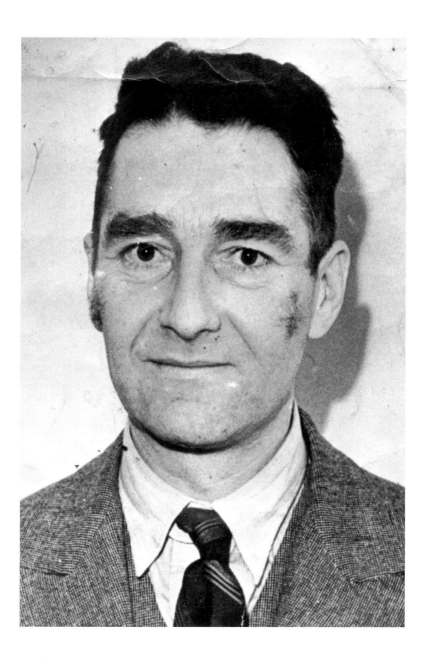

A photo given to the authors by Pat Rose showing Crabb in the period prior to his disappearance. Note the tufts of hair on the cheeks which Crabb retained in later life.

After Crabb's disappearance in 1956, the Soviets Navy embarked upon a programme to develop their underwater diving equipment and operational diving units.

The coffin alleged to be Crabb's was carried, draped in the Union Jack. There was no official Naval presence and no recognition of Naval service.

A photo given to the authors by Pat Rose showing Crabb as a young man. It was at a time when he moved in the art world and began to mix with those who were to be exposed as Soviet spies.

The Soviet leaders Marshal Bulganin and Premier Krushchev being greeted in Portsmouth following their arrival aboard the Soviet cruiser Ordzhonikidze. The following day, in broad daylight Crabb made his dive and made history.

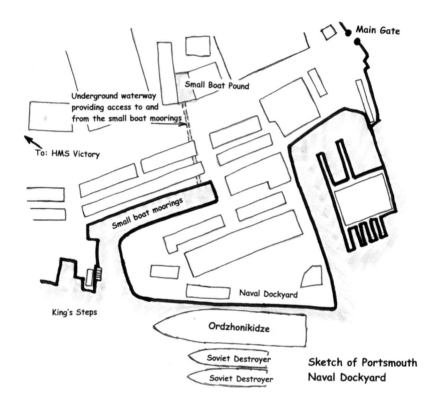

Main Gate

Small Boat Pound

Underground waterway
providing access to and
from the small boat moorings

To: HMS Victory

Small boat moorings

Naval Dockyard

King's Steps

Ordzhonikidze

Soviet Destroyer

Soviet Destroyer

Sketch of Portsmouth
Naval Dockyard

A sketch of Portsmouth Naval Dockyard.
It shows the various places referred to in the book.

the body. The authorities were aware that Sydney Knowles would have knowledge of any identification marks that Crabb may have had and so dispatched members of the Preston CID to interview him in order to obtain accurate details of any marks or deformities that Crabb had. Knowles told us that he gave details of two scars and provided a rough drawing of what they looked like and where they were located. The policemen left, instructing Knowles not to discus the matter with anybody.

On 14 June, King re-examined the remains and located scars. In particular he said that there was a scar on the left side of the left knee which was an inverted Y. The remains were photographed in the mortuary, however the scar was not photographed on the body. Instead a section of tissue was taken from the remains and then photographed. It was never questioned as to why the scar tissue was removed for photographing when it could have been shown in situ. Again, vital evidence in identification appears to have been handled without care, unless there was no scar *on* the remains. Another twist in the story occurs when Dr King requested an x-ray of the leg below the knee because he had been informed that Crabb had a previous fracture.

The radiologist at Chichester hospital recalls being told that the lower part of a leg had been removed and was being sent for x-ray. The leg arrived in a bucket and was subjected to x-ray, where no fracture was found. Dr King raised concern because if it was Crabb's body then it should have had a fracture.

The body that was recovered had been in the sea for some time or at least in water, but was devoid of a head and the hands. However, the lower torso and legs were in remarkable condition, as stark white remains lay on the mortuary slab. Identification would be a problem, but as the Navy had lost a diver, the first and simplest option was for the pathologist to contact the naval diving medical staff, exchange medical information and they may have been able to determine if the body was that of the missing diver or not.

Surgeon Vice Admiral Sir John Rawlins, who retired from the

Navy some years ago, is very much a diving person and we spoke to him after a talk given by Mike about Crabb. He told us:

"We heard that a body had been found and if it was our missing diver then we had medical records which would help in the identification. I was prepared to accept the body for us to do the examination or I would go to Chichester and assist the civilian pathologist. We received a call from the Admiralty that ordered us not to communicate with the pathologist or anybody else and no medical records were to be released unless ordered to do so by the Admiralty."

Rawlins told us that Crabb did have a previous fracture in a leg and his medical records were kept at the RN hospital Haslar and that had the body been taken to Haslar for post mortem, they would have then been able to make any identification through an X-Ray of the leg and confirm if there was a fracture in it, however he was not involved in this. It was explained to him that a Radiological Report for the remains had been prepared and the testimony of the Radiographer about the body stated that it did not have any fractures. He repeated that Crabb did have a previous fracture. The question was put to him as to why the naval records were not used at the post mortem or at the inquest, to which he replied that the Coroner was told not to ask any questions or to accept any questions; which would support what we already thought, that it was *not* the body of Crabb". Rawlins continued:

"It was a matter of the highest level of the Official Secrets Act and we were to speak to no one about it. It was quite extraordinary because the normal process is to make a positive identification if possible. However, under the circumstance you do as you are told and that was that."

As the final comments from Rawlins clarified:

"We knew that the body at Chichester did not have a previous fracture in the leg. The x-rays we had of our man showed a fracture. I understand that the

body did not have a fracture, so who the body was we do not know, but it was not who they said."

We are to our knowledge, the only authors who have discussed the Crabb case with Sir John. He told Mike that another author had quoted information but had not spoken to him about it. Quite rightly he was disappointed with what had been published and, despite our efforts to discuss the Crabb incident further, he was not inclined to do so.

The question of the x-ray was not raised at the inquest. Crabb's medical records were held by the Navy but were not called and no naval medical person gave evidence at the inquest. In the attempt to establish identification the authorities called upon a select number of people.

At this point the question must be asked as to whether the pathologist was under the influence of the security services. He undertakes a post mortem but of course has little to work on. There was little left to determine a cause of death and even less for identifying who the body was. The legs and feet were for the most part intact and his examination culminated in a basic report and provided no details of any identification marks.

Margaret Crabb was driven to Bognor from her home in St. Margaret's bay, Kent, after a dawn call from Kent police to help in a matter of national importance. Every effort was made to keep her visit secret. She met Det-Inspector Ernest Lester of the West Sussex police on a by-pass outside the town and he drove her to Bognor. She was taken to the mortuary on 11 June 1957, where the frogman's body lay under white sheets, and was asked to study the feet, but she was to state in the inquest that her efforts were inconclusive and she could not be certain that the remains were those of her former husband, Commander Crabb.

Another person who saw and examined the body was Sydney Knowles, Crabb's diving companion for 13 years. He was the ideal witness for, as he told us:

"Throughout the years of diving it was only natural that I had seen the Commander in a state of undress, so I can say that, yes, I would know his body."

However, Knowles described an official visit to his place of work:

"Two days after the body was found I was visited at the swimming pool where I worked, by two people. They were tall chaps in civilian clothing, bowler hated, etc, who introduced themselves as a Colonel and Captain. They said they were members of some Intelligence organisation, but not naval intelligence, MI5 I think. They asked whether I would go and see the remains of a body at Chichester, a body in a rubber suit, since I might be able to give the answer as to whether it was Commander Crabb. They said, 'We believe you have been in touch with CID Preston and they have taken a statement from you, referring to identification marks'. I said I had and they wanted to know how long I had known him, the colour of his hair and so on."

Following that visit, Knowles was invited to Chichester to examine the body. He explained:

"I motored down to Chichester, but before going down I was contacted by the Daily Mirror in Fleet Street and asked if I would give them some information, so that they could build a story around my visit to Chichester. For this they would pay me £45, and £45 was £45 then. I wasn't going to tell them anything people didn't know, that was it as far as I was concerned and I was told to meet their reporter in Chichester.

About ten miles outside Chichester I was stopped by a police car, and the two men who had come to see me at the swimming pool, the MI5 people. There was another car there, and they asked me to get into it because they wanted to talk to me prior to my going down to see the body. I asked them why they stopped me on the road and they said, 'This, as you know Mr.. Knowles, is a very dodgy business, embarrassing to the country'. I wasn't awfully in love with the Russians but I didn't hate them, so I said I would help them in any possible way. They told me that 'when you see the body, when you go into Chichester, you will go into the mortuary. I want you first of all to see the Chief Inspector. He will have a word with you and you will go along with him and into the mortuary and they will show the body. You will then tell him the reasons why you know the person who the body is.' Very well, is this the only reason you stopped me going straight in, 'well, we don't want you speaking to any reporters'. That was not what I wanted to hear. Oh! Just a minute, if I don't I'm going to lose some money here. I've been offered £45 to give a good story after this Chichester visit to the Daily Mirror. 'Well, I'm afraid you'll have to be very careful what you say to them, in other words you say this', and he carried on to say what I could tell them and what I couldn't tell them. He then said to me: 'While you were in the Navy you signed the Official Secrets Act', to which I told them that I signed it twice, but that was well over ten years ago. 'Here's another document we would like you to sign'.

It had Official Secrets Act written on the top, there was small print, on four or five sheets of paper and I signed three out of the four or five sheets at the bottom. It was not the same form that I signed in the Navy appertaining to the Official Secrets Act; it was certainly not the same form. Now I'm wondering if or not this form was the genuine thing. This I don't know, possibly it was, and it might have been a revised form. I signed it in the car and he put the document in the briefcase. Knowles was then told, 'Well, now, you go ahead in the normal way'.

I went and reported to the Inspector. He took me to the mortuary in a car, not my car, in a police car. He took me into a building where the remains were laid out. I identified the body. No, I looked at the body but the scars that I'd described and sketched on the form were not in absolutely the same place as I knew them, either in shape or place. I told the police inspector that this is not the body of Commander Crabb. Commander Crabb's hair was sandy; this person's was absolutely jet-black. What you'd expect to come from either Greek or Italian style of colouring, not the skin, the hair was so dark that it must have been a Latin. No, this is not the body of Commander Crabb. I told him that the scars are very much like them and they are almost in the same position but there is one missing, the inverted Y on the back of his leg, the back of his calf. I said, No, this is not the body of Commander Crabb."

Knowles paused then recalled an earlier part of the visit and explained: *"Oh! prior to seeing the body there was a chap in civilian clothes in there, along with two chaps in a white coats, long white coat. The civilian asked these two people to leave prior to me looking at the body.*

Having said that it was not the body of Crabb the Inspector said to me 'Are you absolutely sure this is not Commander Crabb?' To which I replied that I was as sure as I could be considering the state of the body. The legs, for instance, were like parchment; all the skin was virtually white. I had to stretch the skin to search for scars. It was mummified, virtually mummified and the skin was snow-white. Have you seen a lump of fat off a carcass? It was like that, snow-white. Also, the lower part of the body, on the back of the thighs and back of the knees around the lower part of the legs, not quite near the ankles, was badly marked. It looked as if something had been biting them. Looking at the remains I thought that if the body had been held under the water by chain or cable, or even caught up in some wreckage, that's the sort of identification there would be in the skin. I told him that it is not the body of Commander Crabb; as far as I can ascertain this is not the body of Commander Crabb."

The inspector said: 'Very well. This gentleman would like to say a few words to you'. He then left the room. With the body between us this chap said to me, 'Mr.. Knowles, we know this is not the body of Commander Crabb, but I want you to say that it is Commander Crabb'. I asked why I should say that and he said: 'Commander Crabb was a great patriot. He loved his Queen and Country, and so we ask that you don't embarrass the country and don't embarrass him. If he could speak to you here, he'd say please don't embarrass the Queen and Country'. I replied that he would actually, indeed he would. The gentleman asked: 'Will you go with me on this and sign the documents'. What, the Official Secrets Act? I don't know any secrets. He did not respond to my comment but said 'When you go in court and you're asked, did you identify the body, will you please say, that is the body of Commander Crabb' I replied, Yes."

Knowles was left to travel home holding a secret that caused him a lot of concern. He knew that it was not the body of Crabb, but he was under the threat of the Official Secrets Act, so could tell no one. If he had, who could he tell and would they have believed him?

10

A Secret Service Inquest

Who controls the past controls the future: who controls the present controls the past.

George Orwell   1949

When the bodies of frogmen came into the picture some fourteen months after Crabb disappeared, the one at Chichester became the most controversial because we have evidence of the proceedings. But they are all shrouded in mystery and confusion. It was apparent that the identification of the body found off Chichester rested on the undergarments reputed to have been removed from the body. We have seen that the mortuary keeper did not prepare the body, as he would normally have done. Mr. Bridgman, the Coroner, said that it might be some time before he issued a certificate for the burial of the body, as he would not issue one while identification remained possible. The Royal Navy, who held the medical records for Crabb, was not called to provide evidence. The reason for the delay (when one knows the evidence provided by Knowles) is an unknown factor, apart from the fact that it provided time to prepare for the final inquest which the authorities wanted to pass without problems.

The Secret Service and the Admiralty were keen to manage the

Coroners Court. The Coroner himself would be very circumspect in the selection of 'witnesses'. The Coroner found that he needed Admiralty assistance as he claimed nobody was able to furnish details of Crabb's full names or the date of his birth. What about his ex wife or mother? The problem was that they could cause a problem and would not easily be controlled. The Admiralty would provide 'suitable persons' to give evidence.

In fact, the Admiralty involvement extended to determining that the body would be identified through the evidence of non-military people such as Crabb's ex wife. Heinke would identify the frogman's suit as being one similar to one that they sold to Crabb. They then proposed to produce a man from Newcastle who had come forward to identify a bullet wound in Crabb's leg. He claimed that it was a wound Crabb received in 1944 and the scar was of a special shape. This is the first reference to such a witness and a bullet wound. Whoever the person was, indeed if such a person existed, he was never called to give evidence. Knowles never mentioned such an incident or person.

The Admiralty were keen to participate in the cover up and so to help the Coroner they assigned G. W. Bostock, a temporary Clerical Officer who had no knowledge of the affair and so could truthfully be unable to answer any embarrassing questions. If difficult questions were asked, the Coroner could manage the Court and stop the proceedings once he had the information he required. They instructed Bostock to provide the most basic details about Crabb and to conclude; they thought that this would be a pleasant opportunity for an Admiralty witness to pay tribute to Crabb, albeit through a temporary Clerical Officer.

However, as the date for the inquest approached lawyers for the Navy thought that Lieutenant Commander G. Franklin officer would be called to give evidence. If that was to be the case then it was hoped that the oath and evidence could be held in camera. There was anticipation that the police would be able to get him into and out of the court without the press knowing what was happening and keep his identity secret. There was also concern that the officer would be missed at *HMS Vernon* by his fellow officers and that could raise questions. The options were to provide a cover story by creating some fictitious duty or a few days leave. In addition it was considered that some officers in *Vernon* would need to be told to keep their mouths shut.

In archive papers released by the Government there is a hand written note which gives reasons why the Admiralty did not want Franklin to give evidence. It was thought that if he appeared, even in camera, the press would immediately link him as being the mysterious Mr. Smith and expose him as a target of the press and others. If the Coroner did not ask him to identify where he last saw Crabb the press certainly would. However, if he refused to answer the question the press would draw inference about events that occurred close to the Russian ships. This would have been contrary to the country's interest and particularly what the Admiralty had already said. Remember they had already put out the cock and bull story about Crabb being in Stokes Bay, a considerable distance away from the Russian ships.

There was also concern about the inconsistency of what Franklin would say, because if it had been a Naval operation then he would have reported to his superiors that Crabb was missing and they in turn would have provided a high level search. There was no search, only a massive cover up about the whole affair, and everything was contrary to the public interest. The note concluded that if he was called then he should be restricted to providing evidence confined to the fact that, he helped Crabb get into the water and that the clothing found on the body that was recovered belonged to Crabb. The outcome was that Franklin was not called.

On Tuesday, 11 June, at Chichester Magistrate's Court, Mr. Bridgman opened the inquest. The only evidence submitted was the detailed list of equipment found on the body, which comprised: one frogman's two piece suit; one pair swim fins; two sorbo pads; one pair bathing trunks; one pair of nylon socks; one pair of blue combinations (top missing); one pair of nylon combinations and one piece of an undervest. The proceedings were adjourned.

The Admiralty had sent Lieutenant W.Y. McLanachan from *HMS Vernon* to assist with identification of the body, the rubber suit, flippers, and underclothes. It is a mystery what constructive evidence could be obtained from an officer who had not actually worked or dived with Crabb. He only stated that he saw a frogman's rubber two-piece suit, swim fins, which were similar to Royal Naval issue type and an assortment of undergarments. He could not say that they belonged to Crabb, nor could he identify the body and he did not say that the diving suit and under garments were not Naval issue.

On Wednesday 26 June 1957 the inquest was resumed. Dr. King was called to give evidence of his findings from the post mortem examination. On 10 June 1957 he had made an examination of some human remains at Chichester Public Mortuary and, when he saw them, they were clothed in a frogman's suit. Above the waist, parts of the body, including the head had disappeared, although certain bones, including the left humerus and both scapulae, remained. The abdominal cavity was empty, except below the waistband of the suit. The organs had undergone extensive post mortem change, including a change known as adipocere, which is a wax-like organic substance formed in the body fat in corpses, but they were recognisable. He identified a photograph as being of the remains and said that another was an actual size photograph of the feet. He had found the measurement of the feet to be 8.75 inches, which was small for an adult man. He also found that there was a condition called hallux valgus, which was a condition of the toes in which the big toe was turned outwards. The joint of the big toe was enlarged and disjointed. With regard to the hair on the body, the pubic hair was intact and the colour was clearly a light brown and in certain lights when dry it had a gingerish tinge. He thought the deceased was rather a small man in the region of 5'6". The legs were in a good state of preservation and he would describe them as being muscular and well formed, and apart from the feet, there was no deformity. They were quite straight. From the adipocere, he concluded that the body had been in the water for at least six months and could well have been in the water for at least fourteen months.

On 14 June 1957, Dr. King went to the mortuary and examined the remains again. On this occasion he reported a scar, left side, left knee, in the form of an inverted Y. A photograph was taken at Chichester Police Station, in his presence, of the portion of the skin bearing the scar. Why did the coroner not question the fact that in Dr. King's original report there was no mention of any scars on the lower part of the body, when in fact two vital marks for possible identification were on Crabb's body. Did Knowles' drawings of the scars' locations have any bearing on this change in the statement? In other words, was a scar which had not been there previously been 'created' to try to conform to what Knowles had said? Or was Dr. King intimidated into adding material to his testimony?

Margaret Crabb gave evidence about her marriage and divorce, saying that during the short time of their married life he was serving in the Royal Naval Volunteer Reserve and shortly after they were married he became a Commander. She described him as a short man and said he was not as tall as her, her height being 5'5. His legs were very straight and muscular and the hair on his body was very light brown, inclined to ginger. His feet were small and his big toes were very unusual. They appeared to be what she thought were hammertoes and were raised high off the ground. The photograph of the body's feet was shown to her, and she said that they were not as she remembered them. She thought he took a size six shoe. She continued that on 11 June 1957 she went to Bognor Mortuary and saw the remains of a human body but she could not identify the feet as those of her former husband although she was not able to say definitely that they were not his feet. It is recorded that Margaret Crabb could not say whether or not her husband had been circumcised 'as sexual relations were not normal'.

Her statement made to the police at Chichester states:

"I married Lionel Kenneth Crabb on the 15th March 1952 whilst living at Birchington, Kent. We lived together until April 1953 when I commenced proceedings for divorce and my husband did not defend the petition. The decree was made absolute about December 1954.Whilst we were living together he was serving as a Lieutenant Commander RNVR (I believe a diving officer) and attached to HMS Vernon. I cannot be sure whether my husband had been circumcised or not as sexual relations were not normal and our marriage was of short duration. It was because of my husband's abnormal sexual behaviour that I divorced him."

John Randall provided evidence of his find and stated that on 9 June 1957 two other men accompanied him in his fishing boat as he went down the Harbour from Bosham until he got to a point where he saw a black object floating in the water, about 30 yards from the boat. It was just surfacing, with the little running tide showing it just above the water every few seconds. He then immediately saw it was the shape of a body and on examination he formed the opinion that it was the body of a person in a rubber diving suit. The ridges he had seen in the object were the two waistband ridges. They towed the body in to Pilsea Island and then reported it to the Royal Air Force Station at Thorney Island. He then returned and waited for the arrival of the police.

Police Constable Ronald G. Williams, stationed at Southbourne, stated that at about 12 noon on 9 June 1957 he went to the Royal Air Force Station at Thorney Island and accompanied the Station Medical Officer to Pilsea Island. On the beach he saw some human remains. They were part of the body of a man dressed in a rubber frogman's suit. The head, upper portion of the body and the arms were missing.

Detective Superintendent Alan Hoare of West Sussex Constabulary said that he had been in charge of enquiries in connection with the body that was found in Chichester Harbour on the 9 June 1957. He made enquiries from all the Police Forces on the South Coast from Cornwall to Kent and from those enquiries he had been informed that no other person dressed similarly to the body recovered had been reported missing. On 23 October 1955 there was a man reported missing after diving in the River Dark, but his clothing was in no way similar to the clothing in this case. Why, one wonders did Detective Superintendent Hoare make no mention of the body found earlier by Harry Cole?

The Managing Director of Heinke and Co Ltd of Bermondsey London, Mr. Eric James Blake gave evidence and stated that his firm manufactured, among other things, underwater swimsuits. He knew Commander Crabb and on three occasions his company had supplied Crabb with underwater suits, the last one being on 11 October 1955; this suit was unusual in that it had a neck seal and did not have a hood, for normally such suits were sold with hoods. He had seen the suit found on the deceased and said that this was designed about January 1955. During the ten months between the time it was designed and the time a suit was sold to Commander Crabb in October 1955 they sold about fifteen suits identical in all respects to that found on the deceased. The suit he had seen at Chichester Police Station was identical to the one sold to Crabb but he was unable to say, of course, whether it was the same suit. Thus, if a cover-up had been undertaken, other suits were available. The purchasers of the other suits were not sought, to see where their suits were.

George William Bostock, a temporary clerical officer in the Department of the Admiral Commanding Reserves, at Queen Anne's Mansions, London SW1, gave his evidence. He said that it was part of his duty to keep records of Royal Naval Volunteer Officers. One of the files under his control related to Commander Lionel Kenneth Philip Crabb and this record showed that he was born on 28 January 1909. He entered the Navy and on 30 April 1948 he was released with the rank of Temporary Acting Lieutenant Commander. He was recalled to active service on 12 October 1951 with the substantive rank of Lieutenant Commander and on 30 June 1952, he was promoted to the rank of Commander. On 8 April 1955, he was finally released from active service and, since that date had not been employed in the service of the Navy or done any training.

As the court was dealing with a body and not the career of Commander Crabb, why were his Naval medical records not requested? They would have given valuable information in the identification of the body, especially since they would have contained details of any feet abnormalities. If you do not want the truth to be known, you do not provide factual evidence.

Sydney Knowles gave straightforward evidence to the Coroner. He was, at the time, a swimming pool supervisor. He had joined the Royal Navy in December 1939 and he first met Commander Crabb in 1941 when he did underwater work with him. In the winter of 1945, they were serving at Leghorn and the Captains of the ships had been instructed to have rolls of barbed wire placed below the watermarks of their ships for protection against Italian frogmen. Early one morning Crabb and Knowles were going below the surface to search for limpet mines and to investigate the American ship, the *John Harrison*, to see that mines were not present. As they were going down, a tug came along, casting up a wash, which threw both of them against the barbed wire of this ship. When they went back to their launch, Knowles noticed that Crabb had sustained a wound on the side of his left knee. He dressed it for him. About three weeks later, when he was working with Crabb again, he noticed a scar that was in the shape of an inverted 'Y'. This was the scar Dr. King reported after his second examination of the body. However, in his statement to the police, Knowles had also reported a second scar, roughly the size of an old sixpence, on Crabb's right thigh, which had been caused by a seawater boil. This evidence was not produced at the inquest.

Knowles testimony also said that after the war he saw Crabb from time to time and knew that he was living at 2a Hans Road, London. He was also quite familiar with the clothing that he wore when diving. He wore a two-piece rubber suit with a neck seal instead of a hood. He used to wear a pair of maroon swimming shorts and he had two sets of combination underwear to wear alternately, one khaki in colour and the other blue. He also used to wear blue socks. Knowles was not able to say from the photograph shown to him whether the feet were those of Crabb.

Apart from the second scar, which was not recorded by the pathologist, Knowles also stated that Crabb had been trying out diving suits manufactured by Heinke of London. When they were together on a diving job at Tobermory, Crabb was wearing Italian Tenth Flotilla MASS fins and a Heinke two-piece diving suit. Knowles stated: "He never wore British fins. He hated them." Sydney had told the police: "He damaged his fins in 1954 at Tobermory and I loaned him my Italian fins. When I last saw him in the *Captain's Cabin*, I asked him when he was going to return my fins? He replied, 'I can't at the moment. I shall require them, but I will let you have a pair when I go to Italy on business re-the book (autobiography) and visit the Italian frogmen's headquarters'."

Italian fins are much lighter than the British Naval type. The left fin is marked 'Sinistro' and the right one is marked 'Destro'. The fins on the body, which was recovered, were of the British Naval issue type, so why was this evidence not raised? The Italian fins belonging to Knowles were never found amongst Crabb's belongings after his disappearance, and it is evident that he would not wear British fins if he had Italian ones available. Knowles also said in that statement, Commander Crabb did not have hammer toes. His feet were quite normal and in healthy condition.

The Coroner recorded an open verdict, as it was impossible to determine the cause of death. Based upon the evidence provided, the feet, the scar, the colour of hair and the rubber suit, he determined that the body found in Chichester harbour was that of Commander Crabb. The death Certificate issued on 28 June 1957 stated the cause of death to be 'Not Ascertainable. P.M.'

The family was told that the body was presumed to be that of Commander Crabb, and even though the Coroner's court was given no firm evidence that it was his remains that had been found, a death certificate was issued. No member of Crabb's family was called upon to identify the remains, though, which is very strange. Even his mother was never asked to look at the body, and she would certainly have known about his toe deformity and could have made a useful contribution to the vital identification process.

On Friday, 5 July 1957, the body of the *unknown* man was buried at Milton Cemetery, Portsmouth. There were no official representatives of the Royal Navy at the funeral, and neither Sydney Knowles nor Pat Rose attended. The funeral was without full military honours and the headstone placed on the grave was engraved: *In Ever Loving Memory of My Son Commander Crabb. At Rest At Last* There were no first names, no date and no mention of his decorations; this was a strange epitaph under any normal circumstances, but then the circumstances were not normal. Beatrice Crabb never returned to the grave for she did not in her heart believe that her son Lionel was buried there. She had been told that the body found was his, but she never really believed the authorities.

Mrs. Crabb stated:

"They say it was the body of my son, and so I suppose I must believe them."

However, in later years, before she died, she told Pat Rose:

"My son Lionel is not buried there."

Knowles wrote to us saying:

"Crabbies mother referred to the body as, that poor creature at Milton."

About eighty people, mainly women, attended Requiem Mass for Crabb in Portsmouth Roman Catholic cathedral. Naval uniforms were conspicuous by their absence in the cathedral. Mrs. Beatrice Crabb, his mother, headed the family mourners. James Gleason, author of *The Frogmen,* which included references to Crabb's wartime exploits, organised the funeral on behalf of Crabb's mother. Most interestingly his swordstick, with a card attached, was placed on his coffin, but it was not buried. The card contained the message, in French:

"I was there at the fight, so I will be there at the glory."

The senior officer who stopped Knowles when he was en route to Chichester mortuary had identified himself as Col. Malcolm. He told Knowles that he ordered two MI5 officers to go to Portsmouth Police HQ and organise the removal of the pages from the hotel register, which was done by a local police officer. He had sworn Knowles to secrecy on the identification of the body, and had confirmed that the remains were not those of Crabb, but it was part of a massive cover up.

Knowles told us:

"During my interrogation with Col Malcolm I disclosed that Crabb was going to take another person with him, but would not say who it was. He replied, 'We have been aware of this for some time, thank God he didn't go'."

11

Spetnaz

Let us not be deceived — we are today in the midst of a Cold War.

Bernard Baruch 1870 -1965

Crabb's role in the Navy during the early 1950s revolved around secret underwater work. This included the development of specialised, purpose-made miniature demolition devices for the disposal of bombs and mines. The objective was not having to resort to total demolition. He was also very interested in the development of underwater mini-submarines and swimmer vehicles. He worked with the Royal Marines' Special Boat Squadron teams in developing techniques for covert operations. Despite his age, he was physically fit enough to carry out diving operations. He was skilled in the art of locking out of and back into submarines whilst they were submerged. He had been part of a team that attempted to penetrate a Russian Naval base, to undertake a secret underwater spying operation. He was taken there and collected by a submerged submarine. Within the organisation that gathered the naval intelligence, Crabb, a Commander RN, was fairly junior in rank, but was always regarded with respect and some awe by those his senior. Of course only a few knew who he reported to. Those that did were aware of the consequences of conflict with Mountbatten.

The covert operations undertaken by the Special Boat Section

(SBS) in the 1950s are not discussed, or even hinted at. This adds fuel to the inevitable question as to whether Crabb would have been a worthwhile prize for the Russians at that period. The answer must be positive. Those who really knew what he was doing up to the time he disappeared agree that his knowledge and experience would have been of the highest value to the Soviet Union, but only for a limited number of years. Developments and advances in the underwater aspects of warfare were evolving so swiftly that his knowledge of British methods would have become outdated. However, he could have continued to undertake trials and work with diving teams, all of which would have met his desires.

In the 1950s, SCUBA diving as a sport was virtually non-existent anywhere in the world, but especially in the USSR. Then, in the space of three years, the 'sport' of SCUBA diving was developed. It was in late 1956 that the first section in the USSR Central Sea Club (CSC) was opened for the training of SCUBA divers, and courses were soon established for underwater swimmers and instructors. An English article in a Soviet magazine explained that other sections were established in Leningrad, Sevastopol, Odessa and Vladivostok, as well as other cities. The fact that this major event happened almost 'instantly' in 1956, and involved all the places where Crabb is reported to have served, is interesting.

The Soviet Navy had studied in great detail, and with some admiration, the operations carried out by units of British frogmen, charioteers and midget submarines during the war. The Soviets were impressed with the raid, which required midget submarines to penetrate a well-guarded Norwegian fjord. This allowed the crews to set explosive charges below the German battleship Tirpitz. They took a great interest in and had deep respect for the divers who swam ashore prior to amphibious landings, to destroy landing obstructions and remove anti-landing mines. They also had a keen interest in the divers who were involved in countering enemy attacks and removing mines from both the underside of ships and from the bottoms of captured harbours and ports. From those early post-war days, the Russians have foreseen the great advantages of having specially trained free-swimming underwater operatives, able to undertake operations supported by midget submarines.

In 1945 the Soviets only had 'hard hat' divers with heavy equipment and reliance on surface supplied breathing air. They had no free-swimming combat swimmer units, midget submarines or elite specialist amphibious formations capable of undertaking covert underwater operations. Britain did, and they led the world, having gained a good deal of knowledge from the Italians. The Soviets greatest weakness in 1945 was in underwater mine warfare. This is an area where one has not only to consider the mines, but also the fact that they lie in water, and very often that water will be full of murky silt, which means that all handling has to be done by touch.

Mine phobia was a key factor within Soviet thinking during the Cold War and they placed much emphasis on this area of operation. Their interest extended to a careful study of all existing types of mine and they encouraged regular handling of them by the units concerned, enhancing their ability to clear paths through minefields to deal with explosive devices fitted to underwater targets and to place mines during underwater attacks. The Russians needed to train their *Spetsnaz* swimmers in the art of attacking maritime targets by attaching mines to them, and in undertaking reconnaissance missions, during which enemy mines laid for defence purposes might have to be neutralised.

Admiral Gennadiy Zakharov became well known in the country as second in command to the chief of the exclusively land-based security forces of the President of the Russian Federation. He talked to Yevgeniy Zhirnov, a columnist from the magazine *Vlast*, about his service in one of the most secret sub-units in the Navy, the Naval sabotage sections. For thirty years Gennadiy Zakharov trained *Spetsnaz* troops in Naval sabotage. In the article he states:

"In the GDR, not far from the port of Rostock our German friends had

captured the English frogman Commander Crabb. He became well known at the time of Khrushchev's visit on a ship to England. There had been an attempt to examine the parts of our ships that were underwater. Either we were just lucky, or perhaps every crewmember wanted to distinguish himself, anyway a frogman was spotted by visual observation. They stationed ratings with binoculars along the ship's sides. There was no kind of hydro-acoustics at all. At that time our leader was already busily combing over his bald spot, after all, at that time we had neither underwater saboteurs of our own nor methods of combating them. With regard to combating saboteurs, we have in fact not thought up anything radical since then. There is visual observation, when every unidentified object is checked out as a possible enemy. Then there is prophylactic observation; grenades are thrown into the water according to a schedule. And our third measure is to turn the ship's propellers. Then, when we started to have military swimmers, as they were called to distinguish them from us, at every Naval base, they began to inspect the water area and the ships in it."

He continued to state:

"... (Crabb told his captors) that he had been to Klaipeda to hand over a consignment to English agents in Lithuania. He said that he had towed the container with the consignment behind a super-miniature submarine. The committee members gave me a copy of a plan drawn by him personally showing how he reached the spot where he unloaded. When I consulted a map it turned out that his picture was very close to reality. If the man had not actually been there, he could not have reproduced with such exact detail his plan for getting back to shore. But I decided to take it further. I said: 'Perhaps the man simply has a phenomenal memory? Could it be, he was simply preparing for the trip but didn't actually do anything? We needed to follow the route ourselves.' Everything fell into place. The final proof was tests on the seabed in the hollow, which Crabb had pointed out as his mooring place. The result was positive: a boat had lain there ..."

Admiral Gennadiy Zakharov provides sound evidence of Crabb being behind the Soviet Iron Curtain. Wanting to delve further into the Crabb matter, we began to make enquiries. The outcome was that we would not be allowed to know where Zakharov was and would certainly not be allowed to meet him, let alone discuss anything about Crabb.

Voyska Spetsial Nogo Naznachenniya, or to give it its more common form, *Spetsnaz,* was a very closely guarded secret from its inception. Details of its units, both naval and army, were published in *Operation Spetsnaz, the aims, tactics and techniques of Soviet Special Forces* which was a book I co-authored with Bruce Quarrie in 1989.

Prior to Crabb's disappearance in 1956 the new underwater units were being formed under the greatest secrecy. The new frogman and mini-sub units would be recruiting and training. It takes time to form such specialist units if they are to be effective. Crabb would not have known about *Spetsnaz* because the West did not know, such was the secrecy. However, if the Soviets needed some underwater mine expertise then he was a valuable man.

By the end of the 1950s each of the four Soviet fleets had a naval *Spetsnaz* brigade assigned to it, operating directly under the Third Department of the Intelligence Directorate of the GRU. Because *Spetsnaz* was part of the GRU, the principal military intelligence organisation in the former Soviet Union, the ordinary citizen knew nothing about it and, it is said, neither did most serving military personnel. Indeed, it appears that most *Spetsnaz* units were unaware of the existence of other units, as great precautions were taken to cover up their operations, organisation, strength, function, deployment and even existence. *Spetsnaz* troops were denied all contact with civilians or other troops, and all candidates selected for the units were subjected to checks for loyalty and, upon entry, had to sign a form similar to the Official Secrets Act, the breaching of which was punishable by death. Little wonder that the West had no detailed knowledge of developments.

To aid the cover-up all *Spetsnaz* troops wore the same uniforms as the normal Soviet units alongside which they operate. In the case of the naval *Spetsnaz* units, they wore the same uniforms as worn by the

Soviet Naval Infantry. Midget submarine crews wore the same uniform as Soviet submariners. In the effort to maintain their anonymity, the *Spetsnaz* brigades did not have separate bases where they could be identified but had guarded compounds within the Naval Infantry bases. There were four *Spetsnaz* intelligence units, again one being assigned to each fleet.

A brigade consists of up to 1,300 troops and was formed with a headquarters (HQ) company, three combat swimmer/frogmen battalions, a parachute swimmer battalion, a midget submarine group, a signals company and a number of support units. The combat swimmer battalions were for the most part trained in underwater sabotage, mine clearance and intelligence gathering whilst the parachute battalion performed low altitude drops, combined with amphibious or underwater tasks in the seizure or destruction of maritime targets. The training of these elite troops took place at a number of locations within the Soviet Union, one such centre being at Odessa. The particular relevance of this is that it is alleged that this was one of the places where Crabb was identified as being, because it specialised in training men to deal with underwater mines, and with demolition.

A glimpse the West had of *Spetsnaz* frogmen came on 27 September 1983. A message arrived in the office of Sweden's Coastal Defence Group at Vaxholm that an observer at a defence station on Stockholm's northern sector had observed unidentified combat swimmers on an island close to the station. Reaction was immediate: police, coastguard and military forces were alerted and ships and helicopters swiftly dispatched to the area. After a long search, however, they were unable to find any trace of the intruders, or of the submarine, which must have brought them close to the coast.

The man who had spotted the swimmers was questioned intensively, for his evidence was critical. He had traveled from his island home to the mine control station on another island, using a small boat. After landing, about 10.30am on a fine, clear morning, he was making his way to his post when he saw something in the water, some distance from the beach. At first he thought it was a seal, for they are quite common in the Baltic. To get a better view, he climbed onto the roof of a building, and from this vantage point could see clearly that it was not a seal but a man. He then spotted a second swimmer, and finally a third man crouched on the beach amidst some rocks. The three men were in line.

In his testimony, he estimated that the furthest swimmer was about a hundred metres offshore, and said that the three men were roped together. Only the man on the beach could be described in any detail. He was dressed in a black diving suit and had two cylinders on his back with two hoses going to his mouthpiece. It was later determined that this must have been of the closed circuit 'rebreather' type used almost exclusively by military divers.

The Swedish observer climbed down from the roof and started walking back towards the beach, at which point the diver on the shore waded unhurriedly back into the water. The three frogmen then submerged and disappeared from view. To begin with the observer thought the divers must be part of the Swedish Navy's 'Rangers', but when they failed to reappear after some time he decided to put out an alarm.

The man was questioned by SAPO, the Swedish security police, who are highly skilled in detecting lies or anomalies in witnesses' statements, and they accepted his evidence as factual. He had been a serving officer since 1970 and was a trusted guard and reliable observer. What concerned the authorities was what these divers were doing so close to the mine defence station, one of the posts from which the mines off the coast would be activated in time of war. The post is a particularly important one, controlling a channel leading into Stockholm harbour. The building itself was built of rock and concrete and overlooked a stretch of water which was freely used by merchant shipping but in which diving was prohibited because of the possibility of one of the mines being detonated by accident. The channel floor was also laid with cables connecting the mines and with underwater sound detectors. The obvious conclusion drawn by the Swedish authorities was that the three men were engaged in reconnoitering the inshore defences and using the rope connecting them to measure distances.

Six months later, on Saturday, 3 March 1984, there was an even more dramatic incident in which Swedish forces fired on unidentified divers, this time in the vicinity of Karlskrona naval base. The incident was featured in the Stockholm press (Reuter) on 5 March 1984 under the headline. *'Swedish troops hunting a foreign submarine fired at frogmen seen emerging from the sea yesterday on the tiny island of Almoe.'* The Swedish Navy had been hunting an elusive submarine for three weeks, and was on the alert for both a mini-sub and its parent vessel. As a result, ground forces were also deployed, scouring the coastline with tracker dogs. Late on the Saturday evening a number of frogmen were spotted on the shore of Almoe island and, after ascertaining that there were no Swedish divers in the area, permission was obtained to open fire. No casualties were observed and the frogmen disappeared beneath the waves without making any attempt to shoot back. Amazingly, swimmers were seen again in the dim light of the following dawn, and the Swedish troops opened up again, but without seemingly hitting anyone.

One theory is that the swimmers were from a midget submarine which they had been forced to evacuate after such a prolonged underwater vigil. They would then have tried to lay up out of sight before making a rendezvous with their mother ship. Another possibility is that they were on a deliberate reconnaissance mission. Whatever the truth, they disappeared without trace, and no submarine was physically discovered.

Nobody could doubt that Crabb would have been a valuable asset for the Soviets. There were people in Britain, in place and under the control of the KGB or GRU, who could provide information about him and his activities. There were also people in positions of authority who could have influenced his capture or defection. Consider the option, it is after all to be kept secret for 100 years.

12

Pandora's Box

If you open Pandora's Box, you never know what Trogan 'orses will jump out.
Enest Bevin 1881 - 1951

On Sunday 29 April 1956, it is claimed that the Danish authorities officially issued a report that Commander Blanders, the captain of a Danish destroyer, had stated that his ship had been shadowing the *Ordzhonikidze* and the two escorting destroyers when a helicopter landed on the cruiser. The Danish crew observed through binoculars that two men boarded the helicopter. One of the men was being 'led'. The radio officer aboard the Danish ship recorded two coded messages whose contents indicated that the helicopter was arriving to take off a prisoner, and requested fighter aircraft cover, which was granted. From this evidence it is alleged that Denmark had officially stated that a prisoner was removed by helicopter from the cruiser. This was the day before the British press announced that Crabb had died in Stokes Bay in Portsmouth. The Danish Navy informed us in a letter that they had no knowledge of a Commander Blanders and no record of the incident. But of course that is the answer we would have expected, whether the story is true or not.

A key piece of evidence produced by Bernard Hutton was what he claimed to be a Russian dossier that he received. He claimed that it had been smuggled out from behind the Iron Curtain and told of Crabb's capture and interrogation by the Soviets. The evidence portrayed in the dossier explained how he agreed to serve in the Soviet Navy and that Commander Crabb became Lev Lvovich Korablov, a Soviet Naval officer. Hutton copied the dossier and translated it before returning it to the Eastern bloc underground movement. Because Hutton was a Czechoslovakian émigré, who had established himself as a reporter within a London newspaper group, he was credited with having good underground contacts in Russia and Eastern Europe. As a man of repute, having devolved good information in the past he submitted the dossier as being conclusive evidence. It suggested that Commander Crabb had been captured by the Russians at Portsmouth, taken to the Soviet Union, brainwashed, and forced to join the Soviet Navy. Was the dossier a complete fabrication, put together by Hutton or an organisation that sought to exploit Crabb's name, for whatever end? Or was it a genuine document that was secreted out of the Eastern bloc into the West, for long enough to be copied, before being returned to its place within the files of the Soviet Secret Service?

When Hutton made public his valuable contribution to the ongoing story the security services were interested A twist that supported Hutton's case came from Sir Percy Silitoe, who, having read the contents of the dossier, confirmed beyond doubt that it was virtually identical to the one held in the files of the British Authorities. Silitoe was a former long serving police officer who was appointed head of MI5. This was during the service's most difficult years of 1946-53, when Soviet spies were being unearthed at an alarming rate. Openness about his position with MI5 often caused consternation with his superiors and associates in the US secret service. We have found no evidence that his statement was other than genuine and therefore the case that Crabb was captured, defected or possibly *sent in*, is further strengthened.

Hutton's report states that Crabb was taken from the water and held captive aboard the cruiser. The Russians then waited for any response from the British, but none came. We have seen how the Official Secrets

Act silenced those who, reputedly, saw the capture. In due course the KGB told Crabb that a body had been found, identified as his, and then buried. It was said that he would have known that the authorities wanted the story of his disappearance to melt away. This meant that he faced a long term in the Soviet Navy. If he had been sent on a spying mission it would soon have been apparent that he was not going to be extricated, but left to his own devices. On that basis the Russians would not have told him anything about their infiltration of the British Security Services, nor that they set up his capture. However, Crabb knew the extent to which that the Soviets infiltrated the UK. A mystery almost as large as the Crabb affair itself was the flow of anonymous messages into the West over the years. Who were they really from? Was it conjecture or fabrication?

The West German newspaper, *Bild Zeitung* dated 29 June 1957, stated that Commander Lionel Crabb, the British frogman, was in fact alive and was being held in Moscow's Lefortowo prison, and that his prison number was 147. The story continued to declare that Crabb had been captured in Portsmouth, whilst investigating an automatic steering mechanism which enabled the Soviet vessels to manouvre quickly, and that Crabb had been offered a place in the Soviet Navy.

A high-ranking soviet official disclosed, quite openly, to a French politician in a Vodka-banquet: "Crabb is with us, he is our legitimate prisoner."

The French left wing party member was asked to inform Crabb's ex-wife that her former husband was well and she would see Crabb again in several years. The Soviet official continued: "We had, without doubt, the right to arrest Crabb". Then continued:

"*The waters surrounding our ship had been made extraterritorial for the duration of the visit by Bulganin and Kruschev and therewith declared as our sovereignty area. We were therefore allowed to arrest without question any detected spy and bring him to the Soviet Union for examination.*"

The Frenchman wanted to know if there would be a trial.

"That is possible. However, Crabb is sitting at present in Moscow Lefortowo prison. He has been designated the Number 147. Officially, he has no name."

The information indicated that they had taken Crabb's exploits very seriously. He had admitted that he had been supposed to spy on the underside of the Soviet ship in Portsmouth harbour. According to information given by the Soviet official, Crabb had told them that he wanted to find out certain things about the Soviet ship. After a few days, explained the Soviet official, Crabb became very open and gave them many details about his underwater activities.

The Colonel responsible for Crabb's interrogation is alleged to have suggested to Crabb that he could take up a position among secret service men and enter a special department of the Red Fleet for a length of 10 years. This was the length of the prison sentence, which would have been given to him if he declined to co-operate. They told him that after that period he would be able to return to his home country. The Soviet official, Admiral Tribuze, is reported to have held a long conversation with Crabb, in private. He gave him his word of honour as an Admiral, that the contract would be kept quiet if he agreed to their proposition. Tribuze probably also told him that he would not be expected to do anything against his country.

The French politician responded by asking if Crabb had assumed his position:

"Not yet"

"Isn't his soldier pay enough" was the follow up question.

"No, it is not that. He has been offered £1,000 (over DM1,000) a month. I've heard that Crabb, who is a reserve official, wants authorisation from the British Government to work for them for the length of the expected imprisonment."

The politician continued to probe:

"Of course, that cannot be expected because London will not admit that Crabb is in captivity."

The Soviet official disclosed that Crabb had been caught within a hair's breadth. The exact course of events could not be described. But, he stated:

"I know that Crabb had not reckoned with our new alarm system against submarines and frogmen. However, if Crabb had stayed under the water for a few minutes longer, he would have been able to get away and been out of our extraterritorial waters."

Questions continued to be asked when *Bild* newspaper correspondents pursued the story and spoke to Russian sailors ashore in Copenhagen, Denmark. They stated that a British frogman had been captured and had been taken to the Soviet Union, held in the hospital of the *Ordzhonikidze*, which was closed to the crew during the journey back to the Soviet Union.

An article in the Soviet magazine *Sowjetfotte* gave brief details of the Crabb operation, stating that he had wanted to examine the underside of the Soviet cruiser, but it provided no details of his capture by Russian frogmen. It did however declare that Moscow had evidence that revealed that Crabb had been working for the American Secret Service and not the British. This revelation could have been a Soviet misinformation operation, designed to cause friction between the British and Americans.

Reuters issued a statement from the *Narodny Trudovoy Soyuz* (The People's League), who were Russians devoted to the destruction of the Communist system by establishing active cells within the Soviet Union. They have provided much genuine information and so were a credible source of information. They had learned from sailors who were aboard the cruiser when it visited Britain that somebody very important, but unknown to them, had been held in the hospital of the vessel and that no member of the crew was allowed near the area.

News of Crabb/Korablov, the small, stocky diver with a large protruding nose and a strange accent, was reported in the *Ostrreussenelatt*, the newspaper of the East Prussian refugees living in

West Germany, which had a vast network of informants in Communist East Germany. It made the statement that Crabb was alive and reported that he was in Boltenhagen. The story was circulated and made headlines in the World's press. Because of the media reaction and the interest in the Crabb affair, he was removed from the base and returned to Russia to be kept out of sight. No doubt the authorities were interested in finding out how news of Crabb's existence at the base leaked out. The next report indicates that Crabb had been posted back to Sebastopol, to the Red Navy Black Sea Fleet Command, where he became Commanding Officer of the Special Task Underwater Operational Command which, if true, meant that he was assigned to a *Spetsnaz* operational swimmer/diver unit.

For Crabb it would have been a revival of the Italian days. It was the thing that had inspired him most, the challenge and the adventure. There was no war, but he was part of a great military machine, designing, developing, training and equipping divers and swimmers. He would have been in his element. In 1957 a new model of an oxygen underwater breathing system, the IDA-57 was introduced and was a great success, passing all of the tests and was suitable for military use. It remained in service until 1959 as the underwater breathing system for work under water up to a depth of 20 metres. The IDA-59 was then introduced, which had a second cylinder with a heliox mix that allowed safe diving to deeper depths.

During the first part of his induction into the ways of the Soviet Navy, Crabb would have maintained a very low profile, with security observation continuous. To those around him, he would have been the Naval officer with the strange accent and pronunciation. Some might also have thought it odd for a man of his age to be undergoing training courses. Once the initial phase was complete, he would have had his diving skills and knowledge tested. During this time he could well have been given numerous items of equipment to test and report on. It could be assumed that any reports given would have been critical and scathing to the extreme, but the Russians would have listened and analysed. They would also have been testing him to assess his attitude to his new role.

Crabb was a hero, his wartime service and decorations showed that. The Russians made a policy of introducing veterans of the Second World War to new intakes of Soviet servicemen; the veterans give lectures about their struggles defending the motherland against great odds and with huge losses. It was designed, to implant in the young recruits the idea that it was now their turn to defend their land against the aggressor. In Crabb's case, he could have lectured about the defence of Gibraltar, about Italy and new advances in underwater warfare. The students were the trusted ones, the Soviet Union's new elite.

The underground organisation in Eastern Europe and the Soviet Union, which had provided Hutton with the secret dossier, now began to provide precise details, albeit irregularly, of Crabb's career. According to Hutton's informants, Crabb visited each of the Soviet Navy's main fleet bases, all of which were in the process of establishing *Spetsnaz* swimmer units. It is of great interest to note that all reports coming out of Russia told of his involvement with special task divers/frogmen; this information was made known long before the West had any knowledge of the *Spetsnaz*.

It was claimed that Crabb was sent to the Soviet Naval Command at Odessa. This is the base where the Soviets developed their underwater mine and explosives warfare training centre. It is therefore a main centre for the *Spetsnaz* combat training, in demolition and mine warfare. This may well have been Crabb's first contact with the *Spetsnaz* operational staff and he would be aware that these divers and swimmers were different to those he had met previously. They would have worn normal Naval uniform, with nothing to denote that they were part of an elite force. Hutton's contact then reported that Crabb had been sent to Sevastopol, which was the base for the Black Sea Naval Command, and was out of reach of European underground organizations. At Sevastopol it was claimed that Crabb took command of the Special Underwater Operation Group, which was certainly *Spetsnaz*. However, it very much doubted whether he would ever have command such a unit.

Crabb is reported to have served at the Frogman Squadron of the Naval Training Command at Kronstadt. The base is on an island close to Leningrad (St Petersburgh) and is a training centre for Soviet frogmen. It is also a base for the Soviet Naval Infantry, which would include a unit of the *Spetsnaz*. He moved to Arkhangelsk Operational Command, which is part of the Northern Fleet, where he would have undergone winter and cold-water diving operations. This was a maximum security Soviet base where he could be kept under close surveillance. It would also have restricted any possibility of escape or rescue. Reports on Crabb's service state that he was transferred to the Baltic Sea Operation Command to take command of the East German Volksmarine Underwater Unit. Again he would never command such a unit. He was said to have been in charge of training divers for special tasks at the secret Naval base of Boltnhagen, near Lubecker Bay. These East German divers were part of the country's amphibious assault troops and would be used to clear mines and obstructions from possible landing areas in the event of war. Sydney Knowles told us that Joe (Bernard) Hutton had been in contact with a West German General named Gelen, who told him that Crabbie was in the Baltic.

After the publication of *Frogman Spy*, we received a package bearing German postage stamps; it contained a photo of Crabb's grave at Portsmouth, and a letter. The writer explained that he was a former East German who had managed to seek asylum in the West (The wall was still in place, dividing Germany into East and West, at the time of his escape to the West). Once he was out of the East he was intrigued by the vast volume of spy books and the detail that they contained. He had copies of the books that Bernard Hutton had written about Crabb, he also had details about *Frogman Spy* but did not have a copy. He travelled to England and visited the Sally Port Hotel and the grave in Portsmouth. At the Imperial War Museum he obtained details of *Frogman Spy* and the address of the publisher, which allowed him to write to us. The initial content of his letter was of how impressed he was with the book, but it was his offer of research assistance that caught our attention. Receiving a letter out of the blue from a former East German was, to say the least, unsettling. However, the way ahead was simple, we replied saying that we would be interested if he was able to undertake some research. With no information forthcoming from the British authorities about the Crabb incident we needed to turn our attention to the Eastern Bloc. To this end he would be of value and would produce an honest, if not protracted, response to investigations.

The wall may have gone but the barrier was still there and change would be slow, perhaps he concluded, by one or two generations. The peaceful revolution was good for the Communists because it gave them time to burn documents. They could enter the new system with their past 'sensitive' documents lost. It was explained that many old Communists and secret service people, in particular the Stassi were behind desks in the new Germany. News reports in Germany stated that little groups of the East German secret service were still working and some directly for the KGB. The reports claim that the KGB was attempting to infiltrate and build up a new network in Germany. The West German security service obtained a lot of names and information but the Stassi was so large that it has been impossible to investigate, leaving them time to blend into the united Germany. The problem we encountered was that our contact was not a professional researcher and because of the past he was inhibited in some aspects of investigation. He chose to be known as Romeo.

In January 1993 Romeo made the journey from Munich to Northern Germany and the former Naval base at Tarnewitz. The base was in the former East Germany and formed part of the sea defences in the Baltic. He was soon to be face to face with Klaus Brehmer, a small man walking about in worn out civilian clothes. He had brown teeth from drinking too much coffee and smoking cigarettes. Romeo thought him not to be very intelligent, and would, before 1990, have been classed as a typical GDR character. Established within the Communist system, sitting behind a desk and having considerable power. The good days gone, he had little reason to help what he saw as the new system, unless it was of personal value to him.

The base had lost its former glory and was almost deserted, but Brehmer remained as a caretaker and had a small desolate office. Once, it had been his seat of power, but now that was gone. Romeo's presence did not surprise him and he immediately referred to Romeo as the young man from Munich. In the office he made coffee and then opened a safe, from which he removed the only contents. They were the papers and photographs that Romeo had sent him. Among the photographs was one taken from a newspaper cutting with the headline, 'Buster' Crabb still alive: Picture starts new mystery.' Brehmer had been at the base since 1959 and had risen to become the head of VS Vertranluche Dienstsachen, the place where all classified documents were handled. He explained that the base had been used in connection with the testing of V1s and V2s until the British and Americans captured it in 1945. Because it was in the Russian sector it was handed over and became a base for the East German Navy.

Brehmer reflected back upon the question of a British Naval frogman and as to whether or not he was at the base. His immediate response was to say that he had never seen any secret papers or a frogman as they were based in Kuhlungsborn. He then explained that frogmen undertook exercises three times a year, in which they had to make an underwater swim and enter the base unseen. Over the three-day period, the men stationed at Tarnewitz had to defend the area. He did not know of any Russian advisers but went on to say that during the frogmen's operations, Russians were at the base. However, the GDR Naval personnel did not have any dealings with them. Romeo continued the conversation to draw Brehmer out and was told of the frogmen's exercises when they swam ashore and attempted to take over the base before the defenders caught them, and through the exercises he recognised a "prisoner" as being a frogman he had seen before.

From that statement he continued to explain that frogmen belonging to the Stasi, the security service, were at the base. They were only responsible to one man, an officer from the Stasi. Although he wore conventional uniform, he had the authority that overruled others at the base. From the description, Romeo concluded that they were *Spetsnaz* Soviet Special Forces. Bremer told him that he had spoken to one man who had served as a frogman and shown the papers that Romeo had provided. The response was that he did not remember a man call Crabb or Korablov, but was not willing to make any comment about any frogmen, anywhere.

Romeo asked Brehmer what he thought of the Crabb story that was reported by Hutton and by *Ostpreussenblatt*. He replied that the photo taken at Boltenhagen is not very good and he would like to see the original photo. He said that the case was not over for him because he would like to know who had taken the photo. It was possibly somebody who worked for him, a trusted member of his staff. That person had betrayed him and the unit. His voice gave the feeling that he knew more than he had said. Romeo told him that we were going to write a book about Crabb at the base, to which he responded that if we wrote it claiming that Crabb had been at the base, then there would be some influence to stop its publication. He told Romeo that many strange things had occurred in the area and that the Stasi and West German Security Service worked together. Sometimes special areas of the border were cleared of the normal troops and the space was filled with Stasi forces and a deal was carried out with West Germany, such as the exchange of persons over the border. He was able to identify at least four places where this occurred. Romeo returned the conversation to Crabb and asked him if he thought it was true that he was in the base. Brehmer said that the Stassi had published information about Crabb in East Germany. He gave Romeo the impression that there had been strange goings-on at the base and perhaps the most important indication was his reaction to the photograph, which is claimed to be Commander Crabb, alias Koroblav.

Before leaving the area to return to Munich, Romeo was given the name and address of a man who had worked at the base, and he visited him. The man could not remember any frogmen being stationed at the base, but he said that they used to come for training purposes. They would arrive and establish a separate camp, where they stayed in tents. They came for military exercises where they fought the base from the sea. They also carried out long distance swims, and dived using special underwater equipment, as well as carrying out demolitions. The frogman team stayed for six weeks at a time, remaining separate from the base personnel and not mixing with them. They lived on field rations and he recalled that sometimes they would sneak over to the shop on the base and purchase hot sausages. Otherwise the only time they were seen was during exercises.

He told Romeo about visits in the 1960s by groups of special frogmen from the Stasi, who were also kept separate from the staff on the base. Even the lorries and cars that transported them, with Berlin number plates, were not parked in the normal car park, but parked somewhere else in the base. They did diving exercises in the Boltenhagen sea and inland lakes. They were tanned, fit and had diving equipment that he had seen no other frogmen have, and they looked like real underwater fighters. If Crabb was there, it was not common knowledge, but then the frogmen were kept separate. However, special frogmen did operate at the base.

When Romeo had explored all options of investigation available to him, another researcher used his contacts to seek information. The focus was on Crabb's alleged activity as an instructor of East German frogmen in the late 1960s and his transit to Czechoslovakia via Dresden (receiving travel documents and later treatment at a local military hospital). The East German State Security files (Stasi files) and the Military History Archive in Freiburg (formerly Potsdam) were the two main archives to be searched, as the training of East German frogmen could be recorded in either of the two files. The issuing of travel documents could be found in the files of the regional Stasi headquarters in Dresden.

Obtaining official files was dependant on other people searching the files and was necessarily a selective process. Not only are a certain number of documents not yet accessible (due to the files not having been opened) but Crabb might not have entered any official files simply because he was not German. There would have been secrecy as he would have been a major security risk. Contact was made with people in the area of the Baltic coast and in Dresden who were either frogmen or military men themselves or who worked for the Stasi in Dresden at that time.

The Federal Office for the Files of the Former State Security stated that no record was found with regard to Lionel Crabb or L. L. Korablov:

> *"Concerning your enquiry about the cooperation of L.L. Korablov / L. K. P. Crabb with the State Security in Boltenhagen and Dresden I would like to inform you, that we do not hold any material in our files, which we could provide you on the basis of the law on the publication of State Security files. This information is based on the current knowledge of our department."*

Does this mean that, like the British, they have information on file but are not allowed to release it?

It is unlikely that Crabb's training activities would have been recorded in the East German Stasi files; as a Russian adviser he would not necessarily have entered a German state security system. However, the Dresden files may have given evidence of any travel document issued.

The Freiburg military archives of the East German People's Army and Navy, formerly held in Potsdam, have now been merged with the West German military history files (Bundesarchiv Militaerarchiv Freiburg). It was identified that the Kampfschwimmerkommando 18 (Military Diving Unit 18) was the only existing unit at the time. The unit was founded on the 7 December 1959 and was permanently based in Kuehlungsbom. The only relevant file, an alphabetical list of members of the diving unit between 1962 and 1977, did not mention either Crabb or Korablov. However, it was determined that a non-permanent member, such as an external adviser, would not have been registered in a file containing only permanent members of the German staff. It was highly unlikely that a soviet adviser would have trained German divers since all soviet advisers were officially withdrawn from the East German forces in 1958.

Kurt Klingbeil, founder of the Kampfschwimmerkommando 18 and commander of that unit from 1959 until 1968 has stated that his unit was the only military diver unit at the East German Baltic coast at the time, confirming the statement of the military archive in Freiburg. They were based at the secret Naval base in Kuehlungsbom and, as part of their military exercises, they would set up provisional camps along the Baltic coast and attack other Naval bases at night for training purposes. Tarnewitz and Boltenhagen were among those targets, but clearly the divers were permanently based at their training camp in Kuehlungsbom.

Klingbeil stressed that throughout his military career there was no other instructor or adviser other than himself. He stated that there was no need for external advisers anyway because Germany had a history of successful diving missions in the Second World War. He was one of the World War II divers who continued to live in the East of Germany and share his knowledge with the People's Navy. Klingbeil admitted that, starting in 1968, some fully trained members of his unit left to build up a frogman unit that belonged directly to the Stasi. And there is a possibility that Crabb was involved with that new unit. An attempt was made to locate members of the unit but they operated in isolation from the other frogmen in Kuehlungsborn and so nobody knew any of the members by name.

At the Regional Office for the Files of the Former State Security (Landesbeauftragter) in Dresden, it was found that the Russian military hospital where Crabb was allegedly treated has been demolished and all the patient records were either destroyed or are in Russia. Of two former members of the state security in Dresden that were contacted, one of them worked in the department which would have issued travel documents, but he drew a blank. An interesting point concerns the story that an East German underground movement could have smuggled a photo of Crabb at Boltenhagen out of the country. It was considered highly unlikely, although western secret service members readily believed that underground movements existed in Eastern Europe. Commentators state that there was certainly no such thing in Eastern Germany.

Official records show no evidence that Crabb was ever in Germany and neither the official Stasi nor military archives contain any material related to the names Crabb or Korablov. However, this is not a surprise because Stasi and military files would, as a general rule, record activities of Germans cooperating with the State security. Occasional activities of Russian advisers, or advisers acting on behalf of the Russians, would not necessarily be recorded. The former commander of the East German divers training unit in Kuehlungsbom provides a sound argument against any activity of Crabb at the Baltic coast. Not only did he never see or hear anything of Crabb or any other external adviser in the relevant period, he convincingly claimed that it wouldn't have made any sense to use a person with Crabb's profile. However, the existence of a separate Stasi frogman unit since 1968 still raises some questions and it cannot completely rule out that Crabb was actually there.

The next report indicates that Korablov had been posted back to Sebastopol, to the Red Navy Black Sea Fleet Command, where he became commanding officer of the Special Task Underwater Operational Command, which if true, meant that he was assigned to *Spetsnaz* operational swimmer/diver unit. Six months after his arrival at this unit, he met Ken Elliott, an Englishman. The year was 1967.

The story begins when Pat Rose, accompanied by her friend Sylvia, were at the Nagg's Head, where she had first met Crabb. They joined Len Cole, the publican, in his lounge along with a long-standing friend of Len's. Len asked Rose if a name for Hutton's new book had been decided upon. She said it had, and that it was to be called *Commander Crabb is Alive*. The man began to laugh, then said to them:

"You don't mean Commander Crabb, you mean Captain Korablov".

They were shocked:

"What do you mean? That's the name in the book and it hasn't been published yet."

The man looked round at the company, then said:

"I was with Crabb."

Rose was shocked and wanted Hutton present if the man was to say anything important. She was about to go on holiday, but the man told her not to worry, but to call him when she got back to arrange a meeting. He gave her a business card showing the name Ken Elliott and the occupation of Director of Lucas Ltd. The company address was an office in Grosvenor Street, London, and had a Mayfair telephone number. Bernard Hutton gave a false name in *The Fake Defector* to protect Elliott's identity but, owing to subsequent events, Rose divulged it to us. It has been established that Ken Elliott worked in the overseas service department of Lucas Ltd travelling to the USSR, and that he left the company to live abroad. No further trace of him has been found.

The meeting between Pat Rose, Ken Elliott and Bernard Hutton took place at the Nagg's Head, where they found a quiet corner to sit and talk without interruption. Elliott made it clear that they should not speak about the meeting nor quote his name, for he had to go back to the Soviet Union. Then, looking at Hutton, he asked for his word that the tape with his voice on it should be erased once he had taken the details of the story from it. The formalities over, Elliott began his story. He described the events that took him on business to the Soviet Naval base at Sevastopol. He was accepted by the Russians and had certain freedoms, but always had a state security controller with him, whom he referred to as *the shadow*. Walking through the base after having conducted some business, they went past a ramp where a group of divers were loading equipment from the water into a lorry. *The shadow* told Elliott, with some pride, that they were from an elite special diving unit. Elliott nodded with approval and replied that they would have to be well trained and need to have good instructors. *The shadow* stated that they had the best, a unique leader, and indicated a short stocky Naval officer as the leader. Elliott looked at Rose and Hutton in turn and told them that this is how he first met Captain Korablov or, if calling him by his original name, Commander Crabb.

Rose wanted to know what he looked like. Elliott thought for a moment and described Crabb as wearing the uniform of a Red Navy captain; he was rather small, about five feet six inches tall, aged in his fifties, with very thick eyebrows, a rather prominent nose and hair on his cheekbones. He explained that it was a face that he would not forget. Asked if he had followed the Crabb affair with any special interest, he confirmed that he had. As he travelled extensively in Russia, if Crabb had been captured he hoped to meet him. Following on from that, Elliott was asked about his reaction to the headless and handless body that had been found in the sea fourteen months after Crabb's disappearance, and which was buried as Crabb in Portsmouth. Elliott replied that he didn't know anything about that event as he had not been in the West at the time, and didn't remember seeing anything about it in the Eastern bloc or Soviet newspapers.

Hutton moved the conversation to the meeting in Sevastopol. Elliott described how he and *the shadow* went to the officers' mess and saw Crabb/Korablov. With *the shadow* present, Elliott engaged the small man in general conversation. He became certain that the Soviet Navy officer he spoke to was Crabb. He briefly considered the possibility that he could have been a double. The more he spoke the more certain he became that it was Crabb, but he could not challenge the man because the *shadow* was present and all talk had to be of a general nature. Rose asked if they spoke in Russian; Elliott said that they did, and that was one reason he was so certain that it was Crabb, for the man was certainly not Russian. He paused before continuing to explain that the man spoke Russian but with an unmistakable accent.

Then Elliott came to the important part of the conversation. He told Rose and Bernard Hutton that he was *persona grata* in the Soviet Union, however, he was kept under constant surveillance, especially at military bases and other sensitive locations. On one particular day, though, *the shadow* had been called away, leaving the two men alone together. Elliott took the opportunity to ask Korablov point blank whether he was Commander Crabb. The man did not reply immediately but then asked Elliott if he had to ask awkward questions. The two men sat looking at each other, then Crabb looked round to ensure that nobody could overhear them. He asked Elliott if he expected to go to England in the near future. When Elliott confirmed that he did, the man asked if he would contact Rose and pass on a message for him. Elliott agreed.

Crabb told him that he wanted to put her mind at rest, and told Elliott that he might contact her through the Nagg's Head in London, for the landlord, Len Cole, would know where to find her. Elliott already knew Len Cole, but did not bother to tell Crabb this because time was short. Crabb told Elliott that, to prove it really was him he should tell her about the scar on her head, from a car accident, and how her hair grew in a grey streak from the scar, which was why he called her his 'grey witch'. Elliott said that the man then suddenly became tense and stated that he regretted giving the message and that he had been mad to do such a thing. Rose confirmed that what Elliott had said was correct; as only she and Crabbie could link the accident, grey streak and the name 'grey witch'.

Elliott felt from meeting the man that he was happy doing the job of diving and with the high rank he had reached in the Soviet Navy, but that he did not think kindly about his former country. Elliott then went on to describe Crabb's mannerisms, the way he smoked and coughed, and his gravelly voice. These were details which could be known even if he had not met the man or been briefed very thoroughly. Hutton examined Elliott's passport.

Rose asked Elliott if he would be going back to Russia. He told her that he was due to go back soon but that he would be back in England in September; he was going to get married, and told Rose that when they next met he would introduce his new wife to her. It was agreed that Rose should telephone him in September. By then he would have tried to get more information about Crabb and if possible set up a contact link. Rose asked Cole how long he had known Elliott, to which he replied that it was some 20 years, but that he did not know much about him, apart from the fact that he was in a business that required him to travel to Russia. He was always well dressed, well mannered and never appeared to be short of money.

In September, Rose telephoned the London office of Lucas and asked to speak to Ken Elliott. The person who answered the telephone told her that Mr. Elliott had left the company and was no longer employed by them. Rose was stunned, but she gathered her thoughts and told the woman that Mr. Elliott had asked her to contact him in September, after his overseas visit. Could she tell her where she could contact him? The reply was blunt and to the point: the company no longer employed Elliott and they had no idea where he was. Rose continued to quiz the woman, but she would make no further comment other than to suggest that she should write to the personnel officer, who might be able to help her. This Rose did this on a number of occasions, but all her letters to Lucas went unanswered. After 21 years with the company, Ken Elliott had simply disappeared.

Elliott did not want his name used and Hutton agreed, and in his books referred to him as KM. We established that Elliott had worked for Lucas, but had then disappeared from both the company and the country. It was never clear how he had managed to gain access to Soviet military bases during the Cold War period, for as far as can be ascertained Lucas did not openly trade with the Soviet military.

Prior to Sydney Knowles reading *Frogman Spy,* he gave us some names of people attending the *last Suppers,* and one was called Elli. He was a devout Communist, who spoke fluent Russian. Igor Gouzemko, a former Lieutenant in the GRU, who defected to Canada, stated:

"This man has something Russian in his background. It could have been that he was a white Russian or that his relatives came from Russia. He could have been 100 percent English, but was in Russia on official duties not as a tourist."

Was Elli Ken Elliott?

13

Behind Enemy Lines

It takes your enemy and your friend, working together, to hurt you to the heart:
the one to slander you and the other to get the news to you.

Mark Twain 1835-1910

Until his death, Bernard Hutton continued to receive information from his contacts in the Eastern Bloc, but the most dramatic news he is alleged to have received was that Crabb was going to retire from the Soviet Navy and be released into Italy. The report stated that Italy was his own choice and that the Soviet authorities agreed to it. News from his informants stated that, on 3 or 4 August 1977, Captain Korablov/Commander Crabb would arrive in East Germany (DDR) with two members of the Soviet Security Service. The exact date was to depend upon suitable transport. He would then travel with the two security officers to Italy, where he would remain under their supervision, within the guidance directed from Moscow.

Crabb had arrived in Dresden at approximately 1:00am on the 4 August 1977. With his two Soviet Security officers, he was driven to a house on the outskirts of Dresden which was observed to be used by the East German Security Service (which is in fact the counterpart of, and in part controlled by, the KGB). It was also reported that during his stay at the house, he did not leave the premises for the first five days.

On the sixth day he was escorted on a three hour walk in the countryside. The following day about 8:30am, a black car was observed to stop at the house, where it collected Crabb and his security officers. It took them at speed to the Stassi HQ at Bautzner Landstrasse Dresden where, it was said, travel and identity documents were issued to Crabb.

On Friday 12 August Crabb had reported sick, complaining of severe colic in his stomach and abdomen. It was reported that he felt giddy and his legs gave way when he tried to stand up. He also had a high fever and complained that his body ached all over. His security officers were concerned and a doctor was called to the house. He examined Crabb and then prescribed some drugs, ordering that he should stay in bed for a few days. Crabb's health did not improve and the doctor, who made more visits, recommended that he be taken to hospital for specialist examination. The security officers would have made contact with their superiors in Moscow but it was agreed that he should be admitted to hospital and an ambulance was sent to collect him. The hospital was Dresden Bad Weiser Husch which is about six miles south of the city centre of Dresden. Weiser Husch was a town in its own right until it became part of the city of Dresden in 1921. In 1931 it received the title 'Bad', which means spa and developed a reputation for its healthy environment and spa baths, attracting thousands of guests a year. Of great importance was the world famous Sanatorium of Dr Lahmann, and it became a popular rest centre for those who had undergone treatment at Karlovy Vary. After the World War II the centre declined under Communist control and patients replaced guests. A newspaper article summed up the centre:

"hidden behind a metal fence in Bautzener Landstr is the run down famous Sanatorium of Dr Lahmann...the Soviets are responsible as they turned it into a military hospital."

At the hospital Crabb is said to have undergone checks and x-rays, as well as a thorough specialist examination. The results of these examinations showed that he had ulcers and some cancerous growth in the abdomen, as well as a very low blood pressure. This was both dramatic and worrying news for he had previously been in good health, and nothing had been reported when he had his regular medical checks in the Russian Naval hospitals.

Crabb underwent treatment in the hospital and subsequent reports stated that his condition improved, but there were differences of opinion over whether it should be continued. After consultation within the hospital and with Moscow it was decided that Crabb should not be operated on because of possible complications. However, it was decided that he should at the earliest opportunity be transferred to a hospital at Karlovy Vary in nearby Czechoslovakia, which specialised in his medical condition.

Crabb had remained in the Dresden Hospital for six weeks, and then was given specialist approval for his move from Dresden to Karlovy Vary. It appeared from the report that Crabb was very ill and the delay was made so that he could build up his strength before undertaking the journey. He eventually departed the Dresden Hospital, accompanied by two security officers, on the morning of 30 September 1977, to travel to the Special State Medicine Centre Karlovy Vary. They arrived in the early evening, having made a slow, careful journey, with a number of 'rest' stops. The experienced cancer specialists at Karlovy Vary agreed with the diagnosis found by their German colleagues at Dresden, after having studied the x-rays, medical reports and conducting their own examinations. They prescribed a course of treatment which, if effective, should enable Crabb to live a fairly trouble free life, but he would have to stick to a strict diet. The one thing that did give cause for concern was that the patient's mental state was quite low and he was described as having resigned himself to his fate. Of concern to the centre's staff was the fact that he was losing his fighting spirit and developing a 'could not care less' attitude, both of which would have an adverse effect on his treatment. The next report, alleged to have been received in the West, stated that Crabb had been assigned a psychoanalyst as a member of the medical team treating him. It was said that he was not aware that he was receiving psychiatric treatment, for it was felt that he would have rebelled against it. It is said that further reports were slow to come and it was not until October 1977 that the next one arrived, passing on the latest information on Crabb condition. He had responded to treatment and was reported to be as well as could be expected with such an illness.

Regarding his mental attitude, the message said that he did not speak to anyone and took no interest in any community activities:

"He keeps himself to himself and frequently sits in an armchair, staring seemingly 'unseeing' into the distance. His thoughts are lost to himself."

All evidence had pointed to Crabb being at a medical institute in the town of Karlovy Vary, which is in a country where everyday freedoms were restricted and where foreigners and even locals could not go and ask questions regarding the whereabouts of a Russian Naval officer. In November 1986 we had written to the State medical centre at Karlovy Vary to enquire about the fate of a Russian Naval officer, Commander Lev Lvovitch Korablov, who was reported to have been at the centre in 1977-78. We did not receive a reply, nor did we really expect one, as such a letter would have found its way to the desk of the relevant security service for recording and filing.

A telephone call was received from a man with an Eastern European accent who asked:

"Are you seeking information about a Russian Naval officer called Korablov and why do you want such information?" It took some moments for the question to sink in, as the call was totally unexpected. Mike replied:

"Who am I speaking to?" The question was ignored and the man simply repeated his question, to which Mike responded:

"I am interested to know about the man, as my wife and I are writing a book about a former Royal Naval officer who had disappeared, and we thought that they may have been one and the same."

There was a pause at the other end of the phone, and then the voice said:

"The Russian officer Korablov was the Englishman and he had been 'underwater' in both Navies."

Mike asked who the person was and why should he believe what he said, for it could have been an elaborate hoax. In slow guttural tones he explained that within Czechoslovakia there were anti-Russian movements who stood for various causes, such as religious and speech freedoms, while others such as his own group wanted to expose the sinister aspects of the Russian presence within their country.

Although he had little information on Crabb he wanted to tell us what he did know. He could not explain over the telephone what we wanted to hear. However, if we were prepared to go to Karlovy Vary then he would arrange for us to meet someone who had known Crabb in the Sanatorium. We could see the Sanatorium where he had been a patient. The man told Mike that he would be contacted again, and then the phone went dead.

The next phone call was from a woman with an Eastern European accent. She wanted to know if we were going to make the journey She was pleased when it was confirmed that we were. We gave her our planned visit dates, but much depended upon flights and hotels. The woman would give no name, telephone number or address, but said that she would contact us again. We had contact with a former citizen of Czechoslovakia, who now resided in Britain, who was most helpful in explaining about the system of control within the country and the best way to conduct ourselves. He knew some details of the Crabb affair and considered it perfectly natural that the Russians would grab somebody they wanted and then dump them in a satellite country when they had finished with them. It was explained in detail, many times, that Czechoslovakia was a total police state and had an efficient security service linked to the KGB. The people could move about the country as they pleased, but to travel outside was a different matter. At the time 'Glasnost', as preached by Michhail Gorbachov to the West was a sham, and the people remained controlled and oppressed. If we sought information about a Czech citizen, that was one thing, but to enquire about a Russian Naval officer, who would have been under the control of the GRU, was quite another matter. We gave him details of our travel arrangements with the understanding that he would do what he could to arrange help in Karlovy Vary.

The final phone call from the anonymous woman was brief and to the point. We gave her details of our visit, and she laid down one major ground rule: people in Karlovy Vary would contact us and we were not to photograph them or do anything that could put them at risk. Naturally we accepted the conditions. We were to travel as tourists and in the event of an unpleasant situation arising we hoped to get away with being inquisitive English. The people we would meet could face very long prison sentences or worse. There was the added factor that enquiring in detail about a Russian military person would be considered spying.

We left London on a Czech national airline aircraft, which was not without some humour. Inside the aircraft a wire ran the length of the cabin, for paratroopers to hook their static lines to, so that when they jumped from the aircraft their parachute would open. Members of the cabin crew came round and gave each passenger a drink; beer for the men and orange juice for the women.

Arriving at Prague's Ruzyne airport we descended the steps from the aircraft and joined the queue. Eventually we were confronted by a poker-faced, uniformed official who looked at our passports and visas; handing them back he nodded for us to proceed. We had already seen the woman standing nearby holding a card with our name on it and after we introduced ourselves she took us to one side to examine our passports and visas, then used a rubber stamp in the corner of our visas. She said that we should go through the principal passport control and collect our luggage. After passing through customs she would be waiting for us. Who was this person? We did not expect to be met because we had written directions and bus tickets to get to our destination. Was this the result of our letter to the medical institute? As we had not booked an organised tour holiday we suspected the latter. Passport control and customs examined our visas and the stamp, before making their own official stamp, with no questions or demands.

Entering the arrivals hall we saw many people waiting for travellers, as well as placard-carrying tour guides, each wearing a small badge with the name of the guide and organization they represented. Our 'guide' came over to us, no longer carrying the card bearing our name. As far as we could determine she represented the official tourist organisation. She told us we would have a two-hour wait for the bus, followed by a journey of two and a half hours, but if we were interested a taxi driver would take us directly to Karlovy Vary and she would return to us the pre-paid bus fare. The cost of this taxi fare was a figure that we could hardly refuse; it was, in fact, cheaper than the bus. Accepting her extremely generous offer we followed her to a taxi; not one of the normal airport Skoda taxis, but an up-market estate car. The driver spoke very good English also, something we later found to be uncommon. We got into the car but were now more on guard as we began an hour's journey to the town of Karlovy Vary.

As the car sped along a virtually traffic-free road, our 'guide' told us all about the virtues of the Socialist system, intermingling her commentary with questions about, why we were going to Karlovy Vary for such a short time, and had either of us been ill? Why didn't we stay in Prague, as did most tourists, especially in the autumn? Apart from the general questions came those of a more direct and searching nature, did we know anybody in Karlovy Vary or any Czech people in Britain? What work did we do?

Mike said, 'diving', not elaborating any further. Using that word to a foreigner who is not familiar with the subject, would normally receive a shrug or a request for further explanation. Our 'guide' immediately asked Jacqui about the dangers, as it was a high-risk occupation. It was as if it were a subject she knew a lot about. At no time during any of our tourist visa applications or through speaking had the subject of diving or underwater swimming been raised. She knew though, and we concluded that she could only have one source of information, the Czech secret service.

As we entered Karlovy Vary, our 'guide' turned to face us and, as the car slowed down to almost stop, she pointed out one large building and told us that it was the Sanatorium Imperial and was a special centre for the treatment of Russians. Why make a big issue of identifying that building?

The car stopped at the Grand Hotel Moskva, whereupon our 'guide' said that she would go to the local travel office and tell them that we had arrived. It was late afternoon and we checked in at the hotel reception. Accepting that the rooms were fitted with listening devices to record our conversation we said very little. We soon left the hotel to take our first look at the town of Karlovy Vary. The travel office was not far from the hotel and was securely closed and in darkness. As we walked back to the hotel we observed the 'taxi' which had brought us to Karlovy Vary. When the occupants realised that we had seen them, the car sped past us with the 'guide' and the driver ignoring us. However, the passenger in the back was more than interested in us, as we watched the car disappear from sight.

To gain a grandstand view of the Sanatorium Imperial we made our way towards a conical-roofed viewing point on the hillside, the Mayeruv Gloriet, which was directly opposite the Imperial. We shared the climb with other visitors and quite possibly members of the Czech secret service, but waited for them to leave before we proceeded to photograph the panorama before us. The main focus was the Sanatorium Imperial, which was brought into close and stark relief with a telephoto lens.

A man appeared who, upon hearing us speak, asked in an accented voice if we were English. When we said we were, he looked across at the

Imperial and told us straight out that we were looking at the place where Crabb had been. We didn't respond to the statement but continued to look at the distant building. The man seemed to us to be typically Czech; he was one of the crowd, never standing out, just blending with those around him. He gave us no name, and it was again made clear that neither he, nor anybody he was with must be photographed for the risk of identification was too great and they would face severe prison sentences - after the KGB had finished with them.

A woman who had worked at the Sanatorium and looked after the man was willing to talk to us and tell us what she knew. We would then see that the Russian and English Naval officers were one and the same. Two other questions were on our minds, the first being: If he had died at the Imperial where was he buried? Was he laid to rest in the town's graveyard? It was explained that the Russians brought people to the Sanatorium, and that most recovered, but if anyone did die, the body would be returned to Russia. We would find no graves of Russians in Karlovy Vary. Secondly we asked whether as Crabb was said to be of the Roman Catholic faith, the Church would have any information. The man answered by telling us that Russian Naval officers would not be allowed to display any religious convictions, especially in front of the Czech staff. The arrangement for meeting the woman required us to visit the J.Gargarin Colonnade each day at 11am and wait for one hour. If nothing happened then we would return at 2pm and again wait for one hour. Doing this would be perfectly natural and would establish a pattern for anybody watching us.

The Colonnade is a long modern building where five pillars deposit healing waters from the thermal springs and visitors or patients can fill cups and drink and relax. The times we were told to be there were the busiest and, with the entire building full of people milling about, it was a very suitable place to arrange a meeting. The man's parting message was simple and clear, they would contact us, we were to wait and be patient. He disappeared as quickly as he had arrived; our link with the anti-Russian movement was made. The travel company, who had such concern through the 'guide', had no real interest in us at the town's office. The staff, who spoke English, albeit not fluently, attempted to answer all questions, but when we enquired about the Sanatorium Imperial, they said that they did not speak English and did not understand.

The Sanatorium Imperial was set in open park-type grounds, with no security wall or guards, and we took the opportunity to gain a close look at what was alleged to have been Crabb's last home. It was a large, well-kept building, the product of a bygone era. A large notice written in Czech, Russian, English and German demanded that every visitor must report to the reception. The reception was at the front and all other doors were firmly closed, displaying a 'go to reception' notice. Many of the lower level windows had bars; we did not know if they were designed to keep people in or out. As we moved freely around the grounds we photographed the building.

The colonnade was full of people, of different nationalities, cultures and social status mingling around the water spouts. It was a focal point for visitors. A high hubbub of noise was produced by a number of languages, all lost into one. Having purchased our spouted cups, we sat on the seats which surrounded the glass windowed walls and watched the flow of people and sipped the warm mineral water. It was a well-chosen spot, for nobody could overhear our conversation, or record or photograph the meeting. All parties could, if danger approached, move off to mingle in the crowd and become 'lost'.

We had to visit a few times before a woman, who blended perfectly with the general melee, moved up to sit beside us, sipping the waters from her newly purchased cup. She asked us in English if we liked the water and were enjoying our stay. We had met the contact, the person who was to say that she had been with Crabb in his last days.

Her story began with the war, when as a very young woman, she remembered the German troops and how they were 'liberated' by the Russians, who had replaced them and taken over control of the country.

She became involved with medicine and because she spoke Russian had got a job at the Sanatorium Imperial. Her involvement with the medical profession had required her to learn English, although she could not remember very much, for it was not used very often. All questions as to what job she actually did in the Sanatorium were to no avail. She told us that she was employed at the Imperial dealing with Russians, who treated the Czechs as second-class citizens (which is, in fact, how the Russians viewed the situation).

The one Russian who was different arrived, as best she could remember, about Christmas 1977. She said she could link the date through a personal family happening. He was a small man, who had come to be treated for what she remembered to be internal medical problems. In the beginning he was not noticed and she could remember little about him, but recalls that he was polite, which was unusual for a Russian, and did not mix with the other patients.

She told us that she did not remember the name she had been told (Korablov) for it was a long time ago and patients came and went, and the staff were moved about to limit any familiarity or gathering of information about patients. The man did not seem to be getting any better, seemingly having lost the will to live, but drugs and the curative treatment prolonged his life. He lost weight and she recalled that it made his nose look larger, and made a sign of a hooked nose. She laughed when explaining about the bushy hair on his cheeks, which he flatly refused to allow the barber to shave off. It was grey, as was the thinning hair on his head. He would sit for hours and stare at the distant hills, lost to himself, speaking little and sometimes not at all to some staff.

The day he spoke English he really surprised her, as she was only one of a very limited number of staff who could understand any of the language. He seemed to trust her and told her that he was really English. That confused her, for she could not understand what an Englishman was doing as a Russian Naval officer, even though she knew the Russians to be devious.

We asked her if he said anything about England, to which she replied that he told her that he was the only diver to have served in the English Navy and the Russian Navy and to have medals from both. We clarified the word 'diver', to ensure that she understood it; yes, a diver was an underwater swimmer, she knew what a diver was. We asked her if she reported the fact that he spoke English to anybody else. She explained that some of the Czech staff knew that he spoke a language, which she understood, but they did not. At no time did she report the fact to the senior staff, either Czech or Russian, for fear of repercussions.

Did he ever discuss England and any of the people he knew? It was a very important question, but she explained that often he was in pain and when he spoke English, she did not always understand what he said and she was busy, so did not have much time to spend with him.

Every detail she told us about the elderly, grey-haired man, with an emaciated body and a drawn hawkish face, accentuated by the large hook-shaped nose, certainly gave us the impression that it could have been Crabb. The woman told us that for a while she moved elsewhere in the Sanatorium and lost touch, but in 1981 she was transferred back to the section and was very surprised to see that he was still alive. During one of her last short conversations with him he told her that he had been captured by the Russians and made to serve in their Navy. He had waited to go home, by which she thought he meant back to Britain.

At no time, in any of our dealings with the organisation, did we provide any details about the Crabb affair, and the only name we ever used was Korablov. During 1981 the woman left Karlovy Vary, so she did not have the final answer, but said she thought he must have died shortly after she left because he was very ill. She anticipated our request as to whether any files might be at the Sanatorium, and was adamant that all papers on every Russian were kept secure, and left with the patient, alive or dead. Her parting words before disappearing into the crowd were that she considered that Korablov must have died in 1981 – in fact the year the alterations had been made to Crabb's headstone in Portsmouth.

Romeo was intrigued with our visit to Czechoslovakia, which was prior to the border being opened and the decline of the Communists. On Monday 28 October 1991 he travelled to Karlovy Vary to see how things had changed and to see if he could obtain any information. Starting from the hotel in which we had stayed and had now changed its name from Hotel Moskva to the Grand Hotel Pubb, Romeo walked to the Imperial Sanatorium and where we had only been able to walk around the outside, he entered the building and noticed that most large notices were written in Russian, but he was not challenged by anybody. A girl was sitting behind the reception desk, accompanied by a young man playing a guitar, neither were interested in him. Unchallenged, he went upstairs to the top floor and found at each floor two corridors with numbered doors and a few rooms being identified as being for treatment. During this time he only encountered a few members of staff, but did not speak to anybody. When leaving, he encountered two groups of Russians, but his knowledge of Russian was very limited, even though he had had to learn it at school for six years. After finishing school, he burned all Russian books and banned the language from his mind. As a consequence of the demise of Communism, the Imperial is no longer state owned and the Russians do not have control or a monopoly. The change described to us was dramatic, compared to our visit where State rule was evident everywhere.

Romeo returned to Karlovy Vary on 7 January 1992 armed with the name and address of a doctor who resided and worked in the town. We had had communication with a doctor in the town who had made enquiries on our behalf, but had not been successful. He explained in a letter that, because the Russians had been in control of the Imperial there were strange goings-on and a lack of information had to be expected.

It became very apparent that the way a name is spelt or has some small sign can be important and this was the case when Romeo searched for our doctor. He located the street and walked along looking for the house. The doctor's house was secured by the roll shutters on the ground floor windows. Behind the house in the garden there was a large satellite dish. The doorbell had a space for the name but it was blank. The outcome was that he did not make contact with the doctor.

It had been possible to receive satellite television for about five years (late 1980s) and it was not restricted. The programmes were received through the satellite Kopernikus, which required a dish of about 60 centimetres in diameter. Years ago the reception was not as strong and so dishes of 1.8 metres diameter were used. This size would be the same as that seen at the doctor's house, which would mean that the owner was privileged or wealthy.

On the way to the Imperial for a return visit, Romeo passed a group of what looked like and talked like Russians. This would indicate that the Russians were still in evidence in Karlovy Vary and at the Imperial. The building was still a bit of a mess, but while the large notices in Russian had gone, there was evidence of refurbishment. Walking round the inside, Romeo found that the renovation included floors, doors and walls, which were being cleaned or painted. Making enquiries with the lady on reception about records of patients, she was unable to assist but thought that there were archives. The reception manager was unavailable but Romeo was provided with her name and address. It included a telephone number, which was interesting as only very few people in the East had a private telephone as this lady did. She was on reception and very important. One thing that Romeo was able to confirm was a quote from a German travel guide: 'After 1945 the Imperial became the 'headquarters' of the Russians'.

We continued our quest to trace the man at the Imperial, but the letter we received probably answers the lack of information:

"26th August 1993,

Dear Mr. and Mrs. Welham,

Thank you very much for your letters concerning the fate of Comm, Crabb / Korablov. Unfortunately I was not able to get any information about his stay in K. Vary / Imperial 1981. All documentation and case sheets of the patients in Imperial are discarded after 5 years...but don't forget that until now Imperial is covered to some extent still with some mystery.

Yours sincerely,

Dr. Vaclav Sima."

14

War with the BBC

To forbid us anything is to make us have a mind for it.
Michel de Montaigne, Essays, 1595

Throughout the years many have approached the Commander Crabb affair with a view to exposing the truth of what happened in 1956 and 1957. All have fallen foul of the authorities, who have gone to extreme lengths to reduce the impact that books or films may have. One such case occurred in 1972 when a producer with the British Broadcasting Corporation (BBC) had the audacity to want to make a television programme about Crabb. He had located a witness who it was claimed, could confirm what happened in 1956. The problem was that the new witness was a former Royal Naval diver and that information would send shudders through the Ministry of Defence. Under the release of official information, the following records clearly illustrate the concern that the Crabb case raised at the time, and is a situation that continues today.

The BBC 'episode' began when David Darlow a producer with the BBC sent a letter, dated 9 February 1972, to the Ministry of Defence which stated:

"Dear Mr. Jack
As I mentioned on the telephone, I am investigating the possibility of

making a thirty-minute television programme on the mysterious disappearance of Commander Lionel Crabb in 1956. The programme would examine each of the various theories put forward, and would consist very largely of previously published material. We would hope to break some new ground...But, first of all a breakdown of the programme itself:

Crabb, the legend – heroic service during and after the war (library film) – his strange personality – the sudden disappearance.

The political background – B and K's visit – the Russian cruisers – Khrushchev refers to a spy – talks end coolly – Eden's denial of espionage operation – body found by fisherman – inquest.

The Sunday Times Theory: Crabb hired by British Intelligence – physically unfit – dived under cruisers, died of blood poisoning – trapped underwater in Langstone Harbour – drifted free fourteen months later – positively identified at inquest.

Bernard Hutton's Theory: Crabb dived under cruisers – captured by Russians – interrogated – alive in Russia today.

Official Version: Crabb died testing new apparatus in Stokes Bay – now confirmed by another diver, colleague of Crabb's, who says that he and others actually went under Russian ships.

As you can see, almost the whole programme consists of widely published material. The only new information arises with the diver who claims that Crabb did die in Stokes Bay. Whilst this does confirm the official version of Crabb's death, the man, nevertheless, is reluctant to appear on television for fear of reprisals by the Ministry of Defence. In particular he fears that his Navy pension (he is now retired from the Service) might be jeopardised.

My own guess is that the criterion by which you would assess this matter is 'whether or not it would tend to endanger national security', and in that case I think you would agree that the passage of time has rendered this incident harmless. It can have little relevance to present-day security operations or organisation.

I should welcome your observations on the programme, and look forward to hearing from you in the near future.

Yours etc..."

Under normal circumstances the making of a programme about the Crabb incident should not, by that time, have caused a great deal of trouble. This is particularly so when a former diver was to state that Crabb died in Stokes Bay. This supported the official version, especially when it was widely accepted as not being the case. The first record of the BBC letter circulating within the MoD was not until the 4 April 1972 (letter origination as 9 February 1972). It was very evident that the Navy did not like the idea of the programme and clearly did not know how to handle the situation. All of this was despite the passage of 16 years. Their responses were to be based on the presumption that it would not have improved the image of the Navy or the Intelligence Services. Further, it might conceivably tell the Russians something they did not already know. It is well known that in the eyes of the Russians, British Intelligence, have in some instances, left a lot to be desired over the years. The Russians knew all they wanted to know about the Crabb operation, after all they were involved.

Documents reveal that the focus of the MoD internal debate was on any disclosure by individuals who could expose failings with the authorities. However, because the BBC were not asking for active assistance in the making of the programme, there was little they could do to stop it. If they were approached they could refuse to co-operate and discourage the production. They could make it clear that the responsibility for any illegal or improper disclosures would rest firmly with the BBC and the individuals concerned. The idea that the MoD would indemnify them, collectively or individually, in advance against either proceedings for improper behaviour under the Official Secrets Act, or review of a service pension was ruled out, even if faced with political and practical difficulties.

It was proposed that the MoD should write to Mr. Darlow to clarify that the Ministry of Defence could only note that the BBC was proposing to make a programme about the Crabb case. They would not wish to assist in its preparation or be associated with it. They would not comment formally on the hypothetical possibility of any individual being proceeded against under the Official Secrets Act or for any other reason. They would point out to the BBC that they and the individuals concerned would be responsible for any illegal or improper disclosure.

The MoD would never indemnify anybody for giving out any information gained whilst in service and they would certainly threaten to withdraw pensions to anybody who made comments. The authors know individuals who were threatened with just such action if they spoke about Crabb. One problem was that the BBC's letter had not been dealt with speedily. There was reluctance to widen the consultation with the special circumstances of the Crabb case and the possible implications for the Services Press and Broadcasting Committee. There is no record of what the special circumstances were. Is it not banal that we are discussing a frogman who according to the authorities was not a serving officer at the time of his disappearance and not operating on behalf of the Navy? Why then were the MoD so concerned about a civilian?

In a memo dated 5 April 1972, the question of service pensions clarified the situation in that, under the Admiralty Pensions Act and the Forfeiture Act, the Department may at its discretion suspend (and restore later) or forfeit a pension on account of misconduct by the pensioner; conviction of a service offence connected with the Service; a grave criminal offence or any other criminal offence resulting in sentence of imprisonment exceeding six months. From that clarification it was considered to be unlikely that if the BBC's (anonymous) diver took part in the proposed programme there would not be any action concerning that individual's pension.

The memo clarified the position that the diver remained subject to the Official Secrets Act and, depending on what was said, he might lay himself open to prosecution for unlawful disclosure of information. Let us again be very clear on this point, the MoD, through Government channels if deemed appropriate, would stop an individual's pension. If that did not suffice and the situation was of such a serious concern then physical termination of the individual would be an option. The State in its widest sense will do *anything* to protect their interests.

By 6 April 1972 there was a view that it seemed to be yet another case in which the Ministry of Defence should neither give assistance nor be a hostage to fortune. A memo dated 11 April 1972 clarified that the only 'D' Notice relevant to the case of Crabb is 'D' Notice No 10, British Intelligence Services. It was acknowledged much had already been published on Crabb, some factual, much speculative, and it was doubted whether any significant new light could be cast on the affair concerning Crabb himself.

Then there was confirmation that it is a fact that a naval team from *HMS Vernon* did dive under the Russian ships and that the new evidence would be from one of these divers. The operation was kept secret and a revelation could have political and security difficulties.

On 13 April 1972 Sir James Dunnett, GCB, GMG made it clear that he was disturbed about some of the possible implications of this enterprise, not least the apparent emergence of a man, still living, who claimed to be able to throw fresh light on the whole affair. This need not amount to much; alternatively, however, it could be the beginning of quite a lot of trouble, with obvious implications in terms both of security and of relations with the Soviet Union.

In 1961 the Soviets sold their 'super' cruiser to the Indonesians and in 1972 the vessel was scrapped. The Soviets knew there was at least one underwater operation against the ship and had complained. So what were the obvious implications?

A Cabinet Office memo dated 13 April 1972 identified that from the contents of the letter from Mr. Darlow, the un-named ex-naval diver had already committed a *prima facie* contravention of the Official Secrets Act. This occurred in telling Mr. Darlow that he and others actually went under Russian ships.

It was on the 13 April 1972 that a draft letter from the MoD to David Darlow of the BBC was eventually produced and made available. The basis of the letter was very clear in that it was unlikely that there was to be any way in which the MoD could assist the BBC. The opportunity was taken to remind Mr. Darlow and the BBC that if they proceeded with making the programme, they would have to be very careful. This was because any illegal or improper disclosure would place responsibility on the BBC, as well as any other persons concerned or appearing in the programme. The MoD was not prepared to comment on the possibility of action being taken against any individual. However they did advise that any script that was produced should be cleared by the Defence Press and Broadcasting Committee, who would be able to advise them of any 'D' Notice angles.

In true form, a committee considered the draft on the 19 April 1972 who deemed that the letter should go from the Navy but thought that its general tone was not strong enough. They asked for a harder line to be taken in the revised draft. That was produced on 19 April 1972. It now contained the threat that should there be any improper disclosure of information, the responsibility would lie with Mr. Darlow and the BBC. This would also extend to any other persons concerned with, or appearing in, the programme. The Navy would not comment on the possibility of action being taken against any individual apart from the statement that 'any person or persons... should very carefully consider their position before contributing to your programme'.

Another memo followed a meeting under the heading of SECRET - UK EYES ONLY on 20 April 1972, which focused on a number of issues. It was deemed difficult to persuade the BBC to completely abandon the programme on security grounds. This was because of the amount of material that had already been published on Commander Crabb. However, it was considered that the new material might well be damaging. This raised an important point and it was considered that the reply from the Ministry of Defence to the BBC Producer should be amended, to avoid giving the impression that the subject was exceptionally delicate, but at the same time discouraging the whole project and especially the production of new evidence.

On the 27 April 1972, a memo to the Prime Minister provided a brief update and raised the matter of the diver. He was told that the BBC professed to have obtained certain additional information from another diver who was still alive. However, he was reluctant to appear for fear of reprisals by the Ministry of Defence! The BBC stated that this individual whose identity they are not prepared to disclose, would say that Crabb died in Stokes Bay. This, so far as it went, was in line with the official version of Crabb's death, i.e. that he died while testing new apparatus in Stokes Bay. But there could, of course, be no certainty that this diver witness would necessarily confine himself to this story when he appeared in front of the cameras.

There were two options that arose:

1. The diver used the Stokes Bay ploy as a means of working with the BBC. He would then add to that when filming.
2. If Stokes Bay was his story then;
   a) he did not take part in the operation or,
   b) he was planted by the MoD to find out information about the programme.

If Crabb died at Stokes Bay then there could be no alternative version and if somebody said otherwise then the Navy would have a defence. The problem was that Crabb did not die in Stokes Bay and there is sufficient evidence to show that. Any diver who claimed that, when on camera would be ridiculed and would be of no value to the programme.

Having received no communication from the MoD, it was on the 22 May 1972 that the BBC raised the issue of the diver again, to seek clarity of his personal situation with regard to the programme. The memo identified that Mr. Darlow, the BBC producer concerned, telephoned Admiral Denning seeking an assurance that the diver would not endanger his pension rights if he took part in the programme about Commander Crabb. The response was simple in that Admiral Denning was in no position to give such an assurance.

That same day a memo stated that the Prime Minister raised the point as to the amount of time it had taken the Ministry of Defence to deal with the original request. The evidence shows that it was two months before the matter was brought to the attention of the Central Staffs in the Ministry of Defence. It was appropriately summed up in the last paragraph:

"I am afraid this is one of those cases that happen from time to time when a number of people, not knowing quite what to do with the issues before them, shuffle the papers between themselves."

(Official Document)

We must again draw the reader's attention to the fact that according to the MoD and the Royal Navy, Crabb was supposedly a civilian and carried out the dive as such. Those same organisations tell us that it was a private venture and nothing to do with the military. What was the high secrecy aspect in 1972, some 16 years after the incident?

There was a welcome reprieve for the MoD on 23 May 1972 when Mr. Darlow contacted the MoD to say that the BBC had run into problems. It was because the diver's wife was deemed to be a neurotic. She was against her husband taking any part in the reconstruction of events concerning the Crabb case. Under the circumstances, Mr. Darlow thought it unwise to progress things at that time.

Then a twist in the MoD communications was recorded on the 26 June 1972 involving a telephone conversation on the 20 June from an individual who had returned from holiday. Before going on holiday, he had made it known that he had discovered that the original informant was not a member of the naval team which operated against the Russian Cruiser. However, he had been put in touch with an officer who had been. This diver was unwilling to talk without security clearance. He was told that he could not be given security clearance and that any approach to the security authorities would make the point that no military personnel should be involved in the programme.

Then a Memo dated 27 June 1972 brought more doom to the MoD. It stated:

"*I read Houghton's articles in the Sunday Express (June 11 1972) with a sense of horror and revulsion in no way diminished by the knowledge that this man is going to make more out of treason (the publishers being all poised, I gather, to promote the book into a best-seller) than many a serious historian earns from a book based upon a lifetime of research.*"

(Official Document)

Under a newspaper headline 'How Russian Undersea Sentries Caught Frogman Buster Crabb' is a story put out by Harry Houghton, a Soviet spy.

He claims that for the first time in any publication in the West, he could tell the true story of what happened to Commander Lionel Phillip Kenneth Crabb. GM, OBE, RNVR This is where hardly a year goes by without some new rumour about the frogman who vanished while on a mysterious mission under the Russian warships in 1956.

He claimed that one evening in the early spring of 1956 he went for a drink at the Crown Inn at Puncknowie, in Dorset when a woman who worked at the underwater Detection Establishment at Portland arrived. They knew each other quite well, and he also knew that the man with her was her current male friend from the local shallow water diving team.

After a drink or two the boyfriend excused himself and left the table and Houghton commented that he seemed very quiet tonight, quite different from what he had imagined him to be. The girl said that he was a bit fed up, as he had been training for something special which had then been called off.

Houghton claimed that the *Ordzhonikidze* had been fitted out with two wire jackstays running the full length of the ship below the waterline as a support for Soviet underwater sentries to hold on to against the strong tides they would encounter in Portsmouth Harbour.

Six men would guard the ship's bottom at all times and all states of the tide. In spite of waiting for Crabb, the underwater sentries lost him in the murky waters of the dockyard. Some minutes later he was encountered again and during the ensuing struggle his oxygen was turned off for long enough to make him pass out. His unconscious body was then hastily hauled on board and carried below out of sight. By this time he was recovering consciousness, but on being taken to the sick bay he passed out again. After medical treatment he recovered and, in answer to questions, began to make a confession. During this questioning he collapsed and died. Houghton claims that this was verified later by a man he met a couple of times in Dublin and also, later still, by Gordon Lonsdale. From each of these three sources the story did not vary. The intention of getting Crabb on board was twofold: to find out what the British wanted to know about the ship, and to be in the position of humiliating them by making a signal that someone had been caught on the ship's bottom and would the British Navy please come and collect him. Unfortunately, that bit went all wrong. With Crabb dying on their hands, the Russians could now find themselves being accused of his death, which had not been in the plan at all.

It was a delicate situation. What were they to do with the body? It was decided to put him back in the water, lightly secured to the hull by a fine cordage, so that by the time the ship had got underway and proceeded a mile or so the cord would chafe and the body would come adrift. As things turned out, the body remained in the sea for 14 months, probably entangled in a submarine cable or a wreck. It appears that, during interrogation, Crabb had disclosed that he had entered the harbour with a small limpet mine secured to him. In accordance with his training he had automatically slipped it from his body and let it sink to the seabed when he was pounced on. They were not going to blow up the cruiser, but British Intelligence wanted to know if the Russians had caught up with our sophisticated ASDIC programme, and particularly whether the cruiser was fitted with the equivalent of a certain type of ASDIC.

This story was ill founded, apart from the part that describes that Crabb was caught by the Soviets and taken aboard the ship. There are naval witnesses who provide evidence to support this. The story claims that Crabb died and that his body was put back into the water and tied to the underside to be dumped at sea. This would not have occurred because of the naval observation. Remember, the Navy had full observation on the vessels day and night for the period they were in port. The question of Crabb carrying a limpet mine would have had no value and would never have occurred. Imagine the outcome at the height of the Cold War of a mine exploding on a Soviet warship after having visited the UK.

Six underwater sentries guarded the hull of the cruiser in dark, murky water with the impossible task of stopping an intruder from getting to the ship. This further discredits Houghton's story, one of pure fabrication.

For the MoD things were hoting up by the 3 July 1972, when Mr. Darlow informed Vice-Admiral Sir Norman Denning that his diver informant had not, as claimed, been involved in the intelligence operations. However, Mr. Darlow had been put in touch with an officer who had been involved but who was not willing to co-operate with the BBC without security clearance.

Admiral Denning identifies that, from his conversation, Darlow had unearthed the true story concerning the operations of the naval diving team and was told that any introduction of this aspect would be contrary to 'D' notices.

A MoD memo dated 7 December 1972 identified that if Darlow managed to persuade his contact to talk, being a serving officer in Vernon, all sorts of pressures could be put on him to make him keep his mouth shut. It was for the Security Service to pinpoint the officer concerned and tell him to keep quiet. This clearly shows the language of determination to stop serving or former naval personnel speaking about MoD matters. Remember, at this time it was a 16-year-old story which would be of no value to either side, unless of course there was something to hide, and of course in Crabb's case there was.

In a memo dated 8 December 1972 more information flowed about the BBC's new informant or contact, who was apparently still serving in *HMS Vernon*. One presumes from this that, if it is true, he could be identified without too much difficulty and warned off by the MOD. However, it was known that to take action against a Serving Officer on the basis of information volunteered would be a delicate matter to handle.

A memo dated 30 January 1973 gave details of a meeting between the MoD and the BBC, which now set out a very clear picture of the programme that the BBC wanted to produce. The main focus of the meeting was about the naval diving operation, which was separate to that of Crabb. David Darlow met with the Navy on 25 January 1973 accompanied by David Mills and Tom Mangold who were respectively to produce and present the Crabb programme if the BBC went ahead with it.

Darlow explained that, although the Crabb programme had started as a BBC South project, it had now been accepted for full network screening, probably on BBC2. The BBC wished to go ahead with it if at all possible because they believed that the Crabb affair was still of great public interest. In addition they had obtained new evidence, which, in their opinion, discredited the accounts put out by Houghton in his book *Operation Portland* and in the *Sunday Times Magazine*. From this new evidence they claimed, that naval personnel had undertaken a separate operation. They had dived under the Russian Cruiser and had found no trace of Crabb or of the equipment said by Houghton to have been placed on the hull of the ship by the Russians themselves as a counter to possible underwater activity.

The focus was firmly on the 'serving senior Naval Officer' who claimed to have taken part in this operation and was prepared to tell his story in front of the cameras, provided he could be assured that he would not be putting himself or his pension prospects at risk by so doing. Darlow wanted to know if this 'serving senior Naval Officer' would be allowed to appear and tell his story subject to what he said being vetted by the Navy or MoD. In fact, they offered the opportunity for representatives to be present when the interview was recorded so that the MoD could stop anything being said that ought not to be said.

This is where the story becomes unreal. For a serving senior Naval Officer to discus on camera an operation would place him in breach of the Official Secrets Act. He would face a military court, prison and loss of pension. Unless he was a Soviet spy and after his revelations, they were going to look after him, then this 'serving senior Naval Officer' can have no credibility. This has got to be an MoD spook making life difficult for the BBC.

The MoD made it clear that the 'serving senior Naval Officer' would be in breach of the Act if he imparted information, classified or unclassified, which he had acquired through his service unless the release of that information had been specifically authorised. This prompted the question of whether, since all this had happened almost 17 years previously the 'Naval Officer' could be authorised. Darlow made it very clear that the 'serving senior Naval Officer' had not so far told him anything and would not do so until he had received a clearance.

Whilst it may be true that the 'serving senior Naval Officer' had not said anything so far, it was clear that Darlow had got hold of a fairly detailed story from someone. Having clearly devoted a lot of time and effort to the programme, he was anxious to get on with it and was plainly disappointed with the result of his meeting with the MoD; his colleagues on the other hand seem more ready to grasp the implications of what was said and realise that they are likely to get into very deep water if they were not very careful.

David Darlow wrote to the MoD on 31 January 1973 providing options for proceeding with the programme. First, he thanked them for the meeting with the Director of Naval Security regarding a documentary programme on Commander Crabb. He then identified that the problem he faced was making an authoritative and definitive film which would be of real archive value. At the same time there was a need to bring a real perspective to the affair, which had been grossly distorted in the past. He clarified the point in that there were two ways of presenting such a programme; the first was with official co-operation, and as far as possible in the voices of those concerned. It was accepted that for security reasons it might not be possible to fully-disclose certain details. The second was for the facts of the Crabb affair (insofar as they were known) to be told by the BBC reporting team, acting without official co-operation. There were six key points to be addressed:

1. Houghton's story was to be discredited by new information that had come into the possession of the BBC;
2. That an espionage operation was planned against the Russian warships by a specialist team of divers from *HMS Vernon* in Portsmouth;
3. To identify who gave the order? There was a strong possibility that it was carried out on an unofficial basis, without Whitehall's knowledge;
4. Were they seeking important information on the Russian's sonar equipment fixed to the underside of the ship;
5. Was there any evidence of the preparations listed by Houghton such as patrols of underwater sentries clinging to stay wires that had been rigged to the ship's hull;
6. The BBC knew the names of some of the men who took part in this operation but the Official Secrets Act forbad them from divulging them. Why? The Navy acknowledged that, after 17 years, national security was no longer at stake.

The situation for the MoD had now become serious, as it was clear that the BBC intended to make a programme whatever the MoD decided, and they might or might not use serving naval personnel not even former naval personnel.

The Prime Minister was appraised of the situation that, after a period of silence, the BBC had revived the project and they were on the track of fresh information which could be embarrassing. Their original ex-naval contact had second thoughts and had distanced himself from the project. However, they claimed to be in touch with a 'serving senior Naval Officer' who was prepared to disclose information provided that it did not expose him to disciplinary action. The Ministry of Defence had failed to identify the naval officer.

The whole situation raised the stakes to the point where the MoD, if it was possible, wanted to prevent the programme from appearing. It might be necessary to make discreet representations at a high level. The MoD would stand by the situation of refusing all official co-operation to avoid being drawn into some discussion about the unauthorised operation, which could have been very damaging indeed.

A section in the official documents has been removed because it would probably have led to the identity of the senior Naval Officer whom the Government and the MoD were desperate to conceal.

The MoD then made their position clear in a memo to the BBC dated 19 February 1973. They could not offer any indemnity to any naval officer or rating, whether serving or retired, to divulge official information. This meant that no naval diving person could appear on the programme without putting himself at risk. It was made very clear that no authorisation had been given or would be given for the release of information beyond that already published about the Crabb episode of 1956. There would be no official cooperation in the making of a programme.

On the 20 March 1973 a memo to the Prime Minister advised that the MoD would make one more attempt to dissuade the BBC by discreet, but direct representations at a high level. It was anticipated that this would involve an approach either from the Foreign and

Commonwealth Secretary or the Secretary of State for Defence to the Chairman or the Director General of the Corporation. There was some concern over the latter point. Should it become known that an approach had been made and been refused, it would create curiosity and suspicion in the media and public arena.

Then, on 23 May 1973, it was acknowledged that having been denied MOD co-operation and not allowed to interview witnesses on the programme, the BBC decided to go ahead with a documentary using their own resources and actors. Darlow had a new informant who had given much useful information and they would want to make sure that it was cleared, but implied that he was unwilling to be deterred by anything else.

The BBC never made a programme about Crabb. Clearly all efforts were made at producer level, but the ace up the sleeve for the MoD was to approach at a high level. What the BBC discovered was that there was an official diving operation that was planned and separate to Crabb's dive.

Commander Stan Currie-Davis told Mike, in lengthy discussions about Crabb, that there was an official diving operation carried out against the *Ordzhonikidze* whilst it was in Portsmouth in 1956. The sister ship the *Sverdlov* had been inspected the previous year when it visited Portsmouth. The big difference between the visits was the Russian leaders who were carried on the *Ordzhonikidze*. Stan said that it was a matter of course for divers to have a look under visiting warships and that Commander Joe Brooks had led the team. The operation had gone without any problems. The team had been dropped off and swum with a slow current along the underside of the *Ordzhonikidze*. They were then picked up once clear of the ship and the lookouts.

Mike first met Commander Joe Brooks when he operated a commercial diving company. He had lost both legs in a diving incident and was the only commercial diver known to continue to work underwater with such an impediment. Mike recalls one meeting when working on the river Humber, where two diving contractors worked side by side. The owner of one of those companies was Joe Brooks who had been a Commander in the Royal Navy. We learned that he was proud to have led the team that inspected the underside of the *Ordzhonikidze*. He did question what Crabb was doing, as it was not to examine the underside of the ship, because, in his words, 'The serving professionals did that job'. During the Humber job, a member of a civilian diving team had dived to check some work. The diver, ex Navy, went down but did not return to the surface. A diver from our team went below and found him trapped. I recall that he had lost his mouthpiece. He was cut free and recovered to the surface, where we got him onto the support boat. Efforts to revive him failed and he was taken to Hull hospital, where he was pronounced dead. It was a devastating blow for Joe, and the subject of diving and diving incidents were spoken about. He recounted the divers he had worked with who had died. He spoke briefly of the Crabb incident and I recall that he said that Crabb did not die. When challenged as to what happened, he just smiled and changed the subject.

Mike learned from a number of sources that Joe led the dive under the *Ordzhonikidze* and that nothing untoward was found. On the other hand Crabb carried out his dive breaking every rule of the combat diver operation for undertaking a covert operation against a ship. Why? It is a simple answer, he was sent not to return.

15

In the Line of Duty

It is always the best policy to speak the truth unless, of course, you are an exceptionally good liar.

Jerome K. Jerome 1859-1927

During the post war years, the Royal Navy needed to know all about Russian mines and that was a task which befell Crabb. He was a real life 'James Bond' and engaged in the acquisition of mines from whatever source. This included legitimate foreign travel, or more illicit and covert means. Lieutenant Commander Stan Currie-Davis a former diving and mine warfare officer, worked with Crabb in this role, operating at the base known as the Underwater Counter Weapons establishment (UCWE), at Portland. Stan explained his role working with Crabb.

"We would be sent off to a country that had some maritime mines that they could not identify. We had to make them safe and bring them back to the UK. Sometimes we went to places where we should not have been to locate mines and recover them."

He then added,

"Crabbie was in his element doing this, and he had permission from

somebody high up. I never officially knew who that was but it was not hard to guess who."

Pressed further as to who it was he replied:

"Mountbatten."

With the mines they obtained, they investigated them and found ways to dismantle them, so that they could produce procedures for others to follow. This would allow others to render them safe when encountered.

Currie-Davis knew Crabb well, perhaps as well as any member of naval personnel did, and at Christmas 1954 both were at Portsmouth, but Crabb had nowhere in particular to go for the holiday period. He invited him to spend Christmas day with him and his family, but Crabb declined, saying he didn't want to impose on their family day. Currie-Davis had already invited another officer over for the day, so he asked him to persuade Crabb to join them. Crabb relented and joined the group, having a good day, Currie-Davis recalling that he was great company, playing games with the children.

Currie-Davis was sent to another diving position, leaving Crabb to his mines, and it was a year later, in 1955, that he saw Crabb again and noticed a deterioration from the old Crabb. Although he visited Portsmouth fairly regularly, Currie-Davis thought of him as a very lonely and sad 'old man', old by naval standards, where a new generation of young divers had qualified and filled the posts of the wartime personnel. He explained:

"His attitude seemed to be of a respected naval hero trying to cling to the past and still enjoy his well deserved reputation, which quite frankly didn't mean a thing in civy street"

(A civilian outside the Navy).

He made it known that he was not happy about having to leave the

Navy to become a civilian. On the other hand Currie-Davis explained that it was a funny business altogether, because nobody really knew what he was up to and he spent a lot of time in London towards the end of his service. He could well have been working for a secret department; he just went about doing his own thing and did not report to anybody in the normal chain of command. He had been promoted to a full Commander which was most unusual because all but a few of those from the war were no longer required, let alone promoted, particularly in the underwater units, which sought younger members. When Currie-Davis was asked if he thought that it was Crabb buried in Portsmouth, he responded that it was a dangerous subject and declared that he did not want to comment. He explained that he had too much to lose, and he did not mean a naval pension. This was another case of a person fearing for their life if they spoke out of turn.

Mike drew a parallel between Crabb and Currie-Davis because both had been involved with the secrecy of underwater mine warfare and covert operations and both sought to retain some adventure once they were deemed 'old' by naval standards and put out to become civilians. While Mike did not have first hand knowledge of Crabb's post war activities, he did have first hand experience of Currie-Davis's post military exploits. Some of these exploits are described to show how Government offices use former military personnel. Once they became civilians, or were retained on reserve they could be used as a Government contractor or reporting officer, using their civilian occupation as a cover. If it was successful it was 'well done old boy/girl'. But if it went wrong then it was 'it's nothing to do with us'.

In one situation, Mike became personally involved. In the early 1970s he was travelling through Nigeria to Lagos for a flight back to the UK. He looked down the barrels of Nigerian soldiers' guns as he presented his documents at Warri airport. It was a small provincial airport, and there were soldiers everywhere as the country was in the last phase of a bloody civil war. He was traveling on a British passport and Nigerian military pass and so was speedily cleared through the officialdom by an army officer, to board a small aircraft bound for the capital.

Lagos airport was the focus for a strong military presence and the pass, combined with the obligatory bribes, called "dash", ensured that he was cleared through the arrivals desk and met by a company agent who transported him to a hotel in Lagos. As arranged, he met Currie-Davis in the hotel foyer and, while they were pleased to meet each other again, Mike was aware that Currie-Davis was very distressed. Although he would not go into great detail about his problems, it soon became very evident that he had to get out of the country quickly. Currie-Davis worked for a commercial company trading in Nigeria, but was also employed as a 'reporting officer' for a British Government Department, the Cabinet Office. You could say that 'reporting officer' was a less dramatic term title than 'spy'.

He gave Mike his ticket for the Lagos to London flight the following morning. Then, in a quiet voice he explained that he was also on the flight. However, he had not been given a return air ticket by the company, which was a method employed by companies at that time to ensure that people did not go home until the company was ready to let you go. Of course, the Cabinet Office would not help, as there was no official connection with the individual. Currie-Davis did not have enough money to purchase a ticket and had to do a deal so that he could obtain an air ticket through the Swiss Air office, having made a good contact with the Swiss Air Manager. The problem he faced was how he could board the flight without being stopped, arrested and thrown into prison.

Mike was booked into the airport hotel and it was agreed that he would go and check in as normal, and Currie-Davis would join him the following morning, having lost his minders. They would then make the short journey to the airport and check in together. The following morning they entered the airport building to confront the first barrier, a group of aggressive looking soldiers. This was not as bad as it may seem because most of the soldiers were not very bright. It was common to have a passport examined when it was upside down. It was a case of remaining calm and remembering who had the guns. Currie-Davis composed himself, as he was visibly concerned. They approached the soldiers and Mike selected a very large sergeant, sporting a bright red beret. He was armed with a sub machine gun. He handed over two passports, each with an English five-pound note in it, as well as his military pass. With a great deal of pompous authority, the sergeant scrutinised their documents, removed the money and handed the documents back. He signalled for them to pass. They endured the trials of passing through customs with the usual bribes. For Currie-Davis the wait was agony, watching for any sign of the thugs looking for him. Eventually the flight was called and they boarded the aircraft. Sitting at the rear of the British Airways jet as it lifted into the clear blue sky above Lagos provided a magic transformation, and Currie-Davis, grinning, a lot more relaxed, ordered the drinks. He reported to the Cabinet Office, the company head office and returned to Nigeria.

Apart from the exploits in Nigeria, in which Mike played a part and had first hand knowledge, Currie-Davis was, throughout the years, employed in various sensitive areas of the world under what may be seen as 'strange circumstances. In a pub in Lincolnshire he entertained us with details of some of his escapades in times when things went wrong. We could imagine how Crabb must have been, always seeking adventure and danger, believing that those in authority would be in support when things went wrong. However, that was the biggest mistake both men made.

* * *

Crabb was a frogman and that was the only really successful thing that occurred in his life, and he was at home with other divers. One man whom he would have had a working relationship with was Professor

J.B.S. Haldane. He was with the Admiralty Underwater Experimental Unit and engaged in the development of human torpedoes, midget submarines and mine counter measures equipment. He undertook valuable experimental work in the physiology of diving, especially the effects of breathing pure oxygen underwater. After the war he remained in experimental diving and he undertook research into deep-sea diving techniques, leading to Britain obtaining the world record for a deep dive. While Haldane was at the forefront of diving, Peter Wright explains, in *Spy Catcher,* that Haldane was supplying all details of the diving experiments to the Communist Party of Great Britain who, in turn, passed them onto the GRU in London. It takes little imagination to speculate that details about Crabb's activities would have taken the same route. Therefore, one of the most secret military places in Britain in the 1950s was the Underwater Counter Measures Establishment at Portland. The Soviets had established an effective spy network in the base which did untold damage to British and NATO secrets. It is worthy of note that of all the British armed services, it was the Navy that appears to have been the most effectively penetrated. Little wonder the Americans would have raised concerns about Lord Mountbatten.

Soviet spy, Harry Houghton, served twenty-three years in the Royal Navy, to retire as a Chief Petty Officer. He was employed on the clerical staff of a Naval research establishment and was sent as a writer to the British Naval attaché in the Warsaw Embassy. Drink and women became his downfall and he was soon entrapped in the Soviet spy system, and he was returned to England to take up a post in 1952 at the Underwater Counter Weapons Establishment at Portland. He was not alone for long, as he forged a friendship with Ethel (Bunty) Gee, who also worked at the base. Like Crabb, he also purchased a caravan, and when not in the drinking scene, he and Gee, spent time at the caravan. In 1956, his contact in the Soviet secret service proposed to expand his 'business' venture to include spying, for which there was money to be made. He was put in touch with his British controller, Gordon Lonsdale. Houghton had to elicit the assistance of Gee, and to do this he introduced Lonsdale to her as a US Navy Commander, and so the penetration of a most secret Naval base had been made, with the transfer of high-grade Naval intelligence.

Houghton and Gee were arrested while handing over secret papers and film to Lonsdale, and they served fifteen-year prison sentences for spying, through gaining secret information from the Underwater Weapons establishment. When they were released from prison they married. Houghton stated in his book about his spying activities, *Operation Portland* that Crabb was captured by Russian divers and taken into the cruiser through a wet compartment. He also claims that Crabb gave some details of the operation he was to have carried out, then died. The Russians, unable to return him to the British, deposited his body in the water when the Soviet ships left port. During questioning about his spying activities, Houghton tried to do a deal but this was not accepted, and so it is alleged that many of his statements should be regarded with some scepticism. He is also alleged to have deliberately created some mystery in the book he published in order to enhance its readership.

Gordon Lonsdale, groomed by the KGB, entered the London scene in 1955, to take control of the Portland spy ring. He came from Canada. His real name was Konon Trofimorich Molodi, but he was given the name of Gordon Arnold Lonsdale, who was a genuine Canadian of Eastern European descent who had disappeared in Finland during the Second World War. There is no evidence that Crabb knew Lonsdale, but Lonsdale was the Soviet controller of the spy ring of the Portland base where Crabb was working. For his spying activities, Lonsdale received a prison sentence of twenty-five years, but after a few years he was exchanged for Grenville Wynne, who had been imprisoned for his involvement with Oleg Penkovsky, who passed secret information to the West.

It is said that the Soviet Government intended to change Captain Korablov into *'Kapitan Krab'* and exhibit him publicly if there was a breakdown in Soviet-British negotiations. The story states that Whitehall maintained its determination not to give in to Soviet pressure. This led to foreign newsmen in Moscow being 'leaked' information about a KGB plan to exhibit Commander Crabb publicly. The *Sunday Express* published a front-page dispatch from their Moscow correspondent, Mr. Roy Blackman, on 22 June 1969.

'Crabb in Moscow Spy Spectacular?'

"The fantastic suggestion is being made that the Russians may be planning to present before the world Commander Lionel Crabb, the British frogman spy named as 'Kapitan Krab' of the Soviet Navy. This information came from sources close to the Russian Foreign Ministry in Moscow."

The *Express* story continued with details of the events in Portsmouth and reports that he had been captured by the Russians and taken to the Soviet Union to serve in their Navy. Blackman considered that the Russians were testing Britain's reaction and were about to embark on a major propaganda coup. The same sources that released this information predicted in 1967 that the spy Kim Philby was about to make a statement, and he did. Blackman also considered that if the Russians held Crabb, this could be the time to produce him - when the negotiations over a swap between Gerald Brooke, and the Russian super spies, the Krogers, were getting nowhere.

The Foreign Office were asked for their view on the statements, and responded that they never commented 'on stories of this kind'. However, other press correspondents corroborated Mr. Blackman's story. On the 2 June 1969 the foreign Office categorically denied that there was any question of an exchange of the Krogers for Brooke. On the 24 July 1969 Gerald Brooke was released and flown home from Moscow; he had served four years of his five-year sentence for distributing anti-Soviet leaflets. Russia's super spies Peter and Helen Kroger, who had served only eight years of their sentences, were granted freedom on the 14 October 1969.

It was Soviet defectors that produced evidence throughout the years that Crabb had been captured and taken to the Soviet Union. When the KGB officer Anatoli Golitsin defected in Finland during the early 1960s he provided his interrogators with more than a hundred leads on past and present agents. He said that he had read scores of NATO documents sent by agents to Moscow. As part of the investigation he was provided with genuine and bogus papers, and he picked out the right ones. He had indeed seen secret NATO papers. Most importantly, he also gave details of how Soviet Naval intelligence knew that Crabb was to make the dive and had planned his capture. He said that, through information received by agents in Britain, the Russians had details of the planned dive and his capture when alongside the ships. The plan involved a Soviet agent at a high level in the secret service or Navy. He revealed that Crabb had been placed high on the list of wanted people, as he was a most experienced and knowledgeable expert on almost every type of underwater mine and explosive, and indeed underwater warfare in general. Facts revealed by Golitsin on other matters proved to be so reliable that there was no reason to doubt the information about Crabb.

Another of the defectors to the West was Soviet Naval officer Lieutenant Vadim Andreyevich, who, on the 5 January 1962 claimed to have served with Crabb under his Soviet name Commander Lev Lvovich Korablov, and was able to provide such precise information and detail that it indicated that Korablov and Crabb were the same person. However, the Admiralty and Government departments still maintained their silence and at no time was any of the evidence acted upon. The British never denied that Crabb had been captured, nor did the Russians ever deny having captured him.

It will be seen that Britain has long been a hot bed of spies, defectors and cover-ups to a degree that it has become very difficult to determine between fact and fiction. Whilst the Cold War period was the pinnacle of such activity, if anybody comes near the truth then the Establishment clones are paraded to dispel any evidence, and if that fails then termination is not be ruled out. The world of spies, defectors, traitors and the Establishment is a murky and dirty one.

* * *

Sydney Knowles told us that Crabb was training somebody in underwater swimming as he was going to take him on the operation. In the end, the person did not go with Crabb. Remember, Col. Malcolm told Sydney,

"Thank God he didn't go".

The question is who was that person? One explanation that must be explored, involved one of the most dangerous spies of the period, Kim Philby. Following the Second World War, Philby continued his espionage work. However, whilst working in the USA, the CIA pointed the finger at him. They claimed he was involved with Burgess and Maclean and they wanted him out of the USA because he was linked to possible Soviet spies. Philby then broke off all links to the Soviets, so by 1954 he had not had any contact with Soviet intelligence for over four years.

Philby was born on New Year's Day 1912 in the Punjab. He was named Harold Adrian Russell Philby, but he was nicknamed Kim after the Rudyard Kipling hero. Ironically, the story of Philby relates the exploits of an Irish boy who grows up in India and works as a spy for the British. Philby sought a better future for the masses and was easily recruited into the Communist movement, at a time when Blunt, Maclean and Burgess, along with many others, were brought under Soviet control.

It is said that Philby became one of the most treacherous spies in history, described as an unrepentant traitor. He caused untold harm to his country and brought about the deaths of co-workers, as well as many innocent people on both sides of the Iron Curtain. In his own book *My Silent War,* published in 1968, Philby wrote:

"In early manhood I became an agent for the Soviet Intelligence Service. I can therefore claim to have been a Soviet Intelligence officer for some thirty-odd years, and will no doubt remain one until death. Some writers have spoken of me as a double agent, or even as a triple agent. If this is taken to mean that I was working with zeal for two or more sides at once, it is seriously misleading. All through my career, I have been a straight penetration agent working in the Soviet interest. The fact that I joined the British Secret Intelligence Service (SIS) is neither here nor there: I regarded my SIS appointments purely in the light of cover jobs, to be carried out sufficiently well to ensure my attaining positions in which my service to the Soviet Union would be most effective. My connection with MI5 must be seen against my prior total commitment to the Soviet Union, which I regarded then, as I do now, the inner fortress of the world movement."

If Philby was a dedicated Communist, how did he get into British Intelligence? It wasn't difficult. In the thirties, intelligence was a 'gentleman's' game and when it came to hiring, a gentleman was given preference. The right school tie, last name or family connections were enough to open the door. The ancient heads of intelligence couldn't imagine that an English gentleman would ever betray his country. The fact that Philby was clever, courteous, efficient and quick-witted certainly helped his progress to the upper echelons of the intelligence community.

There were, however, plenty of signs of Philby's true colours. His first wife, Litsi was a militant Communist, and so were most of his friends until he went underground. To maintain his cover he divorced Litsi, dropped his Communist friends and joined the Anglo-German Alliance. Philby improved his right wing credentials during the Spanish Civil War, when he worked as a correspondent for *The Times* newspaper. He made a point of siding vocally, and in print, with the Nationalists and was even personally decorated by Franco after being injured in a mortar attack. The connections he made in Franco Spain would help immensely in his future activities.

When the Second World War broke out Philby was assigned by *The Times* to cover the British Expeditionary Force's attempt to stem the German tide. He filed stories as the French and British armies retreated and was eventually evacuated from Bologne. People were impressed and in August of 1940 Philby was welcomed into the Secret Intelligence Service. By this time British Intelligence was well infiltrated by Communists, including Guy Burges, who was one of Philby's interviewers.

Philby proved to be an industrious agent and he was sent to the newly created Special Operations Executive (SOE). At SOE, Philby received field training in covert operations and interrogation methods, all of which would be of value to him in the future. Because of his stammer and poor French he was sent back to SIS. Aged only 29 Philby had infiltrated the top counter-intelligence agency of Britain, which would have pleased the Soviets. Philby was given command of the Iberia sub-section that covered Portugal and Spain. This was an important section because of the myriad agents operating in the region and because of the strategic importance of the Straits of Gibraltar. But for his SIS masters, he quickly improved the efficiency of the administration; he had a clear mind, was a lateral thinker, was good at writing reports and didn't mind doing the boring paperwork. This all occurred at a time when most of the Soviet and British objectives were the same. In doing his job he played a part in extending World War II, by ensuring that anti-Hitler plotters weren't given support by the Allies. It is known that throughout the war there was an anti-Hitler resistance movement operating within Germany. They wanted to kill Hitler and sue for peace and wanted help from the Allies. This information was passed through the Iberian desk and suppressed by Philby. Why? Because the last thing Stalin wanted was for the Allies to reach an agreement with Germany that would have ruined his plans for taking over Eastern Europe.

It is quite obvious now that Philby and the other traitors, such as Burgess and Maclean, were under orders to make sure that any peace proposals from Germany were downplayed or ignored. The fact that Philby had the power and the respect of his contemporaries and superiors in British Intelligence indicates that he had wide-ranging influence in Spain and Portugal, and therefore Gibraltar and Tangier. In *My Silent War,* Philby tells of his successes against the Germans but makes almost no mention of what duties he was carrying out on behalf of the Soviets. He does not mention the Sikorski incident at all; it would have been one of the major events during his term as head of the lberian section and certainly he would have been aware of how Sikorski's death would please Stalin. Philby would have been privy to all reports. He would even have read the German reports which laid the blame for the crash on British Intelligence. Part of the Soviet plan to downplay the Sikorski affair was to act as though it was an unfortunate event, but it made little difference to the future of Poland. Philby followed the line right to the end by simply ignoring it, and failed to mention the Sikorski affair not because he wasn't involved but because he *was* involved. He played a part in the recovery operation, working with Crabb, and carried out an important special operation when the Liberator aircraft carrying General Sikorski crashed into the sea after take off from Gibraltar. Crabb's task was to recover the bodies and the briefcase Sikorsky carried with him. It contained orders, plans and addresses of the highest possible importance and of which there were no duplicates. Every piece of paper was located and recovered.

The Soviets received information that Philby had financial problems as the SIS had opted not to give him a pension, but gave him a one-time payment of £4,000, half paid immediately, and the rest in £500 payments every six months. He had a wife and several children and, with only £2,000 and no job was not in the best of situations particularly given Philby's social circle in the early fifties. Philby's Soviet masters made the decision to help him financially. An agent was charged with locating him, making contact and handing over money. It was identified that such a meeting was extremely dangerous, because if it were discovered, Philby could be arrested, interviewed and prosecuted as a spy and he would have no defence. There was also the concern that he may reveal information that would expose the Soviet spy network in the UK. The Soviets gave serious thought as to how best to solve the problem. Finally the option adopted was to contact Anthony Blunt and use his services, as he was not in the same exposed position as Philby.

Philby was left with £5,000 and the need to prepare for further interrogations and surveillance. It would appear that he was not watched constantly, but the local policeman would appear near his small house in the country, which stood apart from the others, and there was spot checking, to see how often he took trains, where he went, what he did and who he met. Although he had no evidence, he presumed that his telephone was bugged. While he was watched, the authorities did not have the power to stop him leaving the country unless they arrested him, and they would have to have evidence to do that. Of course he did not know what, if any, evidence they did have. It was a game of cat and mouse and if he ran to defect there was no doubt that he would be apprehended.

It was in November 1955 that he was summoned and interrogated by a professional investigator. Of all the British investigators the one he faced was the most aggressive and the interrogation was harsh, but he gave nothing away. Philby continued to live under constant pressure throughout and suspicions remained with him. Whenever a spy story made the press he was worried that reporters would somehow link it to him; it was also in 1955 that Philby's name appeared in newspapers next to the words 'Third Man'. Of course, Philby's name had been circulating for some time and a journalist wrote:

"The name of the third man was known to enough people in Fleet Street to fill England's largest football stadium."

However, no newspaper could actually name Philby and describe him as the 'Third Man' or as a Soviet spy because without substantive evidence there would be a libel action. Not only the media knew who was under suspicion. So did the authorities, however Philby did have friends on the inside who considered him not to be guilty.

The bombshell dropped when, at the end of 1955, a newspaper carried Philby's name in bold headlines. It quoted an MP, Marcus Lipton, who had raised the matter in Parliament as to whether the Government was planning to continue hiding the fact that the not-unknown Kim Philby was the 'Third Man' who had warned Maclean and Burgess, allowing them time to flee. As soon as Philby got home he telephoned Nicholas Elliott at SIS. He was a friend who did *not* believe Philby was a Soviet agent. Philby told him that his name was in the newspapers and he needed to know what to do. Elliott thought that they should leave it for a day to see what happened and then decide what action, if any, to take. Philby couldn't sue the newspaper, the *Evening Standard*, because it only quoted Lipton's statement in Parliament and, according to British law, nothing said in Parliament is actionable.

The following day, Elliott made contact and said that he should wait and only respond when the Parliamentary debates began, which could take up to two weeks. He then made a request that Philby surrender his passport, explaining that, once again, this was a formality. Philby readily agreed, but in reality he had no option. Elliott also asked Philby to come in so that they could carry out another interrogation, only this time he would be questioned by two officers whom Philby knew well, because they had worked under him in MI6 counter-intelligence.

To avoid a confrontation with the media, a car with a driver was sent to take Philby to a safe-house in London, where the questioning was to take place. At this point he was very uncertain, because he did not know if they had any new information on him. He considered he had an advantage with a psychological superiority over the investigators who had worked for him.

The interrogation was just like the previous one and the officers asked all the questions that had been asked before. They covered the whole thing once again from beginning to end and Philby had no problems in answering any of the questions. The big problem with being interrogated, where you are maintaining a cover story, is to remember what has been said previously. The interrogators have the advantage, as they set the questions and have transcripts of previous interrogations. Once they had completed their questioning, Philby was free to go, but they required him to return when they had completed transcribing the tapes of the interrogation and cross-referenced the information. They again met at the apartment and asked questions to clarify some points. He was on guard, waiting to see if they would slip in an unexpected question, but nothing came and so he thought that they had no new information on him. When they were finished they concluded that they were satisfied that he was innocent and that SIS would make the same recommendation to the Minister of Foreign Affairs so that a response could be made to Mr.. Lipton in Parliament.

Philby asked a question as to why SIS concluded that he was innocent, while MI5 were certain of his guilt. The response was that there was no change in the evidence against him and that if he were guilty, he would not have behaved the way he did for the last four years. This meant that surveillance had not given them anything and, indeed, for four years Philby had not met with any of his Soviet colleagues, or any other contacts that could have been used against him. There was no spying, nothing odd or suspicious about his activities. He had made two trips to Spain for holidays and returned twice with no attempt to make contact with anyone suspicious and without an attempt to escape. The decision to break contact with his Soviet contacts and lay low was the right one. His Soviet contacts knew what was happening, and if they felt that he needed to leave the country, they would have re-established contact and arranged it.

In *My Silent War, Philby wrote:*

"Several times in this period, I revived the idea of escape…Finally, an event occurred which put it right out of my head. I received, through the most ingenious of routes, a message from my Soviet friends, encouraging me to be of good cheer and proposing an early resumption of relations. It changed drastically the whole complexion of the case. I was no longer alone."

Up until the time the security services gave Philby a clean bill of health, he was under serious suspicion and at risk of being apprehended. Even then the case was not closed, as there were those in MI5 who still considered him a traitor and sought to expose him. The Soviets would not have wanted him caught, for fear of the exposure of Blunt and the others that were embedded in the Establishment. They would have got Philby home at whatever cost: he was, after all, 'the most successful spy the KGB ever had'. The options that Philby faced if caught were to spend the rest of his life in prison or luxury in the Soviet Union, treated as a hero. The option of escape would have been a priority. His Soviet masters and controllers would also be prepared to bring him home if it was required.

Extracting somebody who was under surveillance would not have been impossible, but for much of the time Philby did not have a passport, as he had surrendered it, so ports and airports would have caused a problem. However, if by 1956 the net was closing in on Philby, an extraction route was available. All the Soviets had to do was get Philby into a safe environment and then, when the *Ordzhonikidze* visited Portsmouth, he could make good his defection. Sydney Knowles told us that Crabb was to take somebody with him on the *Ordzhonikidze* operation but he never knew who it was. Philby was a prime candidate. All he had to do was swim, dressed in a diving suit, to the ship and he would be spirited aboard. Crabb had been giving somebody some training and it was already determined that Crabb was not coming back. When the Russians visited, Blunt declined to take part in the official process of entertaining them, which was most unusual. Did he want to keep his distance, so if the extraction plan was adopted his name would not be linked to the visit. It is stated that Mountbatten was out of the country at the time of the visit, again an unusual situation for the head of the Royal Navy to be in at such an important event. Such a visit by the Soviet leaders would have taken months to plan and prepare for, but the key players were absent.

In considering the options at the time, the Blunt, Crabb and Mountbatten faction could have conspired to undertake such an operation. However, there is not one item of firm evidence and, unless those who could have been involved made a declaration or the official records are opened to the public, then it remains speculation. But, consider what we do know. There was what could be described as an effective pro-Soviet network in our security services, in the military and within Royalty. Two Soviet spies had defected and the Americans were alarmed at the level of Soviet penetration in the UK. The key players were associated with pro-Soviet groups and, as Knowles recounts, they were quite active also with illegal activities. Knowles makes it very clear that Crabb needed to keep involved with diving and, as the Navy did not want him, he would go to where his talents could be used. Crabb was tasked with taking somebody with him on the last dive, but to the relief of the security services that person did not go. Was that person Kim Philby, assisted by Blunt and Mountbatten, Crabb's boss?

16

The Royal Connection

The truth is rarely pure, and never simple.

Oscar Wilde 1845-1900

Crabb was coming to the end of his active military life in the Royal Navy and there were younger, fitter people entering the service. The selection of divers and training was formalised, as were underwater operations. These changes were a problem for Crabb for, as we have seen, he did not conform to normal naval protocol, as he reported directly to Mountbatten. It is without doubt the most important name connected to Crabb's disappearance. There was a connection between them as the latter had undertaken special operations overseas and reported directly to Mountbatten upon his return. It would seem that it was Mountbatten who authorised his promotion to Commander, but we do not know why. Mountbatten's involvement in the Crabb affair was unresolved and there continued to be some very pertinent questions asked in Parliament, in the media and by his mother and friends. It will be seen that Mountbatten's activities were

not without a lot of controversy, for example where the Americans and others alleged that he had damaging links with Communists in the UK and senior people in the Soviet Union.

Percy Sillitoe, former Head of MI5, Admiral Gennadiy Zakharov, who trained *Spetsnaz* troops in Naval sabotage, Anatoli Golitsin, Col Mikhail Gleniewski and Marcus Lipton are among many who claimed that Crabb was in the Soviet Union or East Germany. On the basis of that evidence, the question that must be asked is whether that final daylight dive and capture in Portsmouth was planned and arranged by the pro-Russian Mountbatten. Did he arrange for Crabb to defect or be captured? Was Crabb destined to assist Philby to escape the long arm of the security services? Sydney Knowles told us that Crabb defected, and that the plan was for Crabb to take another person on the *Ordzhonikidze* operation who was not a qualified frogman, but somebody who needed to be taken to the Soviet warship. At the meeting between Knowles, Mike and Gary Murray in London, they contemplated who that person might be and, as we have seen in the previous chapter, Philby was the strongest contender, as the net was tightening around him.

Mountbatten was conveniently touring India and Burma on official naval business when the *Ordzhonikidze* operation took place. Therefore, he did not immediately spring to mind as a conspirator with either the media or public. If the Navy had wanted to undertake an official dive they would have used a Navy team or Royal Marine SBS team to look under the warships. It was current practice by all sides. This operation would not have included Crabb. Mountbatten claimed that, before leaving on the tour, he gave specific instructions that no such underwater operation should be carried out, which implies that he knew that it was at least being considered. However, his second-in-command, Admiral William Davis, maintained that Mountbatten gave no such instruction. Mountbatten also said that as soon as he heard about the operation and Crabb's disappearance on his return he ordered the reluctant Admiral Davis to inform the First Lord of the Admiralty immediately. Davis is alleged to have said that Mountbatten did not want the First Sea Lord informed until it became clear that the story was going to break in the press. Because Crabb had no close family links, such as a wife, the outcry from friends was unexpected.

Following the *Ordzhonikidze* operation, the first link with

Mountbatten's name occurred as the subject of a *Daily Mirror* article dated 15 May 1956, which stated:

> "There was a silent figure in the Gallery of the House of Commons last night. He was: Admiral The Earl Mountbatten, the First Sea Lord. He sat in the front row of the Peers Gallery listening to evasive replies by Sir Anthony Eden, the Prime Minister, in the debate on the 'Frogman Blunder'." He heard Sir

Anthony Eden say:

> "I deplore this debate and I will say no more. I have not one word more to say than I announced on Wednesday. I am not prepared to discuss these matters in this house." Eden repeated that what was done in the affair of Commander Crabb was done without the authority of Ministers." He emphasised: "That includes all ministers and all aspects of this affair."

The article continued to ask:

> "Does Lord Mountbatten the First Sea Lord know the answer to the questions that the whole world is asking? It was the Admiralty that issued the first official statement that Crabb was presumed dead. The service chief at the Admiralty is Lord Mountbatten. Is he the only man in the world besides the Prime Minister who knows the full facts of the mission and the fate of Commander Crabb?"

Another press cutting, dated 1956, carried the headline:

> *Frogman: who is Eden shielding?*
> "Is it Mountbatten, MPs ask? Some Labour MPs decided last night that the man Sir Anthony Eden is shielding in the case of frogman Crabb must be Lord Mountbatten, First Sea Lord and uncle to the Duke of Edinburgh. Lord Mountbatten is chief of the Navy and of its intelligence service. He lunched with Eden a few hours before the Premier made his stone walling answer to questions in the House of Commons. What evidence there is, points to Lord Mountbatten, said the MPs."

The article continues to say that they would not believe that even the cloak and dagger men who sent frogman Crabb on his spying mission under the Soviet cruiser *Ordzhonikidze* did so without permission from the highest authority. Eden, shaken by the universally critical press over the incident, brought the whole question before the Cabinet, asking the help of Ministers in deciding whether he should tell, or what else to do. In the ten minutes that he refused to tell MPs the facts of the case, his prestige suffered a great slump. He lost much of the goodwill he had won among Tory backbenchers during his successful talks with the Soviet leaders.

It was not just in Parliament that the storm raged. Numerous publications revealed that there was disquiet within the Navy and that Casper John was very wary when taking up his appointment as Vice Chief of Naval Staff. He doubted whether Mountbatten as First Sea Lord was the right man for him to serve under, and his daughter expressed the view that:

"He deplored flamboyance, the self-promotion, above all the deviousness of the First Sea Lord…Mountbatten was known as 'Tricky Dicky' throughout Whitehall."

The revelations also report that Casper John always blamed Mountbatten for the running down of the Naval Intelligence services. They were the equals of, if not superior to, MI6. The service gathered vital Naval intelligence, which if it had been used properly would have more than justified its existence and the cost retaining such an organisation. As has been said, sometimes the people, who seem to love flirting with treachery, or simply delight in intrigue, either switch sides or play along with both.

While Mountbatten was focused on the dissemination of Naval intelligence he had the opposite view of Soviet intelligence organisations, as in his opinion of Lavrenti Beria, the head of the NKVD and Chairman of the Ministry of Internal Affairs (MVD), about whom he said:

"Beria is the man to do business with in Russia."

For those who are unfamiliar with Lavrenti Pavlovich Beria it is relevant to provide an overview of the man who was described as the grandfather of the KGB. He was an early Bolshevik and was given his first intelligence job by Lenin. In the *Dictionary of Espionage*, Christopher Dobson and Ronald Payne describe him:

"From 1921, until the end of his days his entire working career was taken up with the business of conspiracy, espionage-both internal and external, murder and execution. Among his first tasks when Stalin appointed him head of the KGB (it was then called the NKVD - People's Commissariat for Internal Affairs) was to arrange the execution of his predecessor, Nicolai Yezhof...under Beria's control, the KGB became a state within a state, with its own uniformed army and police force, spies, executioners and death squads. It was in charge of industries, labour camps, and publishing enterprises...the KGB became a sought-after privilege for the brightest and most ambitious young men, for though membership carried obvious risks of denunciation and death at the slightest suspicion of treachery, it also offered promise of social advantage, wealth and prestige...Beria worked on the principle that soldiers should be more afraid of the secret police than of the enemy; as a reward he became a Marshal of the Soviet Union. Although feared, he made many enemies, and even though he was among the most powerful men in the Soviet Union when Stalin died in 1953, Khruschev...in a swift and daring pre-emptive move...managed to arrest him and then have him shot. Following his death his infamous NKVD was renamed the KGB."

Of course the main factor is that this was the man that Mountbatten identified as the person with whom he could work. Perhaps it is best summed up by commentators who said that it was a combination of vanity, egotism and a compulsive urge always to get his own way, regardless of others, which caused Mountbatten to become an agent of influence. Often it appeared in favour of the Soviet Union.

The authors of *War of the Windsors* focus on another factor that runs through Mountbatten's career from the earliest days. It is described as a seething hatred of Britain which is said to stem from the humiliating treatment bestowed on his father, his family and himself during the World War I. His father was stripped of his princely status and forced to change his name from Battenburg to Mountbatten. It is alleged that the young Mountbatten held a great desire to teach the British a lesson and that would have been evident through his support for everything Russian. However, he eventually had real influence in 1955 when he attained his 40-year-old ambition and became First Sea Lord. It was a post from which his father had been forced to resign at the beginning of the World War I.

The First Sea Lord is the top job of the Royal Navy; they are the operational head and Chief of Staff, directly answerable to the First Lord of the Admiralty, the Government Minister responsible for the Navy. Commentators identified that there was much interest in the fact that he held the post while concerns were raised, particularly in the USA, but in other countries also, that Mountbatten was an agent for the Soviet Union. If there was sound evidence to support the claims then his promotion to such a high level job was extremely dangerous. The position placed him at the forefront of Britain's defence policy and planning, providing him with access to the most sensitive of national secrets. As commentators make the claims, there is no denial from any quarter, and with such damning statements there should have been some comment.

The question asked by the American CIA is why was someone who was known to associate with Communists and left-wing sympathisers, including, as it happens, his own wife, who was under suspicion in the United States, was allowed to hold such an important post? The British security services knew that he readily associated with homosexuals and that he was an advocate of friendly relations with the Soviet Union.

There is a quote in *War of the Windsors* from in 1956, where Mountbatten stated:

*'If I were Prime Minister I'd go to Moscow tomorrow to meet Khrushchev...
I know they killed all my family but that mustn't stand in the way of getting on
with them now.'*

This was done at the height of the Cold War. In fact Churchill, who
was returned to power as Prime Minister in the general election of
1951, raised the matter with Mountbatten about his 'left-wing' opinions
and associations. However, the Americans went further, and denounced
him as a Marxist.

Richard Deacon, in *The Greatest Treason,* identified that in the early
days of World War II the Americans were worried about Mountbatten
on two counts: first, that he might be in the camp of the appeasers and
would play a role in a compromise peace with Germany.

Deacon also points out that when Mountbatten was identified as a
possible security risk, both in America and Britain, there was no
enthusiasm in Britain for a detailed investigation. This was despite the
fact that American, French and other security services produced
evidence to his having pro-Soviet sympathies. The response in Britain
was that he was a World War II hero whose integrity was beyond
question.

The security service would not consider confronting Mountbatten
because such an action would create a major scandal. Being 'British',
nobody was prepared to go that far. True to form, the fear was more
about what they would uncover. As Deacon further identified, the
Americans had knowledge of information being passed to the Russians.
They could not understand how Mountbatten, a homosexual and
companion to Peter Murphy (see below) could have been in the
military and hold such sensitive positions.

Deacon quotes a CIA source:

*"What we could never understand was how Mountbatten, a known
homosexual and therefore a security risk, managed to achieve the kind of
promotion and jobs he got."*

In the mid-1950s Mountbatten was in secret contact with the Soviet Ministry of Defence. The Naval Attaché in Moscow, Captain Geoffrey Bennett, who handled the correspondence, revealed this to Richard Deacon. According to Bennett, Mountbatten not only disclosed his hostility to US foreign policy to the Russians, in one letter he even stated bluntly that in the event of a war between Russia and the USA: "I should be on the side of the USSR".

This is an unbelievable statement, especially coming from a high-ranking NATO officer. Crabb disappeared in 1956, which was during the period when Mountbatten was probably most active in co-operating with the Soviet Union.

In *The Greatest Treason,* it is identified that at least one, if not two dangerous informants to the USSR were inside the Admiralty. Suspicion rested on two senior British Naval officers who had worked under NATO, one an admiral, the other a captain. This was confirmed to the Americans by the defector, Anatoli Golitisin, who claimed that he had seen photocopies of three extremely secret British Naval plans and stated:

"It was said that the CIA had considerable evidence pointing to a senior officer in the Royal Navy, who had passed information to the Russians. There was some firm evidence that Lord Mountbatten was himself mixed up in all this and was instrumental in playing down the idea of spies in the Admiralty. He kept dismissing our raising of the matter as "American hysteria" and it would seem that some in MI5 fell for his anti-Americanism. What the Americans could never understand was how Mountbatten, a known homosexual and therefore a security risk, managed to achieve the kind of promotion and jobs he got and asked the question as to whether he was ever positively vetted?"

There is evidence that Colonel Mikhail Goleniewski referred to Mountbatten's friendship with Blunt and what he called 'the Soviet Agents Club' at Buckingham Palace. Goleniewski explained that to find out if Mountbatten was passing intelligence to the Soviets, he was made privy to information about the infiltration of the Red Army by the Chinese. Goleniewski reported:

"One of the leading members of the Imperial Underground in western Europe elaborated a plan to use this information in other ways and to make a test to see if Lord Mountbatten was involved in cooperation with the Soviets or not... this information was brought to the attention of Lord Mountbatten through one of his close contacts, and in a way concealing the real task of this operation."

The objective was to find out whether Mountbatten would pass on this intelligence of Chinese infiltration of the Red Army to the Soviets. If he did this, it was calculated that the Soviets would take immediate action. A report followed that four generals who had been mentioned in the Information about Chinese infiltration of the Red Army died or disappeared. It was found that the action was as a result of information that Mountbatten had received in complete confidentiality.

Defenders of Mountbatten will immediately dismiss Goleniewski's allegations as disinformation or imaginative nonsense. But it should be remembered that information he provided led to the uncovering of Philby, Blake, Heinz Felfe the West German traitor, Colonel Israel Beer of Israel, Stig Wennerstrom the Swedish air attache in Washington and many other spies in Britain, the USA and other parts of Europe.

It appears from what the various commentators record that Mountbatten had a complete disregard for all our allies and focused on our enemy at the time, the USSR. Whatever help he gave to the Soviet cause was cautiously done without allowing him to be linked directly to any particular Soviet network. There was another event, not connected to Crabb, but that focuses on Mountbatten's activities at the time.

With information drawn from the web site *Thunder-and-Lightnings* and other contributors on the the internet it was in 1951 that the Warsaw Pact air forces were being equipped with large numbers of

MiG-15s which provided a considerable threat to the aircraft of the Royal Air Force. To counter this threat the Ministry of Supply issued a specification for a new bomber and reconnaissance aircraft. The requirements were very demanding and called for an aircraft capable of delivering a 6-ton nuclear weapon over a combat radius of 1,500 miles at low level and at high subsonic speed. There also had to be a reconnaissance version with a high specification. What was sought was an aircraft so advanced that it was thought impossible to achieve at the time. However, the British Aircraft Corporation (BAC) provided a design for the TSR-2. It was designed to penetrate a well-defended forward battle area at low altitudes and very high speeds, and then attack high-value targets in the rear with close-in bomb runs and precision drops. The TSR-2 included a number of advanced features that made it the highest performing aircraft in its proposed role. The performance of the prototypes was very impressive and the figures would make impressive reading today. The aircraft was of a design and concept that was way beyond its years. It would very probably through a number of upgrades be flying today. A prototype is kept at the Imperial War Museum, Duxford and does not look out of place with our most modern combat aircraft. At the height of the Cold War, this aircraft would have provided a credible and cost effective aircraft with considerable export potential for long term defence or attack against potential aggressors.

The failure of the TSR-2 to enter service was alleged to be due in part to the efforts of the then Chief of the Defence Staff (CDS), Lord Louis Mountbatten. He was against its development and had become famous within the industry for placing ten photographs of a Buccaneer aircraft on a desk followed by a single picture of a TSR-2, and then stating that you could buy ten Buccaneers for the price of a single TSR-2. The vast difference in capability between the two aircraft did not enter into the debate, nor the long term costs or indeed the defence of the realm. It was to be, in part, the end of world class military aircraft design and development for Britain. The damage was deep and in the end very costly.

A BAC delegation had visited Australia and left with high expectations of an export order for the TSR-2; the Australians were very interested in the new superior aircraft. Mountbatten became involved, but because of his negative attitude the Australians lost interest in the TSR-2 and the export prospects disappeared. In addition to Mountbatten's activities, the Labour party, whilst in opposition, were making it very clear that they would cancel the project if they were elected. They were elected and that is what they did.

On 6 April 1965 Harold Wilson's Labour Government cancelled the TSR-2 project. All airframes were scrapped. All tooling was destroyed; on the production line, as workers completed assembly of some airframes prior to their transport to the scrap yard, the tooling was being destroyed with cutting torches behind them. A wooden mockup of the TSR-2 was burned in front of the workers. All technical publications were ordered to be destroyed; even photographs of the aircraft were destroyed. Boscombe Down's official records of test flights were 'lost'.

If the allegations that Mountbatten and Wilson had 'affiliations' to the Soviet Union are correct then the 6 April 1965 was a red letter day for both men and for the Soviet Union. The Australians chose to buy the much inferior US F-111, which cost them 10 times more than they had been told and was to be 10 years late into service. The UK lost its leadership in military aviation and had to order some aircraft which never entered service in the UK and cost a fortune in contract cancellation fees. A mixture of inferior, expensive aircraft filled the gap. How many billions that has cost the UK is not known, but at least the leaders in the Kremlin would have been very happy.

In 1964, Marcus Lipton, Labout MP for Brixton, submitted new evidence to Harold Wilson, the Prime Minister. The information was based on statements made by a high ranking official who was linked with British and American intelligence. The evidence was that British Intelligence had received information some seven years previously that Crabb was in Russia. Wilson studied the report before deciding not to make a statement. How strange! The Labour Party, when in opposition created mayhem in Parliament at the time of Crabb's disapperance but would not say anything when they had the opportunity.

* * *

A number of books identify that Peter Murphy was a major influence in Mountbatten's life. This relationship spanned back to the mid-1920s and was described as his closest relationship. Without any formal position on Mountbatten's staff, Murphy had always been around, apart from when Mountbatten was at sea. It is said that Peter Murphy had been openly and unashamedly a Marxist when he first met Mountbatten at Cambridge and never wavered in his allegiance. Not only was Murphy a Communist and pro-Soviet, he was also known to be promiscuously homosexual. This would have made him a high security risk because he would have been susceptible to blackmail.

Robin Bryans throws some light on the status of Murphy by explaining that John Brabourne, husband of Mountbatten's daughter Patricia, said:

"Few people actually knew what Murphy's role was in Dickie's life, but his real position was a sounding board. He was brilliant at spotting mistakes in something that Dickie was planning, and he wasn't afraid to speak up. Dickie would show him a letter he had drafted and Peter would read it and say what he thought the reaction of the recipient would be."

In 1952 MI5 investigated Murphy at Mountbatten's instigation because of the increasing focus of the American's allegations. The investigation outcome is said to have cleared Murphy as there was no hard evidence that he was either working for the Communist Party or for the Soviet Union. This was of little surprise considering the state of the British security services at the time.

Robin Bryans told us that there had long been concerns about the Mountbattens. He recounted an incident that occurred in 1934 when evidence was given in New York's Supreme Court about a family photograph album belonging to the family. It contained pictures that included children indulging in sado-masochism, homosexuality and bestiality. He further explained that Mountbatten only married Edwina for her vast fortune. On the face of it they were a married couple, but Mountbatten had his live-in friend, Peter Murphy. Murphy had been in the Guards and then at Cambridge with Mountbatten, where they became great friends. Murphy played a very important and influential part in Mountbatten's life.

In interview, Robin Bryans told us that Mountbatten wrote letters that one would not expect a man in his position to do. Mountbatten had asked Driberg, a Socialist MP, to show Prince Phillip around the House of Commons and introduce him to Labour MPs, and on the 14 August 1946 Mountbatten wrote to Driberg thanking him for being kind to his nephew Phillip. He explained that Phillip was thrilled with the day in the house and expressed the view that Phillip was impressed with Driberg. Then in a letter dated 3 August 1947 he wrote to Driberg, thanking him for sticking up for his nephew, Prince Phillip, The Duke of Edinburgh. While letters written by Mountbatten to Driberg and others could be considered rather reckless, it was other letters that gave the greatest cause for concern, as they were addressed to the Soviet Union.

Bryans told us that Driberg had much in common with Mountbatten including a sexual preference for men. He lived in a top flat, opposite Dil De Rohn which overlooked the entrance to the underground gents lavatory. It was here we are told that Driberg procured companions for his homosexual exploits. Also involved in this 'circle' of associates was Anthony Blunt.

Robin Bryans explained that another friend of Mountbatten was an unnamed sailor who was an active member of a paedophile ring. Because of the implications of who knew what, two people had to be silenced, one was the sailor and the other was Robin Bryans. He explains that the sailor disappeared rapidly with a long prison sentence for the sole purpose of silencing him. Bryans was also meant to disappear, but things went wrong and he survived to remain free. He made it very clear to us that Mountbatten did not indulge in girls, only in boys. He further stated that Queen Elizabeth became concerned about reports that the sailor friend had left prison and was talking about old times with Mountbatten. The sailor referred to events that the Admiral of the Fleet had done and places that no Admiral ought to have been to.

Whilst Mountbatten was, on the face of the allegations against him, a potentially serious security risk, he continued to maintain an anti American position. One of the most puzzling of Mountbatten's 'fantasy' stories concerning the disappearance of Crabb was the photocopy of a remarkable letter said to have been written by Mountbatten. It was in the possession of Pat Rose, Crabb's fiancée. It is interesting in that, in all the hours we spent talking to her and the letters and photographs she provided to us, the matter of Mountbatten's letter was never raised. Pat had passed it to Richard Deacon prior to our being involved with her.

On one point however, she was adamant; that Deacon would not quote her on the Mountbatten letter in her lifetime. As she is no longer alive he felt free to set the record straight. Certainly the story has all the elements of fantasy; apparently Crabb was not spying on the Russians, but taking part in a security operation to protect Krushchev and Bulganin against possible sabotage by the Americans. When he made his search under the Soviet ships he discovered American produced limpet mines attached to them. Crabb is supposed to have died while trying to remove the mines, his death being due to the failure of his equipment.

A similar but slightly different account of the Crabb disappearance was given to Derek Jameson in 1986. The story was reported in *Jameson's Week* in the *Today* newspaper, dated 29 March 1986, under the headline 'I spy the signs of a cover up'. He wrote about being shown a letter which was supposedly written by Mountbatten, marked Most Secret. It gave permission for the story to be told one day. Christopher Creighton visited Derek Jameson and produced the letter. Creighton is not his real name and he refuses to have his photograph taken. Creighton told Jameson:

"Crabb died in my arms." He continued:

"It was exactly 0805 hours on the 19th on King's Stairs jetty, only yards from Nelson's Victory in Portsmouth".

He said that Crabb was not spying on the Russians but taking part in a security operation directed by Naval Intelligence to protect the Soviet leaders against any embarrassing incidents. The story continues to say that when he made a sweep under the Soviet craft he made an astonishing discovery. There were American manufactured limpet mines attached to the warships. Creighton, on the spot as an RN Captain in intelligence, claims that Crabb killed himself in a heroic effort to remove the mines. Creighton explained that towards the end, totally exhausted, his equipment failed and he was rushed ashore dying of oxygen poisoning. What of the mines? It was all part of a plot directed by hard-line elements in the KGB to get rid of the all-powerful Krushchev, according to Creighton who explained that the whole thing was covered up by Mountbatten, acting on Eden's orders. When it all went wrong the Premier took the view that it was not in Britain's interests to reveal the facts.

The story continues to explain that Crabb's body was held for five days, and then dumped at sea after a navigation officer weighed up the tides and worked out that ultimately it would be washed up in the Chichester area. Jameson asked the inevitable question: what is the explanation for the letter written by Mountbatten from his country home at Broadlands authorising Creighton to tell this remarkable story? There was no answer.

It is obvious that Creighton knows nothing about military diving, mine warfare or security. The first point is the location of the Soviet warships, which were not in a very accessible location for combat swimmers to undertake an underwater swimmer attack carrying limpet mines. However, it would not have been impossible. Could the KGB have undertaken such an operation? Remember, the Soviets in 1956 were years behind the West in underwater operations and equipment. Could it have been the Americans? What would have been the purpose? To damage Mountbatten's standing and position, a man they had concerns about? The real issue is that the number of mines that would be required to cause enough damage to the cruiser to actually kill Kruschev would have removed half, if not all of Portsmouth That would have most importantly, required dozens of divers to place them. It is also relevant that the sheer size of a cruisers hull makes an underwater search by one diver impossible. When searching the underside of a ship, a team of divers is used and they work to a dedicated search pattern. If a mine is found there are procedures for its removal, because limpet mines are fitted with anti removal devices. Crabb would have known how to search for a mine and even how to remove it, but he could never have done this on his own.

Another most important aspect is that we are expected to believe that there would be an underwater attack on a Soviet warship in Portsmouth. The success of any such attack would have threatened world peace, so would the Navy have allowed such an exploit? The answer is a simple no. Creighton says that Crabb was totally exhausted, but rushed ashore, dying of oxygen poisoning. Crabb could safely operate to a depth of 10 metres using oxygen-breathing equipment. This means that he could have worked under the ship quite safely, without contracting oxygen poisoning, and 10 metres is not a rigid depth, as experienced divers have worked deeper. A failure of the equipment could have produced carbon dioxide poisoning, and Crabb would have been aware of the symptoms, and taken action to surface. He could have received a cocktail from water mixing with the carbon dioxide absorbent, and again from experience he would have known what to do. In fact if he had been in real trouble, he would have become unconscious and sunk to the bottom. In that situation he could not have saved himself and so his body would have been washed out to sea or further up river with the movement of the tide.

A twist comes following an investigation into Creighton's past exploits. Gary Murray undertook it on behalf of publishing clients and, whilst he did not disclose any details of his findings, he did say that the story was part of Creighton's dream world. We were told that Creighton had been awarded the Victoria Cross, but could not be recognised as having the award as it would expose his real identity. On that basis alone his 'letter of evidence' could be discounted.

Another story that was raised from the ashes, only to disappear as quickly as it rose, involves the Ministry of Defence supposedly investigating the controversial war record of Lord Mountbatten. Sonia Purnell wrote in the *Daily Mail* on 7 April 1999 that veterans of *HMS Jackal*, a destroyer under his command in World War II, had demanded to know what happened to ringleaders of a mysterious mutiny against him in 1941. The fear is that they were taken from the ship and shot. The article quotes crewman John Draper, 80, who said:

"There are a lot of rumours about what happened. It is time we knew the truth."

It was 1941 when HMS Jackal helped defend Plymouth by turning its anti-aircraft guns on incoming German planes. The air raids on mainland Plymouth were clearly seen from the destroyer, which was very distressing for the crewmen, largely from the area, who had to watch their homes being destroyed. The article quotes veteran Jo Lewis, 74, of Cardiff, who added:

"The Plymouth men were desperate. They wanted to go ashore, but they weren't allowed."

The problem was that the men wanted to check on their families, but instead Mountbatten ordered his ship out to sea. The ratings protested by slamming the watertight doors and refusing to obey orders, eventually forcing Mountbatten to relent. But when *HMS Jackal* reached Gibraltar a few weeks later, the mutiny ringleaders were flown home and never seen again by their shipmates. The MoD is now examining its records, which, unusually, have not yet been released to the public 58 years later, leading some veterans to suggest a cover-up to protect Mountbatten's reputation.

In *Blitz and Account of Hitler's Aerial War over Plymouth in March 1941*, Gerald Wasley states:

"*On 22 March,* HMS Jackal *having sailed up the Hamoaze to ammunition the ship, returned to the dockside at Devonport. It was then the crew informed the First Lieutenant that they wanted a promise of shore leave before they went back on station. The watertight doors were locked in the face of the naval Officers, who ordered the men to come on deck for 'leaving harbour' stations. Lord Louis Mountbatten was informed of the mutiny. This stalemate lasted until the late afternoon, when the crew were granted their shore leave. When the men went ashore some were to find their homes destroyed and relatives dead or injured. No court martial was held. However, two days later the destroyer put into Dartmouth harbour, just along the coast. It was here, as one of the crew recalled, 'some of the men left the ship and were never seen again by their shipmates'. It was assumed they had been transferred.*"

The search for the truth spread to Gibraltar, where is was claimed that the men left the ship. The following article was published in 2003 in *Gibraltar News – Panorama*:

"*Plymouth campaigners are appealing to the Chief Minister of Gibraltar to help solve perhaps one of the biggest mysteries of the Second World War and the 'disappearance' of Westcountry shipmates from the Rock nearly 62 years ago this month. City residents are demanding the MoD finally reveals the truth about the fate of Plymothians who 'disappeared' after a mutiny in Plymouth Sound.*"

One veteran said before he died recently:

"Some of the men left the ship and were never seen again by their shipmates".

Kevin Kelway, spokesman for the Plymouth Party said:

"This month marks the 62nd anniversary of the firebombing of Plymouth. And the 62nd anniversary of the uprising against the Queen's uncle Louis Mountbatten, who was in command of the 5th flotilla which included the Jackal. City residents are calling on the Chief Minister of Gibraltar to help find out if the rumours and speculation are true or not? The Rock is where the mystery of the Jackal ends and the time for openness, and transparency by the MOD must surely be now?"

There is clearly some confusion as to when and where the men left the ship. It is evident that the men did leave and there appears to be no records available. The one fact that can be certain is that if the men were removed from the ship and some form of severe punishment was administered, such as being executed, it will never be made public and it must not be a surprise.

Frank Goldsworthy, having retired from being a front line newspaper reporter, was on hand when the Cabinet Papers were made public at the end of thirty years. He reported to us with the following note:

"There is a blank space in the 1956 British Cabinet minutes disclosed this week. It indicates that another 70 years must pass before the British public can be told who sent George Medallist frogman Commander Lionel "Buster" Crabb to spy under the Russian warships which brought Russian leaders Marshall Bulganin and Premier Kruuschev to Britain in 1956."

An official note states that Item One, as an exception to the normal

30-year rule, is to remain "closed" until the year 2057. The main issue in the note is the *who,* and of course details of the events. At the time of the incident, the 'scapegoats' in the security services were named and replaced. That means we may determine that the *who* was not a member of the secret service. Evaluating the names of those who have been mentioned and the positions held, the list of the *who* is very limited. In fact it is so limited that, as alleged by many commentators, the *who,* was Mountbatten. The confirmation and detail as to whether he sent Crabb or assisted in him going to the other side remains the unanswered question. It will remain unanswered, not until 2056 but forever.

17

Crabb's Return?

Whoever treadeth on this stone I pray you tread most neatly for underneath this stone do lie your honest friend...

Anonymous 1683

Milton Cemetery near Portsmouth is a large place and we had entered the office to enquire as to the location of the grave of Commander Crabb. We were shown a map and direction to the row. The staff at the cemetery had obviously encountered many other visitors to the grave, as they had no need to check the records. While we stood at the graveside we became aware that an individual was standing in a distant tree line observing and photographing us. Because he was standing amidst the trees we could not identify who it was. There was no option but to ignore the observer. The grave headstone gave nothing away and before we left, we photographed it. It offered no tangible evidence, but was supposed to be the end of the story. At the time it was the start of our research and the revelations about the body were yet to be uncovered.

We had obtained a photograph of the grave following Crabb's burial and laid it beside the photograph that we had taken on our visit. The original photograph showed the headstone as being dirty and displaying the stains of weathering, which had left marks running from the words of the inscription. The grave had an oblong surround. The headstone in the photograph that we had taken was new, white and with no weathering stains and did not have the surround. As we analysed the photographs we found that not only was the headstone new and clean, but also the inscription was different. It had been altered.

Crabb's mother originally had the headstone inscribed:

IN
EVER LOVING MEMORY
OF
MY SON
COMMANDER CRABB
AT REST AT LAST

This was a very strange epitaph from a mother to a son, as it omitted his Christian names, naval service, decorations and date. She placed that inscription, because she didn't believe that it was her son Lionel buried there.

The new headstone gave dramatic new evidence because it read:

IN
LOVING MEMORY
OF MY SON
COMMANDER
LIONEL CRABB
RNVR GM OBE
AT REST AT LAST
1956

There it was, his rank, Christian name, service and awards. What had happened to cause the change? What message was to emerge from this, because people do not change a headstone without very good reason and there were no really close relatives? Certainly none that we identified would have gone to that trouble.

A Portsmouth newspaper, which had interviewed us following the publication of *Frogman Spy,* published an article on February 16, 1990 about Commander Crabb with a photograph of Crabb's headstones. Apparently the newspaper had published a photograph in 1974, but it was not the same as the current headstone. In a letter to the newspaper a Mr. Lee had taken a photograph in 1985, and when he compared the two he noticed striking differences. The photographs we had were cropped to include the headstone and wording on them. Mr. Lee had a photograph that showed more of the background and states that the 1974 photograph shows the headstone with the *Good Companions* public house visible in the background. But the photographs taken in 1985 and 1990 show the headstone with Milton Road and factories in the background. This is a turn of 180 degrees. Mr. Lee was asking why and when the re-positioning took place.

We had already asked the question when we first contacted the cemetery office to find out why the headstone surround had been removed, leaving only the headstone. It was explained that as a part of a general 'tidy-up' of the cemetery, all additions to graves were being removed, providing permission was given. The owner of the grave gave permission in 1974. We also discovered that the authorities were always concerned that if the headstone remained on the grave of an unknown person, then there remained the possibility, no matter how tenuous, of an exhumation to confirm either way if it was Crabb. To avoid any risk of that occurring it was easier to move the headstone to a new location, which is what they did.

The first part of the puzzle was to identify that in 1981, Barrell's of Portsmouth were commissioned to remove the headstone from Milton Cemetery and take it to their workshops. There, the face was skimmed off and the remainder of the stone cleaned. They then re-inscribed the sparkling white stone with the new inscription. It was taken back to the cemetery and replaced on the grave. The question remained as to who made the commission and why?

Burrell's would not divulge the identity but we eventually

discovered that it was a relation Mrs. Walsh. It was a name that had never been mentioned before. She had been close to Beatrice Crabb, his mother, and after her death took over the responsibility of looking after the grave. She made an arrangement with the cemetery officials to have the grave maintained and have flowers placed on it twice a year, but never visited the grave and so was never identified, as all communication was undertaken by post.

In 1981, the 25th anniversary of Crabb's disappearance, there was renewed interest in the grave to the extent that the cemetery authorities wrote to Mrs. Walsh. They told her that they had received numerous enquiries as to the identity of the person who was maintaining the grave. She declined to be identified and, as instructed they continued to refuse to pass on any information.

We eventually located the woman's son, the Rt Reverend Jeremy Walsh, the former Bishop Suffragan of Tewkesbury. He informed us that in 1981 an unnamed official contacted her and wanted to visit, as he had something important to tell her. He told us that although he was in the house at the time of the visit, he was not privy to the conversation. It was important enough that following that visit she had the headstone removed, re-inscribed and replaced. Why did she do this and who was the visitor? These are questions that she will never be able to answer for she died at the age of 87.

The Rev Walsh said in the *Portsmouth News*:

"My mother felt she should add his decorations to the inscription on the grave stone in Milton Cemetery, but this in no way was meant to acknowledge that the remains buried are the remains of Buster Crabb".

In discussions with the Rev Walsh, having photographed the medals for us, he asked where they could be placed and exhibited. We suggested the Royal Naval Museum and so in 1997 he presented them to be displayed in the Royal Naval Submarine and Diving Museum.

However, the question remains, if the body that was buried in Milton Cemetery was not that of Commander Crabb, then whose was it? Was Commander Crabb buried in 1981, in secret, with only the headstone change as a clue of our man coming in from the cold?

* * *

It was in 1981 when an Aeroflot aircraft touched down at London's Heathrow airport. It was a scheduled flight from Moscow and had arrived on time. At the stand, passengers offloaded through the mobile gantry while baggage handlers' offloaded luggage. There were small items of cargo, identified as being classified 'diplomatic'. This was always of interest to MI5, but they could only watch, record and speculate on the contents. It was part of the diplomatic game between East and West.

On this day, waiting at the aircraft close by the baggage handlers were two members of MI5. They stood with two members of the Soviet Embassy. Also waiting close by, almost hidden from view was an unmarked black van. Two passengers from the aircraft joined the four men. They were members of the KGB. They all acknowledged each other and then waited. The Soviets huddled together and in deep conversation. The last item to be carefully lifted from the aircraft was a simple black coffin. One of the MI5 officers signalled to the driver of the van to join them. The driver put it into gear and drove the vehicle towards the small group and the coffin. He turned the van and carefully reversed it to the conveyor and the waiting coffin. One of the KGB men handed the senior MI5 officer a piece of paper, which he wanted signed.

The text was in Russian and English but that did not matter because the MI5 officer was fluent in Russian. It was merely a document to confirm transfer of the coffin and its contents from the Russians to the British. A signature was applied and the paper was handed back. The KGB man then handed over an envelope, which he stated contained the medical records and other papers relating to the deceased. Then the coffin was lifted and put into the van. It was an operation completed quietly, efficiently and with dignity. Once the formalities were completed the two KGB men departed to re-board the aircraft. The two Soviet officials departed in their official car. The van departed on the next part of the journey, with the two MI5 officers following in an unmarked car.

The coffin began its journey in Czechoslovakia, following a telephone call from the Imperial Sanatorium at Karlovy Vary to the KGB Head Quarters in Moscow. The message was simple; Korablov is dead, followed by a code. The message meant nothing to the KGB officer who answered the telephone, but he knew what to do when hearing the code. It was a high level message and had to be acted upon immediately. He wrote the message on the appropriate form and called a member of staff to deliver it to the appropriate official at once. A senior member of the KGB read the message and asked his assistant to obtain the file that the code referred to. When it was delivered he read the opening brief, which gave him sufficient information upon which to act. This was political and above his level of responsibility and he had to consult with others at the highest level, which he did without delay.

The Soviet political masters reviewed the options. They could use the situation to embarrass the British, but it could reflect badly on them. The outcome they reached was that they accepted the request. It was in the form of a letter which was written by a former senior British naval officer who had links to senior Party members in the Soviet Union. He had been most helpful in a number of matters and had been in command of the deceased when he was spirited out of Britain. The decision was made and the KGB set the wheels in motion that would enable the process of repatriation of the body to Britain.

The head of medicine at the Imperial Sanatorium was directed by the KGB to prepare the body for transfer to Moscow as a matter of urgency. He was directed that the medical records pertaining to the deceased must accompany the body. Doing things in secret and linked to Moscow and in particular the KGB, was not new at the Imperial. It was imperative that all records of the existence of the man departed with him. The deceased body was prepared and dressed in a simple black suit and placed in a black coffin. Once in place the lid was secured and, along with the document file, was transported from Karlovy Vary to Prague's Ruzyne airport for the flight to Moscow. It was an unremarkable event and as the coffin departed the Imperial everybody returned to business. KGB matters were not something to discus with anybody.

The KGB in Moscow communicated with the Soviet Embassy in London and, through the appropriate coding system, transmitted the information about the deceased and the plan to repatriate the body. It would be done very quickly so as not to allow the British time to debate the situation. Their man was going home and that was that. If they argued then the media may well be advised of the fact that in 1956 the most senior naval person in the Royal Navy was involved in the affair and there was a letter to prove it. The next phase was for a meeting to be arranged between a Soviet official and a member of MI5. Emphasis was placed on the urgency and importance of the meeting. When the two met it was polite and very much to the point. The Soviet official handed over a file, which the MI5 officer took and opened. Whilst he scanned the documents the Soviet official explained that, in 1956, a British naval frogman was with the help of a very high ranking naval officer, spirited aboard a Soviet warship in Portsmouth harbour and taken to the Soviet Union, where he remained behind the 'Iron Curtain' until his recent death in Czechoslovakia.

The MI5 officer reflected on what was said and considered the implications for the Soviets of a British frogman captured in a British port and held until he died. Did he defect or was he kidnapped? It appeared that he was sent on an impossible mission. The Soviet official anticipated any potential response and told the MI5 officer to examine the letter. The letter, written in green ink, was addressed to a very senior Soviet official and dated 1956. It stated that, as had been agreed, Commander Crabb was to be returned to the United Kingdom having been a valuable asset to the Soviet Union. Suitable arrangements would be made to allow this to occur without harm being done to either side. Should the writer of the letter or Crabb die before this was achieved, then his body should be returned for burial. It expressed an understanding that secrecy was paramount so as not to implicate either side or expose them to media investigations. The name at the bottom caused the MI5 officer to look up at the Soviet official. He stated that the letter was genuine. The MI5 officer was shocked but attempted not to give his concerns away. In the battle of 'cat and mouse', the Soviet official was relishing the discomfort of his opposite number. After a suitable pause the Soviet official said the body was on its way from Czechoslovakia to Moscow and then it would be transferred to a flight to London. It was planned to be on the scheduled Moscow/London flight in two days. The Soviet Government considered that the arrangements gave sufficient time for the British to prepare. Under the circumstances the MI5 officer had no comment to make and, as he had senior people to report to, the meeting was concluded.

Departmental rivalries were swept away when some Members of Parliament, senior legal figures and senior officers of MI5, MI6 and the Ministry of Defence converged for a meeting. As is normal when a very real problem arrives that could be a political 'hot potato', each department wanted to offload it to another. That was unless there was some glory to be gained. With the story laid before them all that could be seen was trouble. MI5 thought the Navy should deal with the body and the Navy considered it to be an MI5 or MI6 matter. Those representing MI5 stated that it was the then head of the Royal Navy who arranged for Crabb to 'go to the Soviets', so they should clear up the mess. The Navy declared that the operation in Portsmouth was done under the umbrella of MI5 and not the Navy. MI6 stated that the operation was undertaken in the UK and was not their problem. It was decided that, because of the *modus operandi* of MI5, they were the only department that was able to handle the acceptance of the deceased and arrange for the body to be identified, based upon all records that were still held. Once confirmation was made that the body was that of Crabb, they would have a secret burial.

It was identified that there was one major problem that had to be dealt with. There was the one surviving member of the family who maintained the grave. It was a woman and the question was whether she should be told. This was considered by many in the room to be very unwise. However, discrete external enquires had been made and showed that, over the years, she had maintained silence about the grave. It had been decided at Ministerial level that she should be told, but nobody in the meeting was given a reason. It was going to be incumbent on the Royal Navy to meet with the woman and explain the circumstances of the situation. That said, a very narrow brief would be provided and there would be great emphasis placed on the fact that it was a matter under the Official Secrets Act and a matter of national security. To ensure consistency, MI5 would coordinate the entire operation.

A Royal Naval Captain responsible for Soviet Naval Intelligence was at his desk in the Ministry of Defence, Whitehall. A member of staff entered his office and handed him a file which had just arrived. It was sealed and marked Top Secret - Urgent. He opened the file and read the introductory note and then the letter written in green ink. He immediately realised the serious implications of what he had been handed. He called his assistant and enquired as to how the file had reached them. The assistant referred to the MI5 officer who was waiting. He had said that he would wait until the Captain had digested the contents of the file. He told his assistant to bring the MI5 officer into the office and whilst waiting he read the briefing note again. He was reflecting on the letter and its contents when the officer entered. The briefing note explained that Commander Crabb RNVR had disappeared whilst diving under a Soviet warship in Portsmouth harbour in 1956. It continued to describe the finding of a 'body' in the water at Chichester, the 'problems' regarding identification and the naval involvement in the MI5 'managed' inquest. The body was claimed to be Crabb and was buried at Portsmouth. It stated that further information was available if requested, but to note that it was held from public access under the 100 Year secrecy rule.

The situation that confronted the Captain was that Crabb did not die in 1956, but had done so recently in Czechoslovakia and his body was being returned as requested in the letter. Therefore, there was a need for joint cooperation between departments to expedite matters in the utmost secrecy. The two officers introduced themselves and after the usual pleasantries, they sat in the closed office and discussed the Crabb matter and the issues to be addressed. MI5 had identified that the grave was still tended by a relation of Crabb's. It was considered at the highest level for it to be appropriate that she be informed that the body of Crabb had been returned and was to be buried where the headstone currently stood. The Captain thought that it would be best to do what had to be done with the body and tell no one, not even the relation, however the MI5 officer explained that his department had been instructed at the very highest level to do otherwise. The plan was that once the body had been delivered and buried the Navy should inform the woman that Crabb's body had been returned following an operation of national importance.

Of course, no details of the 1956 operation and subsequent activities could be divulged. The officer stated that a full briefing note would be provided; detailing what could and could not be said. The Captain still considered it unwise, as they would have no control over what she might say or do. The MI5 officer concluded that the question was who would believe an elderly woman if she said that the body of Crabb, had secretly been brought home from the Soviet Union and buried in the cemetery, in the original grave? No, it was considered a safe option. If she did speak, the interest in Crabb was long gone, and, if required, the media could be managed at the highest level. They had managed the BBC when they wanted to raise potentially difficult matters. Whether Crabb was a defector or an honourable man, a hero, who was used and manipulated by a person of power and authority, was not discussed.

The Captain looked at the letter, its green ink and name at bottom, so distinctive. The MI5 officer gave a brief outline of what was proposed and said that he would contact the Captain with the briefing note and the official approval to make the visit. The Captain responded that he would await instructions.

The morgue was stark white with two table slabs where autopsies were undertaken. It was out of hours and the building was closed for normal business. Only a handful of selected people stood around the coffin, which was on a trolley waiting for the lid to be removed. The Home Office pathologist had been appointed and was well briefed with the object of identification of the body if possible. Cause of death was not important and there would not be an inquest. That had already been held in 1957. To assist the pathologist there were pre-1956 naval medical records and a selection of photographs of the missing man taken in the years leading up to his disappearance. A specialist artist had in great haste, used photographs to age the person to reproduce a likeness of what the man would look like 25 years on. Also present was an orthodontist who, likewise, had been briefed and was provided with what records were available. Both the pathologist and orthodontist were dealing with the records of a body some 25 years older than the records showed and both were under the umbrella of the Official Secrets Act. They were well aware of the security obligations and their part in the process. They had little to go on with regard to providing conclusive identification.

The lid was removed to reveal an insignificant, wizened elderly male dressed in a dark suit. With as much care as possible, the body was removed from the coffin and placed on a slab. The garments were cut away to reveal the naked body. The initial inspection identified that the nose was large and hooked; a feature enhanced because of the sunken cheeks. The man was short in height, which was in part due to his age, and he was uncircumcised. The big toes had been a major factor in the identification process and the naval records were compared to those of the body. There had been debate as to whether there was or was not any degree of bilateral hallux valgus, where the big toe was turned out. The feet had a slight deformity in the big toes. There were scars resulting from previous operations, probably when dealing with a serious illness.

A portable x-ray machine was brought in and both legs were x-rayed, as were the feet. Although the x-ray from the pre-1956 period was available, it had deteriorated and was of no use. However, the written medical report gave sufficient detail to indicate a previous fracture, and the new x-ray could be used to identify the status of the bones in the legs of the body.

It was reported that there were scars on the lower half of the body and the pathologist sought to locate them. Although the body changes with the passage of time, there was some trace of scars and a photographer moved in to record them. The pathologist recorded the exact location. It was evident that the scars were not going to provide conclusive evidence because of the overall deterioration of the body due to age and illness. However, they may help in the overall identification process. While the pathologist consulted the notes and compared them with what he had found in his initial examination, the orthodontist examined the mouth and teeth and compared his findings to those records that had been provided.

The pathologist and the orthodontist spent time away from the body and reviewed their respective findings. They compared what they found to that provided in the naval medical records. The x-rays were processed and brought to the morgue. The pathologist examined them and then compared them with the written record in the naval records. He found that the old fracture could be seen and matched the description in the notes. The orthodontist concluded that, although dental work had been done in the intervening years, as far as he could ascertain the dental records he had been provided with matched those of the deceased.

Those waiting for the process to be concluded could only watch as the examination proceeded. Time passed slowly, but what was required was a definitive answer one way or the other. The MI5 officer contemplated how they would deal with the situation if there was a negative outcome and the body was not Crabb. He would have been relieved when the pathologist told him that, to the best of their ability under the circumstances, the examination of the body matched the information they were provided with. With business concluded, the body was returned to the coffin and removed from the morgue. Placed in the back of the black van, it continued on the next part of its journey. The MI5 officer telephoned his superiors to confirm what they anticipated to be correct. They had the body of Commander Crabb.

The Local Government Official (LGO) responsible for cemeteries in the Portsmouth area received a telephone call from a Whitehall Government office. The caller identified himself as a member of the security services and requested an urgent meeting to be arranged. He could not give any details over the telephone, other than it was Top Secret and was covered by the Official Secrets Act. The LGO had never received such a phone call and considered that it may be an elaborate hoax. The meeting was to be in his office, so no harm done if it was a joke. The MI5 officer advised the LGO not to mention the telephone call or the meeting to anyone. At the time of the conversation Fuller, the MI5 officer, was en route to the official's office. Speed and secrecy was of the essence.

The LGO was in his office when he was informed that he had a visitor. He identified who it was and arranged for the MI5 officer to be shown to his office. After the initial identification and formalities, the MI5 officer proposed that, because of the confidential and security implications of the matter, it would be best if they left the building to discus matters. Having left the building the MI5 officer explained that the Government found itself in a potentially embarrassing position. To remedy the situation, an unusual course of action was to be followed.

It was made very clear that it fell under the umbrella of the Official Secrets Act. With the secrecy line drawn it was explained that the whole success of the operation lay with the LGO and it was naturally accepted that he would co-operate fully to assist HM Government and the Establishment.

The MI5 officer explained that there was a grave in Milton cemetery for a Commander Crabb. The LGO was aware of the grave, the story and the ongoing saga. The officer continued to explain that in 1957 a body was buried and the headstone erected to Commander Crabb. The original grave surround was removed and the location of the headstone was moved. The MI5 officer thought that the LGO would be aware of all of this. He was not, as this was down to local management and not an issue he would get involved with. The conversation continued and the MI5 officer stated that the body that had been buried was not Crabb. He did not elaborate further and the LGO did not enquire. The situation was that they now had his body and they needed to bury it. It was to be done at the site of the headstone and in total secrecy.

The LGO raised an issue in that the staff would know when they prepared the area and dug the grave. He thought this would cause people to speak and, as a result, gain unwanted media attention. The MI5 officer stated that none of the staff would be involved. It would be an MI5 controlled operation and they would arrange for people to do the job at night and in secrecy. The only person who would know would be the LGO. Because the operation would be done at night they required the LGO to provide them with access to the cemetery. This would mean opening the gates at a pre-determined time, then closing and locking them after the operation was completed. Should there be any unwelcome attention, then he would be in a position to be able to deal with it. He would also ensure that the staff carried out work away from the site of the grave for as long as possible. The LGO was considering what he would say to his family about being at work all night. Before departing, the MI5 officer stated that it would be Friday night and hoped that it did not interfere with any other arrangements, but it was, after all, a matter of national security. There was no opportunity for objections and they parted company, the LGO awaiting confirmation of date and time.

Whilst the black van and a mini bus headed towards the cemetery, the LGO had parked his car a short distance from the main gate in Milton Road. He checked his watch and then got out, and walked along the road where streetlights gave illumination. He had the key to the main gate in his pocket and in the spirit of the cloak and dagger nature of his being there; he had taken the precaution of wearing dark clothing. He unlocked the gate and pushed it open just far enough to allow him access. Once in, he pushed the gate closed. Consulting his watch again he waited until it was almost midnight. He went and opened both gates and stood back in the shadows to wait. Almost immediately the van and mini bus drove in, followed by a car. Looking to see if any other vehicle was coming, and determining that there was not, he quickly closed the gates. The vehicles moved into the cemetery and had switched off their lights. They slowly moved along the roadway that led to the main building, set near the entrance in the grounds. At the building the mini bus stopped, as did the car, leaving the van to continue along the roadway. When it reached the appropriate avenue it turned right, travelled a short distance and stopped. Meantime a team of men alighted the mini bus and walked to join the van. Two men got out of the car and in the darkness the LGO was just able to recognise one as the MI5 officer who had visited him. He was not introduced to the other person. He joined them and walked, without speaking, to join the others at the grave.

The passenger in the van got out and checked with the glow of a red torch beam the headstone. It was located alongside the avenue and close to the van. Once he confirmed the grave, he returned to open the back doors. Inside, apart from the black coffin, were the tools required for the night's operation. When the men arrived they placed screening from the van around the site, to hide what they were doing.

This was a precaution, even though they were in the middle of the cemetery where there was little chance of being spotted. Whilst that was being erected, others laid out a tarpaulin alongside the grave location to accommodate the pile of earth. Two wooden planks were laid either side of the grave area and the first of the turf was carefully cut. This was a critical job, as it had to be replaced and show no sign of having been tampered with. Once the turf had been removed, the men took it in turns to dig out the grave. It was hard work and seemed like a never-ending exercise. For all concerned, except the LGO, the cloak and dagger enterprise was normal and each person got on with the task in hand. Nobody spoke, apart from an occasional whisper of instruction as the task progressed. The LGO had had to reconcile with his family the fact that he was going to be out all night on official business. Of course he gave no hint at what the official business was.

Once the grave was dug down to a satisfactory depth the men moved to the van, and as quietly as possible, removed the coffin and took it to the grave. Others collected the ropes required to lower it. At the grave the coffin was lowered using the ropes to rest it in the bottom. The ropes were dropped down into the hole and the task of replacing the soil began. There were low whispers as some men said a few words over the grave. The MI5 officer, his companion and the LGO peered into the darkness but said nothing. As the soil was shovelled in it was compacted by men stamping on it, so as to reduce any settlement once they were gone. When the soil reached the top, the careful task of replacing the turf began. At the same time the remaining pile of soil, accounted for by the space taken by the coffin, was removed in buckets to be emptied into the van. Once the soil was cleared, the tarpaulin was removed, as were the planks of wood. It remained only for those laying the turf to continue with their task. Stiff bristled brooms were used to sweep away loose soil and blend the grass together where the turf was cut. The last part of the operation seemed to take an age but finally the area was deemed suitable. Then, using watering cans filled from a water supply in the van, they gave the area a soaking. The screen was quickly removed and loaded into the van. A check was made to ensure that the area was in good order and clear of tools. Once confirmation was made the men made their way back to the mini bus. The van passenger guided the vehicle back along the avenue, where it turned into the wider roadway then headed back to the main building.

Moving in the first sign of pending daylight, the van joined the other vehicles. The MI5 officer thanked the LGO for his assistance and got into the car. His colleague still didn't speak or acknowledge his presence. The small convoy was ready to go and the LGO opened the gates allowing the vehicles to move forward and out onto the road. They drove away, leaving the gates to be closed and locked. Once that was done, the LGO walked back to his car, tired and with a multitude of questions spinning in his head. He knew they would never be answered. He started his car and drove home.

On the Monday morning the LGO returned to the cemetery for a visit, a task he did at each cemetery during the year. He told them that he would just have a walkabout and did not want to disturb their activities. He noted that work was being done well away from the site of the grave, and he eventually wandered down the avenue and paused momentarily at the headstone. It was a relief to find that it was in good order. The men who worked on the job knew what they were doing which was the message he relayed to the MI5 officer. He was told that there was only a need to telephone again if anything untoward arose.

The lady did not hurry to answer the telephone, but when she did she heard a well-spoken male voice ask to speak to Mrs. Walsh. She acknowledged that it was her speaking. He gave his name and said that he was from the Admiralty. He told her that he wished to meet with her because he had some very important information. She enquired whether it was about Lionel, Lionel Crabb. The caller said that he could not speak on the telephone, but he could explain if they could meet. After considering the proposal she agreed, but said that her son would be at the house. A day and time were agreed.

She answered the door to greet the man from Whitehall. He was very courteous and showed her his identity, promulgating that he was a Captain in the Royal Navy. She invited him in and, as he entered, he noticed a man. She explained as he followed her into the sitting room, that it was her son. He did not join them. She asked if he would like tea, but he declined. He began by talking about secret operations in general and the dive at Portsmouth in 1956 in particular. He spoke of the disappearance of Commander Crabb and then of the body that was recovered at Chichester. He recounted the post mortem and the subsequent inquest and finally the burial at Milton Cemetery. She did not respond to any of this appraisal, but when he stopped speaking, she enquired as to the purpose of his visit. He said that what he had to say was a state secret of the highest importance. It was felt that the Government and the MoD could entrust the secret with her. Her concern was for news of Lionel as she assumed that he was the purpose of the visit.

The Captain began by telling her that it was not Commander Crabb who was buried at Milton cemetery in 1957. She responded by stating that the family knew this. Beatrice, Lionel's mother never believed it and neither did she. What they did not know was what they (the Navy or Government) had done with him, but they believed that he would come home one day. Unfortunately Beatrice had passed away and so she would not know what had happened. The Captain commented on the fact that the grave was maintained. She responded by saying that she had agreed with Beatrice, before she died, that she would maintain the grave to keep Lionel's memory alive for as long as she lived. This had been done throughout the years, which was a small price to pay and they had kept her identity secret. She asked if Lionel was now at rest in Milton, to which the Captain replied that it was the case. Her next question wanted confirmation that he had been buried at the current site of the headstone. That was also confirmed. She said that because a body claimed to have been that of Lionel was buried there, they had no other information of his whereabouts, so they had only put basic words on the headstone.

Because of the post mortem, inquest and publicity, what could they do, apart from go along with it? Many people knew it was not Lionel, but where was he? Now that he was home she would arrange for the headstone to be changed to include full details with title and honours. The Captain asked if it was necessary after such a long time, but took the view that she believed the Captain and what he told her. After all, why come and tell her if it were not so. No, she would make things right and concluded that she would keep their secret, after all who would believe an old lady if anything was said? She was too old to grapple with any media intrusion. The changes were made to the headstone without incident and so the Crabb cover up had reached another milestone. She had promised Beatrice Crabb that if they brought the body of Lionel home while she was still alive then she would ensure that his epitaph was completed. Crabb was home.

* * *

Whilst this scenario of the return of Crabb to be buried in Portsmouth is fictitious it does not alter the fact that today, this is a case with untold implications. This is not about Crabb undertaking an unauthorised dive in Portsmouth and some people having egg on their face. This is much more serious, possibly in the realms of treason or other major criminal activity, and for that reason it has to be covered up.

Consider the hand written Top Secret note dated 24 January 1978, which identified that the authorities wanted to move documents relating to Crabb into records as a special category. The reason was determined in three criteria:

"1. exceptionally sensitive…disclosure of which would be contrary to the public interest on security grounds.
2. contains information supplied in confidence, disclosure of which would…constitute a breach of faith.
3. disclosures…could cause distress or embarrassment to living persons."

The note concluded that the information should not be disclosed for 75 years, until 2031. We now know that the figure was extended to 100 years meaning that the 'truth' will not be made public until 2056.

In 2010, some 54 years after the event, what possible security grounds could there be? The note says that information was provided in confidence and if disclosed could be a breach of faith. How could that possibly be? Who provided such information and what was it? Who are the living persons who could be embarrassed? Politicians? No; members of the secret services? No; recipients of stolen art and loot? Yes; members of the Royal family? Yes.

There is a link to the USA regarding the unfavourable activities described above and so we made an application to the CIA and FBI, for information under the Freedom of Information Act about Crabb and Mountbatten. The FBI sent to the authors a box of 1,500 A4 pages. The only bits not blacked out amounted to six pages. Clearly the FBI had information about Crabb and/or Mountbatten, but was not willing to share it. The CIA sent nothing and just said that it was in the interests of US National Security not to make available any documentation or information about Crabb and/or Mountbatten. Applications to the KGB for information remain unanswered and a former KGB official acting on our behalf attempted to search the records for information but failed to make progress and without explanation, did not want to search any further.

We endured 'Crabb Watch' our very own spook. Sydney Knowles' telephone was tapped. The conversation was being intercepted by INTERPOL. Were they listening for any names of those who in the past may have been involved with stolen works of art, particularly World War II Nazi loot? Gary Murray had his car tampered with and received a strange response with regard to the cutting, or not, of the crucial nut.

As one last quest for information, we wrote to the CIA on the 16 August 2009. After all, much of the alleged information that Mountbatten was possibly a Soviet spy came from the USA, and in particular the CIA.

We wrote:

"Under the Freedom of Information Act, 5 U.S.C. subsection 552, I am requesting information or records on Commander Lionel Kenneth Phillip Crabb a former Royal Naval diver who disappeared when diving under a Soviet warship in Portsmouth (England) in 1956. It was claimed that he was working for the CIA.

Also information or records of The Earl Louis Mountbatten who at the time was head of the Royal Navy where it is alleged that he was under scrutiny by the CIA for having links to the Soviet Union.

If you deny all or any part of this request, please cite each specific exemption you think justifies your refusal to release the information and notify me of appeal procedures available under the law."

A reply from the CIA, dated 9 September 2009 stated:

"This is a final response to your 16 August 2009 Freedom of Information Act (FOIA) request, received in the office of the Information and Privacy Coordinator on 1 September 2009, for records on Commander Lionel Kenneth Phillip Crabb and Earl Louis Mountbatten. We have assigned your request the reference number above. Please use this number when corresponding so that we can identify it easily.

In accordance with section 3.6(a) of Executive Order 12958, as amended, the CIA can neither confirm nor deny the existence or nonexistence of records responsive to your request. The fact of the existence or nonexistence of requested records is currently and properly classified and is intelligence sources and methods information that is protected from disclosure by section 6 of the CIA Act of 1949, as amended. Therefore, the Agency has denied your request pursuant to FOIA exemptions (b)(1) and (b)(3). I have enclosed an explanation of these exemptions for your reference and retention.

Information and Privacy Coordinator.

FOIA exemptions (b)(1) and (b)(3):

(b)(1) exempts from disclosure information currently and properly classified, pursuant to an Executive Order;

(b)(3) exempts from disclosure information that another federal statute protects, provided that the other federal statute either requires that the matters be withheld, or establishes particular criteria for withholding or refers to particular types of matters to be withheld. The (b)(3) statutes upon which the CIA relies include, but are not limited to, the CIA Act of 1949."

We conclude from this final response that there is information on file and, like the British and Russians, the Americans are not going to share it. There is no time frame given for the release of any information, but it is clearly a matter of importance to the Americans.

A lot of time has passed since Crabb was involved in the smuggling of art and treasures that were sought after by those who had no regard as to their origins. Much of what would have been 'traded' after World War II would have been plundered from conquered countries by the Nazis. That alone is a good reason for those with power and influence, who were among the recipients, to maintain secrecy. Crabb's search for fame and fortune found him associating with some of the most dangerous spy's in British history. He was even working for the then head of the Royal Navy who, it is alleged by the Americans, was providing the Soviets with information.

Prior to Crabb's disappearance, the net was closing in on Philby, Britain's most notorious spy. He had reluctantly handed over his passport to MI5 and whilst facing further interrogation, was preparing to escape exposure. A simple swim to a Soviet cruiser in Portsmouth accompanied by Crabb was a very real option. The security services yet again failed to trap Philby so he didn't go, but it would seem that Crabb possibly did. The new Soviet *Spetsnaz* elite underwater units were being formed and he would have been a valuable asset. Did 'M' send him to the other side?

In Portsmouth harbour Crabb did not 'search' under the Soviet warship. There were no mines, American or others, there was no underwater filming and there was no measuring of the propulsion system. He dived in daylight against all covert operational protocols and left Smith to cover up behind him. There was outrage in Parliament and a media frenzy, all way beyond anything that was to be expected. An 'over the hill' naval hero said to be on a 'folly', had disappeared and 'an official cover up' was put into full swing to protect the guilty. Heads rolled in the security services but they were not the right ones. Those really responsible went undetected, protected by those who had power and influence. When the story did not go away a body in a frogman's suit with no head or hands was 'discovered'. The security services took charge and controlled events. There was a very strange autopsy and an inquest that appears to have been 'managed' by MI5 and the Admiralty for someone what was claimed by them to be a civilian. The outcome was that the body declared to be Crabb was buried as such. The problem is that it was not the body of Crabb and the guilty remain 'officially' un-named and not held to account.

Bibliography

Borovick G., *The Philby Files*, Little, Brown and Company, New York, 1994.

Bryans R., *The Dust Has Never Settled*, Honeyford Press, London, 1992.

Bryans R, *Blackmail &Whitewash*, Honeyford Press, London, 1996.

Bryans R, *Let The Petals Fall*, Honeyford Press, London, 1993.

Bryans R, *Checkmate*, Honeyford Press, London, 1994.

Costello J., *Mask of Treachery*, Collins, London, 1988.

Deacon R., *A History of the British Secret Service*, Granada Publishing, London, 1980.

Dobson C, Payne R, *The Dictionary of Espionage*, Harrap, London, 1984.

Hale D., *The Final Dive*, Sutton Publishing, Stroud, Glostershire, 2007.

Houghton H., *Operation Portland*, Granada Publishing, London, 1972.

Hutton B. J., *The Fake Defector*, Howard Baker, London, 1970.

Hutton B. J., *Commander Crabb is Alive*, Tandem Publishing, London, 1968.

Hutton B. J., *Frogman Extraordinary*, Nevil Spearman, London, 1960.

Jane's Fighting Ships, Jane's Publishing, London.

Jay A., *Oxford Dictionary of Political Quotations*, Oxford University Press, Oxford, 2007.

Knowles S., *A Diver in the Dark,* Woodfield Publishing, Bognor Regis, West Sussex, 2009.

Lacey, Robert, *Sotheby's: Bidding for Class*, Little, Brown and Co, New York, 1998,

Pugh M., *Commander Crabb*, Macmillan, London, 1956.

Picknett L., Prince C, Prior S, *War of the Windsors*, Mainstream Publishing, Edinburgh, 2002.

Sherrin N., *The Oxford Dictionary of Humerous Quotations*, Oxford University Press, Oxford, 2007.

Suverov V., *Soviet Military Intelligence*, Grafton Books, London, 1986.

Waldron T., Gleeson J, *The Frogmen*, Pan Books, London, 1971.

Wasley G, *Blitz and Account of Hitler's Aireal War over Plymouth in March 1941*, Devon Books, Exeter, 1991.

Watson, P., *Sotheby's: The Inside Story*, Random House, New York, 1998.

Welham M.G. & J.A., *Frogman Spy*, W H Allen, London, 1990.

Welham M.G., *Combat Frogmen*, Patrick Stephens, Wellingborough, Northamptonshire, 1989.

Welham M.G., *Naval Elite Units*, Arms and Armour Press, London, 1990.

Welham M.G., Quarie B., *Operation Spetsnaz*, Patrick Stephens, Wellingborough, Northamptonshire, 1989.

Wright P., *Spy Catcher*, Viking Penguin, New York, 1987.